A Bomber Crew
Mystery

In tribute to Jim Westfall 1957–2015,
whose encouragement ensured this book was written.

A Bomber Crew Mystery

The Forgotten Heroes of 388th Bombardment Group

David Price

Pen & Sword
AVIATION

First published in Great Britain in 2016 by
Pen & Sword Aviation
an imprint of
Pen & Sword Books Ltd
47 Church Street
Barnsley
South Yorkshire
S70 2AS

ISBN 978 1 47387 046 8

Typeset in Ehrhardt by
Mac Style Ltd, Bridlington, East Yorkshire
Printed and bound in the UK by CPI Group (UK) Ltd,
Croydon, CRO 4YY

Pen & Sword Books Ltd incorporates the imprints of Pen & Sword
Archaeology, Atlas, Aviation, Battleground, Discovery, Family
History, History, Maritime, Military, Naval, Politics, Railways, Select,
Transport, True Crime, and Fiction, Frontline Books, Leo Cooper,
Praetorian Press, Seaforth Publishing and Wharncliffe.

For a complete list of Pen & Sword titles please contact
PEN & SWORD BOOKS LIMITED
47 Church Street, Barnsley, South Yorkshire, S70 2AS, England
E-mail: enquiries@pen-and-sword.co.uk
Website: www.pen-and-sword.co.uk

Contents

Foreword

They say time is not on our side, and each day we lose more warriors and the stories of the accomplishments of a generation of B-17 crews in the skies of Europe over 70 years ago. We want to understand what it was like for these men to leave the security of their families, homes and jobs to defend a continent across the Atlantic in loud, cold, and vulnerable aircraft – knowing that they may never return. Who were they, and why did they do what they did?

This book peers into their world. It takes the reader on a journey and introduces a mystery that reaches from a small store in Scotland to the skies over Germany and back. Along the way, you will get a glimpse into what it was like to fly over the British countryside en route to war as a pilot or crew member of a B-17. It examines the view from the cockpit of a high-speed German fighter as it stalks the B-17s and explores what it must have felt like to experience post-traumatic stress disorder, or lose a close friend in horrible circumstances. After all this is the triumphant feeling of having survived when the odds were stacked against you.

Having flown Air Force F-16s in combat during three conflicts, I have a profound respect for the men of the 388th Bomb Group who overcame their natural fear with unnatural courage. Combat is different for everyone, but without question, the men behind the 'bomber crew mystery' and hundreds of others like them, were tested to their limits. I too have been shot at by a persistent enemy, but David's insight quickly reminded me of how my experiences paled in comparison to theirs, and just how vulnerable and brave these men were.

As the current President of the 388th Bomb Group Association, I am always amazed at the men who continue to join the annual reunions that have been a source of camaraderie and fellowship for decades. As their numbers unfortunately fade with each passing day, it is even more important to carry on their legacy. David Price does just that, and in an amazing way. Besides learning history that I had not known before, this story moved me;

and I could not put the book down. As I followed the 'clues' to the mystery, I found myself in awe, in joy, and, at times, in tears. David selflessly took on this compelling mystery, and in the process, paid a humble tribute to the men behind it. The mystery continues, so turn the page and join the ride. You won't be disappointed.

Scott Long
President, 388th Bomb Group Association
Colonel (Ret), USAF

The Procession

The B-17 bombers were all now waiting. One hundred and twelve Wright Cyclone engines wheeled and chuntered, propellers spiralling in the early June air. It is early morning and the brown discolouration of the air around the B-17s from the exhausts is perceptible around the lifting dawn. In as tidy a queue as they can muster, they trundle along the peri tracks towards the runway in a pre-arranged waltz, a little correction here, a small turn there, each pilot watching acutely the plane in front; close, but not too close. The runway is reached and, after a short wait, a green flare arcs its message; it's time to go. As the lead plane accelerates down the runway, the next takes its place to take off, a gap of thirty seconds between each rolling, thundering chorus leader.

First Lieutenant Johnnie Colburn waits his turn in the second group, 388-B Group. Today is special because for the Colburn crew it is their first combat mission. Two years of training and preparation consummate into this moment; they are doing what they came here for. Johnnie has officially flown two missions before this, both of them a few days before with a different crew. The first ended abruptly as Johnnie had to abort the take-off because of a technical problem and the second to Boulogne, a short hop across the English Channel, was fairly uneventful. Unknown to them all is that they are about to be written into history, for today is not just any day, today is 4 June 1944. Perhaps for the many thousands involved today, it is another day and, like any war, they have no idea of the workings of their higher command. In some cases, many years will pass before their story is written or understood. The Colburn crew do not have time to think any such romantic notions; they are concentrating. Nobody wants to screw up on their first mission and, although they have rehearsed this many times, the feelings of excitement and anxiety are pushed down in order to get on with the job in hand. What many of them fear is that they will become afraid and in this condition let down their crew.

Eyes scan the instruments in the cockpit – engine tachos, oil temperature and fuel gauges. Ears are fine-tuned to the noises of the aircraft, listening, sensing what is happening and whether it 'feels' right. They are aware too of their heart rate and the expectancy in the pit of their stomachs – they just want to fly; to get on with it.

The queue shortens as one by one the B-17s roll down the runway and ahead Colburn watches B-17 *Wizard of Oz* starting the take-off run, an aircraft that fewer than three weeks later he will fly and see lost in circumstances few could imagine. Almost before the mist of daylight comes between the wheels and the runway of the aircraft ahead, Johnnie knows instinctively it's his turn. He barely need exchange a glance with his co-pilot, Charles (Russ) Weekes; they know the drill and now it's time. Finally. With a firm motion the four throttle levers are moved backwards and the four engines evolve from a deep settling chatter to a musical note. The pilots are still hard on the brakes as the aircraft begins to vibrate from nose to tail. In a few seconds the brakes are released and, as the speed picks up, the whole of their surroundings reverberates with physical sound. The Wright Cyclones produce a deep thunder, a comforting and powerful sound, a tone that guarantees their take-off. The tail begins to lift although perhaps imperceptibly to most of the crew as B-17 44-0691 *Lotta Bull* prepares herself for flight. A loaded B-17 tends to take off with the nose up by some margin. In the tail gun position, 20-year-old Frank Nutt notices the tail lift a little as the tail wheel underneath him loses contact, and he watches the B-17 behind him get smaller and smaller in the dawn as the runway begins to rush from underneath and behind him.

In a Second World War bomber so much can go wrong; in the twinkling of an eye a normal flight can turn into a nightmare. Take-off with a fully loaded aircraft can be particularly hazardous and today *Lotta Bull* is carrying her higher capacity bomb load, some 8,000lb of high explosive. A tyre burst or engine failure on take-off could be catastrophic, not just for the crew but for the whole air base. The omission of a simple detail such as ensuring the tail wheel is locked in its forward position could cause significant problems. As hundreds of bombers leave their bases and become packed tightly over East Anglia, a smudge of oily black smoke coming up from the ground is not an unfamiliar sight. Whether it was from a bomber that failed to take off, one that crashed shortly afterwards or even the result of a mid-air collision during assembly, the funeral pyre of a burning wreck far below is no welcome send-off.

As the wheels of Johnnie Wilmer Colburn's plane leaves the runway the pen of history begins to write, as the first mission of an expected thirty begins. Another unusual thing is also happening, unperceived, unimagined and unintelligible; this moment is the first strand of a simple story that will touch the crew's children and grandchildren in seventy years' time.

Colburn begins the process of coaxing his bomber into safe flight and after a series of gentle manoeuvres it is time to get the plane turning for the rendezvous area. The fields of England, a little grey and hazy today, are a far cry from the burning Utah heat in which the crews trained. Today, the 388th Bombardment Group is providing 28 aircraft in a force of what will eventually be 183 US 8th Air Force B-17s. The ballet of getting into the correct formation is a lengthy but essential part of the plan and only when this process is successful would they set course for their target. The air becomes clearer and bluer, and even the conditions below them are better than predicted. In *Lotta Bull* everyone is doing their job – and watching. Oxygen masks are adjusted and checked; they are now spacemen in a hostile oxygen deprived atmosphere. Not only is the circus of B-17s and their position to be watched, the arrival of their fighter escort is another key element in their rendezvous. The specks in the sky of the arriving fighters is also of concern to the gunners, they have to be certain that these are their 'Little Friends', for, however unlikely an enemy attack may be at this point, this is a war. The fighter escort for this mission is spectacular and the number of P-47 Thunderbolts and P-51 Mustangs is nearly as many as the bombers themselves.

It's a short trip today to a target that doesn't trip easily off the tongue; Cap Gris Nez in northern France. Meaning, literally, Cape Grey Nose, it is close to Calais and therefore the nearest point of France to England across the Straits of Dover, the English Channel. A crew on a first mission could not be closer to England in attacking the enemy and such a trip was known as a 'milk run' in recognition of its comparative ease. Just as the white cliffs of Dover and their welcoming sunny disposition would be a cheery sight for thousands of returning airmen, the discoloured grey of the French coast could warn of tough times ahead. Milk run or not, today would also mark the first day the Colburn crew would come under enemy fire; not from fighters, but from a similarly deadly adversary, anti-aircraft guns or flak. The first signs would be seemingly lazy puffs of black smoke bursting beneath and ahead of the approaching bomber stream. However, the danger was that as the German gunners ranged the height of the raid, the air could become filled with sharp explosions and flying shards of white-hot metal. The days of visual viewfinding in gun control were drawing in and a new technology, radar, was being employed to help the shells reach the height of their foe accurately. Gone were the days of the First World War German anti-aircraft fire known as 'archie', even the nickname suggesting some gentlemanly chance of sport. Today's industrialized gunning was flak; as short, sharp and ugly as the name.

The target today and tomorrow is not cliffs or beaches but the defences that lie on them. Big guns sheltered in concrete bunkers, firing positions and a network of communications formed part of a defensive barrier known as the Atlantic Wall. Devised and executed to stop an Allied sea-borne assault, the defensive structure stretched from the northern reaches of Finland to the border of France and Spain. By this point in 1944 it was overseen by one of Hitler's most accomplished generals, Erwin Rommel. In a gigantic game of bluff, the Allied armies needed to deceive the German high command as to where the landing – known to us now as D–Day – was to be. The Germans had become convinced that the short stretch of water separating Dover and Calais would be the most likely point. Today, as on other recent days, bombing raids were conducted to intensify this belief.

As Colburn and his fellow B-17 crews ran in to their target, they were relieved to see that it was possible to bomb visually. Here was a first view of occupied Europe, and from 23,900ft it looked curiously similar to the friendly country they had left a short time before. The black flowers of flak were now bursting in amongst the bomber formations but there was nothing to be done but fly straight and level. At 2.33 pm, they dropped their bombs and Colburn's crew felt *Lotta Bull* rise noticeably as the weight left them. In the tail, Frank Nutt could see the streams of bombs leaving other B-17s, seemingly slowly, matching the speed of the aircraft before clustering up and dropping horizontally towards the target. It was time to turn for home and home was the 388th Bombardment Group airfield at Knettishall in Suffolk.

Across the Channel on Hillcrest Road, Hythe, in Kent, the windows rattled with the percussion of the explosions some twenty-seven miles away. The residents are used to these sounds and after nearly five years of war they can distinguish the type of explosions and the area they are likely to come from. The noise of the percussion of bombs has faded only a few minutes earlier before the drone of the waves of bombers and fighters becomes distinguishable as they head for the safety of England.

Unlike the slow circling departure, the bombers now pass over Knettishall at lower levels and begin peeling off in the circuit, a roundabout of aircraft preparing to land. Although there is relief at reaching the relative safety of England's green hedgerow-filled landscape, there is still a well of tension in the crew's stomachs. All the training flights had prepared them for most eventualities and possible failures of the aircraft's systems on landing. Now, for the first time, another alien element has been introduced; the enemy has tried to shoot them down. Thousands of shards of metal have been fired into their vicinity. It would take only one to damage something and perhaps they would not know. Johnnie and Russ were running through their pre-landing preparations, but with every action there would be the background anxiety of whether everything was functioning as it should. Were the engines running smoothly, were the flaps coming down as they should, would the undercarriage lower correctly, are the tyres still in good condition? All were questions running through the minds of all the crew as they subconsciously felt the effects of each action through the airframe. As *Lotta Bull* touched down in a straight line and she responded to the brakes, the heartbeat inside the B-17 slowed down a little. It was a simple trip now along the taxiways to the dispersal point, where the engines cut and the props wound down – then silence; or at least relative silence.

The results of the raid were mixed but the Colburn crew were pleased to find their group had hit the target, unlike Group A. This was the first and last time they flew *Lotta Bull* in combat and, although she flew forty-seven missions, her end came in September that year over France on the way back from Germany. With instrument failure in dense cloud, *Lotta Bull* went into a spin and ended up smashed into thousands of pieces in a French field. She was unlucky on that trip but, happily for her crew, they all escaped by parachute into liberated France and were ready to fly again.

As the Colburn crew slept the previous night, 4 June had already delivered its place in history. Even for an unsettled British spring, the force of the inclement weather is an unexpected and sobering threat to General Eisenhower. Plans for Overlord, the Allied invasion plan, are at risk.

Group Captain Stagg, Chief Meteorological Officer to Eisenhower, made the following report at 0415 hrs on Sunday, 4 June to the Supreme Allied Commander:

Wx becoming so unsettled that it is difficult to make any certain predictions for a long time ahead. But Westerly wind at 16 kts set in over the Channel almost immediately with 10/10th cloud at 500' in the UK and over the Assault Area. No prospect of improvement until Wednesday but on the other hand the position is finely balanced and a slight tip in either direction could make a great difference.

At ports throughout the south coast of England, thousands of men were clambering aboard a vast array of ships and many had already sailed. Among the fleet were thousands of tons of equipment, tanks, guns and every kind of vittle necessary to support a huge army.

With many of the invasion ships at sea, Eisenhower had to make the extremely difficult decision; delay the invasion a further day or risk thousands of men and years of planning. Meanwhile, Erwin Rommel had made up his mind that the Allies would not attempt an invasion in the immediate future. The tides and weather seemed set against such an eventuality. Reports of the raids on the Pas-de-Calais did not sway his opinion and he set off early that morning to meet his wife in Berlin for her birthday.

Chapter 1

The Beginning

'Begin at the beginning,' the King said, very gravely, 'and go on till you come to the end: then stop.'

— Lewis Carroll, *Alice in Wonderland*

Wednesday, 7 May 2014

The occasion of your wife's 50th birthday is a matter for celebration but all husbands will recognize the fine balance to be struck between marking the occasion with enthusiasm, yet not emphasizing your partner's march in time. In the face of possible matrimonial disaster, I decided it better that we take a short city break than be at home where all the daily duties can swallow up any day off. We decided that Edinburgh would provide a pleasant location and as we live just outside Carlisle, about 100 miles away, it is a relatively short trip. I should make a note here to specify that is Edinburgh, Scotland, and Carlisle, England. The emphasis will become self-apparent as the subject of this story affects not only both sides of the border, but both sides of the Atlantic.

A pleasant but not too opulent hotel was chosen so we had the opportunity to eat out at nice restaurants in the evening without feeling guilty about the expense. We have a penchant for all things French and found a lovely and realistic French restaurant where we paid to be insulted in the nicest possible way. Our lack of comprehension of the French language made us the target of all sorts of efforts to make us understand by the hosts. Hand waving and some laborious translation of the menu followed before we would generally nod in agreement; after that effort it would be rude to say no. Our trip was marked by the amount we walked. We walked everywhere; then we walked some more. Edinburgh is a city of fine architecture and steep inclines and, given our penchant for combining such activities with regular treats such as coffee and cake, such exercise could be demanding at times. The Castle and Royal Mile provide the tourist with both stunning views and the opportunity to buy tartan scarfs, trinkets, hats and kilts in every second shop. Some are tasteful and fashionable, others trade to the more comical-minded visitors and include tartan hats (known as the tam-o'-shanter) with ginger wigs pre-stitched in. If there's one thing that the Scots do well, it's promote their national iconography, and the sight of tartan and the skirl of the bagpipes is never far from eyes and ears. Space here does not permit the full exposition of the adoption of tartan as theirs by the Scots, but surprisingly the cult of kilts, sporrans and everything dressy in Scottish lore actually originates from a romantic period of the eighteenth century and not from medieval times.

I suppose we are not an unusual couple in that my wife, Trish, likes shops and we both like cafes and browsing the odd antique shop looking for curios. We rarely, if ever, buy much and today, 7 May, is no different. It's mid-morning, we've just had coffee, and a few doors down the street is a small antique shop. It wasn't really my thing at first glance; it had a dark underrated exterior which one might imagine would fit into the set of a Harry Potter movie. It was small, a little crowded and filled with silver and silver-plated items such as cutlery and shiny tea pots. It had the all too familiar musty smell that all such establishments should have if they are not selling more modern imitations.

Squeezing in, we found two Italian tourists of student age together with rucksacks that took up more space than their diminutive stature. 'Do you have any World War One helmets?' one of them asked. I thought it was a strange question in a shop full of silverware, perhaps one of those strange questions that foreign tourists have the tendency to ask. As the owners explained that they did not, my eyes wandered upwards to the ceiling and a selection of military hats, helmets and uniforms. It was clear that not all were for sale, so here was a place with a military interest and that was far more my 'thing' than knives and forks. With the rucksacked duo still blocking all but a flimsy breathing space, I found myself looking up at a display of silverware. Then, it caught my eye.

Dangling from a handle of a large ornate wine cooler was a label and on the label I could read 'US Air Force WW2'. It probably didn't need much else on it to get my attention because if military objects were my thing, aeroplanes were especially my thing. Trish probably thought she was on safe ground in Edinburgh because here was somewhere she was very unlikely to be asked to stand around for ages on a windswept airfield waiting for me to do – well, something and a lot of the time she didn't know quite what. We've been married for thirty years and, although I consider my hobby to take but a few minutes here and there, I know it's hours if I'm honest. Trish's suffering has stretched to being soaked in the pouring rain, reading in a car at the end of some runway or other or being sun-baked at an air show. Now, just when she least suspects it, her husband's brain is about to be scrambled once again with the thrill of an aeroplane chase. So, the story starts for me with a dangling label.

The wine cooler was a chunky piece of metal and it was well engraved. I asked to take it down and I scanned the front which read 'outstanding crew of the month', a crest and then '388th Bombardment Group'. I turned it round and found two crews listed, one under August 1944 and the other September 1944. I knew instinctively that this was a trophy from the US 8th Air Force and, with nine names per crew, a bomber group. At these times, with my possible interest in a purchase, I don't like to show too much emotion as I am aware that all hopes of getting a lower price can be beaten by starry-eyed enthusiasm. Apart from this, I didn't really know a great deal about the US Air Force as I tend to be an RAF follower. Here was an object though that many an enthusiast would donate a limb or a kidney to find.

What I did know was that thousands of American airmen and aircraft populated the east of England in counties including Lincolnshire, Norfolk and Suffolk during the Second World War. They launched huge bombing raids on mainland Europe, not only on German cities, but also on industrial and military targets throughout occupied Europe. The RAF fought by night, the Americans by day in a relentless wave of action designed to destroy both Axis infrastructure and the will to fight. Here in my hands was a tangible echo of eighteen young men, their service and more than a handful of incredible risks.

Politely placing the wine cooler back in its place, I took my leave after expressing some interest and said I would possibly call in again. I remembered only one name, the surname 'Weekes' as it reminded me of the philanthropist aeroplane collector Kermit Weeks in Florida. The spelling of Weekes was different but somewhere in the mix I thought that maybe there were a few dollars to be made as American collectors like this kind of item. This is an early confession, for, having said my interest was in aviation, I found I was falling into the old trap of believing Americans were worth tapping up for a few dollars whenever the occasion arose. For this most base of instincts, I have to apologize, although, in my defence, the American is far more generous in his spending than the Brit.

Getting back to our hotel room, I checked the internet and found an amazingly detailed 388th Bombardment Group website listing every serviceman, every aeroplane and every raid. In short, it was a goldmine of information. Charles R. Weekes was a 1st lieutenant, a co-pilot and listed clearly. I never had a doubt about the wine cooler's authenticity anyway.

The hijack of my wife's celebration was nearly complete and that evening I plotted to purchase the wine cooler. A more impractical article in our home I cannot imagine; having a fridge makes such an item implausible. Perhaps I have just divulged our lack of true grace and decorum, neither 'Champagne Charlies' nor fine diners are we. So, there was simply no reason to obtain a wine cooler other than for the names and the history they brought with them.

The next day, we walked through the city again. Through the streets, passing 'the most pierced lady in the world', one of the many street sideshows, and down to the little antiques shop where the purchase, after a little gentling haggling, was completed. I asked where the cooler had come from but there was no provenance with it, simply the information that it had come from a house clearance in the north of the city. The owner was very apologetic but here was a near seventy-year-old mystery in the making. How did a US Army Air Force trophy find its way so far north and in whose keeping had it been in? Trish is very British and doesn't like the bartering process I enjoy so much so she window-shopped along the street until I emerged. I don't remember too much of the morning, it was very pleasant but, giving Trish an hour to shop by herself, I darted back to the hotel with my booty. The first name on the cooler under 'August 1944' was an unusual looking name; at least for a dyed-in- the-wool Englishman. It read, 'Dong Ong 1st Lt'.

The marvellous 388th history website had every crew under their captains and sure enough the entry on the list read 'Ong 1'. Clicking on the link brought up a crew photo showing eight men under a Boeing B-17 bomber. There, kneeling in the centre, was the crew's boss, the pilot, holding – and I could not believe my eyes – the wine cooler. For an enthusiast like me, and probably any collector who seeks that most sought-after quality in an object, irrefutable evidence of its history, it was another explosive moment. There are few words or expressions to match the experience. It's the fisherman who catches the biggest fish and finds a gold coin in its mouth, the footballer who scores the goal in the final minutes of a match, and the boy who finds his Kit Kat is all chocolate and no wafer. If you ask my friends, they would tell you that I'm not the most expressive sort. I'm a 'glass half empty' type of person – even at times, so I'm told, pessimistic and not given to spontaneous outbursts of anything. Today though, sitting on the corner of my hotel bed clutching a laptop, there were some expressions of delight.

I walked to meet Trish all the more quickly that lunchtime, my head buzzing with just a few facts. I must say, I impressed myself by being able to switch off some of the excitement; I knew that as this was Trish's trip away I must try not to let my discovery take over. However, once back at the hotel I became immersed in the details I kept turning up. The 388th Bombardment Group was based at an airfield called Knettishall in Suffolk, it flew Boeing B-17s, Dong Ong had two crews, Weekes was spelt with an 'E' not without …. A voice suddenly spoke. 'Enough!' came the clarion call of an annoyed woman and, like the addicted gambler, I had been caught at the roulette wheel spending the family allowance. I had to admit it had all got the better of me and, carefully wrapping up the wine cooler, I vowed to learn my lesson and not speak of it again that trip.

We returned to Carlisle the next day and I tried to be a little more circumspect about my enthusiasm for researching every part of the wine cooler's history and those eighteen elusive names. I knew it was probably going to be a long job and, after some initial dabbling around web searching, life returned to a more normal pace. I had also seen the picture of the second crew captained by Johnnie W. Colburn (spelled Jonnie on the cooler). This picture was of all nine men but, on first glance, unlike Ong's crew photo, no wine cooler. However, Johnnie was kneeling in front and had his hand resting on something mostly out of shot. It was round and looked white; indeed, the rim of the obscured cooler. In the meantime, I had been asked to help with a First World War display in our village and my mind was wandering across to the twenty-two names on the village war memorial – a large number for a very small village. I became engaged in the task of searching for their graves and working out who they were and where they lived. The wine cooler sat next to me on my dresser in the office but did not command my undivided attention.

So it was for the next couple of weeks. I got hold of some silver polish, gently cleaned the cooler and realized it was still in pretty good shape. So many plated objects get marked or worn by over-rigorous polishing and, wherever it had been in the last seventy years, it was not over-cleaned. Someone had appreciated it, perhaps it had been in a few hands, but I suspected it was a 'one owner' item once its tenure with the US Air Force was finished.

Through that time in early May I told a few people about the cooler, or as I shall now refer to it, the trophy. Nearly everyone was interested and I thought it would make a good display at my local aviation museum. I had been a volunteer at Solway Aviation Museum for more than twenty years, served time as the chairman and generally got stuck in maintaining old aeroplanes. Based on the old RAF Crosby-on-Eden wartime airfield, there were plenty of roots and links to the Second World War, but perhaps not so many to the US Air Force. Crosby was a fighter training base that trained Hawker Hurricane pilots and, later on, the mighty twin-engined Beaufighter. It wasn't a luxurious posting, being six miles outside the city, and, by all accounts, the paths between the wooden accommodation huts could become wet and muddy. The calibre of the instructors could not be questioned though. They were veterans of the Battle of Britain (as were some of the aircraft) and had that precious commodity; real life battle experience.

One Friday night, our friends, a suitably chilled married couple who are American and Canadian citizens, came to stay over. Having teenage daughters, we were familiar with sleepovers, but now it was the parents letting the teenagers have some space – we had our own sleepover. With the ladies temporarily out of the room and knowing I had to avoid being a bore, I decided to show my friend Jim Westfall the trophy. He was suitably impressed and conversation about the trophy lasted into the evening; the wives being very patient, I felt. A laptop is never far away in our household and before long Jim and I were scanning the early leads on the two pilots, Ong and Colburn. In both cases, we turned up telephone numbers that could be relatives or even the gentlemen themselves. It was at this point that Jim said the immortal words: 'You know, you're going to have to call them.'

All courage suddenly seemed to leave me. Whatever would I say? Even when I collected my thoughts into a pattern of speech, it seemed something that may require a stiff cup of tea before attempting. One thing however was certain; the demand of the trophy was unwavering. There was no way it could sit on my sideboard without me doing something. We also found an obituary for Dong Ong. He had died in 2007, but it named his sons and now

I had a telephone number. There was a number for Johnnie Colburn too but, in that he was born in 1919, I thought it must be an old listing. I started with the Colburn number that night, but there was no answer or, more precisely, the number was disconnected. I must admit it was some relief in a curious way. I decided to sleep on the matter as my courage, what little there was of it, was ebbing away.

Jim was a typesetter and printer by trade and, as we walked in the woods just up our lane the next day, we talked about all things publishing. I had written a few features and articles before and I enjoyed blogging – I had even started, but not finished (yet) a children's book. Jim was talking about small print run book editions and the idea came to me that a book was maybe a good thing. In a vague sort of way, I began thinking that a book about the trophy might be a good idea but what would it have in it? I knew I was going to have to call those telephone numbers, courage or no courage. I didn't know enough about the US Air Force, I told myself, and I was right, I didn't. My interests and study had been, on reflection, somewhat parochial. I enjoyed all things Royal Air Force and, somewhere deep in my subconscious, I considered those Brits obsessed with the US 8th Air Force in Britain a little unpatriotic and gaudy in outlook. Some of this might have been coloured by meeting some camouflage-clad enthusiasts who took to all things American with a passion. One of them, a man of ample proportions, had been detained at a US base in Britain after trying to conceal himself in some grass at the end of a runway. His idea was to get a photograph of an F-117 'Stealth Fighter', at the time a bit of a scoop as they were quite new. This event was well before 9/11 and really at the end of the Cold War. He was recognized in the guard room and known throughout the base as a friendly enthusiast. Indeed, his release with a friendly reprimand was quite quick. So, my experience of the American-centred Brit was not always flattering.

To write this story I was going to have to hang up my bias towards patriotism, my RAF interest and, for a while, immerse myself in not only the history of this US Army Air Force Group, but the culture and ethnicity of America. I was going to have to call and email a whole load of strangers, and the fear of being mistaken for a salesman, con artist or stalker was something I was going to have to overcome.

There was something deeper afoot though. In the book *The Lord of the Rings* the central powerful item is the ring. Lost at times in its history, it is picked up by Gollum, who calls it 'my precious', and it wields huge control on its keepers. There is the pervading sense that the ring chooses its keepers and holds powers and almost its own intelligence. The trophy has no such malign aura but it does demand attention and perhaps its remarkable disappearance for nearly seventy years is a further mystery that demanded an answer. Could an answer be found and could I find the relatives, or enough of them to make any kind of interesting story?

There was only one way to find out and that was to call a telephone number I now had that I felt was a certain link to the first name on the Trophy: Dong Ong 1st Lt. I dialled the number for one of his sons in Indianapolis, Terry Ong. The phone rang, which is always a good start, and it came on to answer machine, so I left a message saying I would call back. I was committed. I rang again the next day and Terry's wife answered. Sometimes in these situations a woman's voice is more calming and I introduced myself and explained my quest, trying not to trip over my words too much.

'Hold on,' she said after a couple of minutes. 'Terry's just here, do you want to speak to him?'

Suddenly, the story was coming to life, not just engraved names on an old piece of silver plate, but real voices and that most endearing element to any good story, human experience told through the lives of those who knew the names and loved them. My conversation with Terry confirmed their family interest and they seemed quite excited at the trophy's re-appearance. I had not fully grasped how important a place in the hearts of their families these airmen had. To me, they were simple engraved names and I rather naïvely thought that my interference in the lives of their children might be a nuisance.

My friend Jim also exhorted me to follow the chase. His words were clear to me: 'You've got to write this book.'

So, from a short visit to a pretty city, I was left with an exciting and demanding challenge; a challenge that would take many months to complete, but a journey of insight and a dig deeper into recent history. I had made one phone call, the first of many, and I knew if I was successful, I would make a new set of friends – even friends I might never meet.

Part of the challenge was dealing with eighteen or more names, each of whom had a different role within a B-17 crew. For the reader of any book, there is the challenge of having too many names thrown at them, yet with the need for historical accuracy, names are an important part of this story.

The Names on the Trophy

August 1944		*September 1944*	
Dong Ong	1st Lt	Jonnie W Colburn	1st Lt*
Earl M Lippert	1st Lt	Charles R Weekes	1st Lt
Ulysses B Ganas	1st Lt	Morris H Neiman	1st Lt
Morris L Fleischman	T/Sgt	Robert E Simmon	1st Lt
Kenneth L Gardner	T/Sgt	Richard T Heslam	1st Lt
Carl N Lindorff	S/Sgt	William R Tobias	T/Sgt
Morris S Gumpel	S/Sgt	George E Kragle	T/Sgt
Arvid J Estrom	S/Sgt*	Leonard W Granath	S/Sgt
Daniel C Visconti	S/Sgt	Frank E Nutt	S/Sgt

* Spellings how they appear on the trophy

Chapter 2

Let Battle Commence

The two most important days in your life are the day you are born and the day you find out why.

– Mark Twain

Dong Ong was only 22 years old but had the lives of nine others in his hands. The Ong crew knew that the invasion was coming. By 5 June operations had stepped up a further gear and elements of the 388th were flying missions nearly every day. It was obvious by the frenetic air activity by night and day that something was going to happen. The talk had gone on for some time on both sides of the Atlantic. The intensity of the hushed conversations and speculation at Knettishall had been fuelled by the recent missions to northern France. There was still strict discipline observed on how these discussions were held as it had been drilled into each serviceman that secrecy was essential. Mission after mission was being flown with B-17s coming and going daily in waves. Not too far away, British air bases had been putting up large numbers of bombers and fighter escorts, too. Lancaster and Halifax bombers took off in the late evening for their night missions, vibrating the metal roofs of the huts in which the Americans have been trying to sleep. The individual aircraft sounds lose their definition as, with so many aircraft airborne, the engines create a low musical note, a throbbing wave of sound. It is a sight and sound they have become accustomed to but, as a new crew yet to fly their first combat mission, the building anticipation is tangible. Their flying training has been intense but, even with returned crews in the States lecturing them on their experiences, it has been hard to come to terms emotionally with what lies ahead. For some, it has been dawning on them that their chances of living long enough to learn the hard lessons of war seem to diminish with every aircraft that fails to return.

There has been no time for lounging around, everyone from the gunners to the pilots has been ground training through the day or getting kit ready.

When they get into a B-17, they recognize the familiar smell, that mixture of damp canvas, oil, hot metal and rubber – a smell they will remember for the rest of their lives and even when visiting a peacetime B-17, it will act as an instant recall of the past.

RAF Knettishall is different from any other Army Air Force Base they have been on to date. Although it is operated by US staff, even the name is a reminder that they were there as guests. All the facilities had been put together by American planners, though, and plenty of thought had gone into the layout, which had seen a launderette, cinema and gym established. The quip is that Knettishall is 'The Country Club of the 8th Air Force' and a sign has been created to that effect. For the newly arrived crew, it takes a little time to acclimatize to the location of their accommodation and to determine the functioning areas of the base. There are a dozen or more dispersed sites, some close to the local village, others effectively out in the fields. If the crews were close enough to the runways to see, there was an instinctive pause to watch take-offs and landings, although at times the view of the aircraft was lost among the huts and training rooms. Damage to the aircraft coming back was commonplace, some peppered with holes, others with whole sections blown away. The landing sounds of a damaged B-17 were often different to a healthy one; airframes whistled with holes and gaps, engines could sound rough and landings were sometimes 'as it happened' rather than textbook touchdowns. Stopped engines and emergency landings were part of the routine. Some aircraft never came back at all and it was a long wait for the ground crews to see if their ship was late, had landed elsewhere or was lost forever. Injury was a constant risk, both on the ground and in the air, and if an aircraft had managed to creep back to base damaged, the crews faced the impending danger of landing with perhaps burst tyres or failed brakes. The hazards also affected ground crews, with bombers landing heavily with bombs still on board and accounts from other bases of aircraft crashing into buildings or vehicles after losing control. In just over a week in May 1944, five 388th aircraft had been lost on raids and, statistically, the chance of completing thirty missions was as low as one in five. Dong's crew never really knew this figure until after the war. Indeed, the speculation was that the loss rate was far higher.

They were about to start their combat careers at a seminal point in history, at a time when, fortunately for them, losses in their group would remain lower than the previous weeks and months. They were still coming to terms with their muted welcome at Knettishall. It seemed few people really wanted to know them and the barrack room bravado that they imagined would greet their arrival was not apparent. The truth was that losses had been grievous; there was not necessarily a lack of respect for these new arrivals, but making friends too quickly could be too painful for the older hands.

Much of Britain was also waiting in expectation of the news of the start of the invasion. Given the vast quantity of men and material, it was impossible not to notice. For years, with Britain being at war since September 1939, the message was carefully cultivated on posters and adverts: 'careless talk costs lives'. Other slogans included the phrase 'be careful, there may be a Jerry under the bed', which was a play on words as a 'Jerry' was a chamber pot. Information in Britain was scarce but German propaganda in the shape of radio broadcasts mentioned the invasion freely. However the broadcasters, like the rest of Europe and indeed the Nazis, had no real idea where the hammer would fall, or when. The most famous, nicknamed Lord Haw Haw, was a British fascist, William Joyce, whose broadcasts from Hamburg began with the catchphrase 'Germany calling, Germany calling'. In contrast to the light, restricted news in Britain, he seemed to know all sorts of detail and would speculate freely on matters that could cause consternation to the public. Although it seemed he had a steady source of information, much of it was similar to a fairground crystal ball reader; he picked on subjects on which he could elaborate. The difficulty for the Allies was that there was a perception that the Germans were willing to say more than they. It is also worth remembering that this was really still the infancy of radio, particularly in relation to the digital age and mass media we now enjoy. The public's ability to be discerning was limited; this was the first time any voice from the radio was trying purposefully to deceive them.

The Americans, too, were targeted, in their case by 'Axis Sally', who was voiced by two people, Mildred Gillars and Italian-American Rita Zucca. Gillars was involved in a radio drama on the night of 5 June that aimed to unsettle the troops by emphasizing the effect of their death back home. By all accounts it was a chilling broadcast but the fact was that the troops were already loaded on transports and on their way. This simply emphasizes how the timing of D-Day had remained a secret; a remarkable feat of secrecy, too. Both Gillars and Zucca were arrested and imprisoned after the war for treason, with Gillars being released in 1961 and Zucca somewhat earlier. William Joyce was far less fortunate and paid for his actions in a manner in which he must have expected; he was tried and hanged for treason in 1946 at His Majesty's Prison, Wandsworth.

Much of the south coast of Britain had become an enormous military camp and the whole of Britain an aircraft carrier with thousands of aircraft ready to take their place in the plan before them. Harbours and ships were filled with every kind of craft imaginable and of 6,939 vessels used on D-Day, eighty per cent were British or Canadian and only sixteen per cent American. The size of the Royal Navy was considerable during this time and, compared to the size of these small islands, it is hard to fathom given the post-war shrinkage, that it was bigger and more powerful than the US Navy. The invasion had been planned and prepared for years and, like a coiled spring, it had been wound up and was quivering with potential energy. The need for secrecy had some interesting personal side-effects, as the creators of the huge Normandy operations map at Southwick House in Hampshire discovered. They were not allowed to return home until after the start of D-Day for fear they might accidentally leak the location.

Amid all the obvious secrecy surrounding D-Day, there remains a tier that is less known, but which thankfully in recent years is becoming more of a feature in understanding the history of the Second World War. From 1939, the British had a specialist unit set up at a country house fifty miles from London, Bletchley Park. Its task was listening to Axis communications and code-breaking. The unit was spectacularly successful in breaking German codes and by 1943 had a bank of what is now known to be the world's first semi-programmable computers, called Colossus. Using these machines to break the German Enigma codes provided the team with a huge stream of information that was translated carefully and checked. The unit not only intercepted all high level German military communication but could identify particular signals operators by their habits and language. By this point in the war, Allied Supreme Command knew that not only had it managed to bluff the Germans on the location of the landing beaches, but that Rommel was heading for Berlin and probably even the number of pretzels ordered by the garrison battery commander at Longues-sur-Mare.

Johnnie Colburn was from Texas, was slightly older than Dong Ong and, at 25 years old, had been married since 1941. For Johnnie's crew, 5 June would prove to be very busy indeed. Having flown their first mission on 4 June, their preparation and training were stretched immediately. The two days, 5th and 6th, merged into one continuous stream of action.

Their mission on 5 June was a diversionary raid to Cap Gris Nez but with weather conditions poor they were diverted to a secondary target. Flying at 19,900ft, they released their bombs at 10.19 am. The cloud cover meant that they bombed on the cue of a lead plane using an early radar device. Often referred to as the Pathfinder Force (PFF), these lead aircraft had their underslung ball turrets adapted with a device often referred to as Mickey but formally known as H2X. The first of a new breed of B-17s were also being introduced that had a chin radome that winched down once the plane was airborne. Despite the new devices, results proved to be poor on this raid.

Rob Simmons, Colburn's bombardier, kept a diary that he later transcribed into a fuller account of the day's actions. I include it here in its entirety:

D-Day, June 6th 1944

A Personal Story of the 388th Bombardment Group's Participation in The Allied Invasion of Normandy

On D-Day the 388th Bombardment Group flew three separate missions, sending 72 aircraft into combat; 71 successfully completed their mission – only one aircraft had to abort. At 0230 hours GMT (Greenwich Mean Time) our unit was to lead the entire 8th Air Force on the first bombing attacks in support of the Invasion! The 388th received the Distinguished Unit Citation for its Outstanding Performance.

This is my story:

Robert E. 'Bob' Simmon, Bombardier on Johnnie W. Colburn's Crew

Today is June 6, 2004. I wonder how many people who participated in the invasion of Normandy are still alive and wonder what they remember of that special day. Many tales of that day's history will never be told as we have lost so many of our military and civilian participants who never put their stories in print or just never wanted to tell their tale, perhaps preferring to forget the terrible things that happened to them and to their comrades or people near them. Many remarkable feats and accomplishments happened that day, and it is sad to think many of those pages of history will never be shared with those who remain to carry on the legacy of American Patriotism.

(Bob Simmon passed away nearly four years later on April 21, 2008 at the age of 86. Thankfully, he captured his role in the Allied Invasion of Normandy in the following account. Robert E. Simmon, Jr. – January 18, 2013)

It was about 2200 hours GMT June 5, 1944 on Station 136, Knettishall, England, the home base of the 388th Bombardment Wing (H), an 8th Air Force B-17 unit of the 45th Combat Wing of the 3rd Air Division, when my crew was awakened to fly a mission. We had only been in bed about an hour. It was very dark out, cloudy and misting just enough to drip off the ends of the Nissen hut that we had as our living quarters.

We had just become a Combat Operational Crew on June 4th when we flew our first combat mission. We flew our second earlier this very day attacking German coastal batteries at Cap Gris Nez, France that had guns powerful enough to reach England – endangering lives not only in the Straits of Dover, but also in Dover itself. These guns had been shelling that city intermittently since 1940.

We landed about noon from that mission so we were fairly well rested when they alerted us once again to fly a combat mission. The officers of our crew, the pilot, co-pilot, navigator and I, the bombardier, lived in a third of the hut. There was enough room for the officers of two other crews to reside there, but we were lucky to have just one other crew sharing it with us. The hut had just one small bathroom in the center rear area. That made it pretty complicated when eight people were all up at the same time trying to do their thing before going to the mission briefing, but we seemed to manage. The flight engineer, radio operator and our gunners were housed in the NCO area in a much larger Nissen hut.

We had little time to attend to our personal ablutionary rituals, prior to having a breakfast, of sorts. Most just drank coffee, juice or had some toast. The juice (orange or grapefruit) was canned, and we all called it battery acid. It was a good thing it was dispensed from stainless steel containers. It sure did have the capacity to wake one up. Food did not seem very interesting to us at that time of the night so it was unusually quiet in the Officer's Mess. We all knew of the impending invasion of France and so wondered if this was the day. No one seemed to know for certain. Any talk of the impending invasion was discouraged, as it was all so highly classified.

I was a bombardier on Johnnie W. Colburn's crew, a member of the 562nd Bombardment Squadron. At 2230 hours, our navigator, Morris H. Neiman, and I, along with the other crew navigation/bombing teams, were transported to the target study and mission planning area of our Intelligence and Operations building to plan the day's mission for our crew.

The route planning, target, bomb load, fuel load and all other factors necessary to execute the mission had been transmitted from 8th Air Force Headquarters to our unit in the form of a Frag (fragmentary) order earlier in the evening. This initial alert data allowed the full complement of the unit's work force to prepare the aircraft and crews for the day's operational mission. It was a complex problem for the Air Staff to make certain all information was included to assure mission success. Each day we were involved with some 2,000 aircraft for each mission which not only included the bombers, but fighters and other required support sorties, such as weather-reconnaissance and radio-relay aircraft, as well as all the sorties the Royal Air Force would engage in.

The initial Frag order required many revisions that were transmitted to the units involved in the day's mission. It took an immense number of people to get this show on the road. And just think of all the numbers of people that were involved with the manufacturing of these war implements and the immense logistical factors involved to support the operations. It is necessary to say that our entire nation had committed their lives in many ways to giving our combat personnel the means to conduct this War. There were so many unsung heroes that enabled us to take the fight to the enemy.

When the routing and Target location were given to us, we immediately knew this could be the day we were all looking forward to, however the term "D-Day" was never used in our pre-briefing. The target was: Gun Installations South of Le Havre, France.

Morrie Nieman, our navigator, did the route planning and made our flight plan which consisted of the flight-plan log, Metro information, all maps and charts necessary, and back-up data to cover unforeseen contingencies. My portion of the pre-mission planning consisted of the route study and study of the impending target and all areas surrounding the target area. My mission package also included detailed Metro information necessary to compute height above the target and True Air Speed so the correct data could be set in the Norden bombsight for an accurate bomb release. It also contained a pre-computed set of data to be set into the Norden bombsight for the planned bomb run. The next scheduled event was the General Briefing. This took place at 2400 hours midnight. The entire crew attended this briefing, which covered all aspects of the mission – routing, weather, radio procedures, assembly tactics, intelligence data that included all information concerning the expected flak areas, and where the enemy fighter intercepts would possibly occur. It covered all facets of the Mission from start engines to recovery at the home base at the termination of the sortie.

It was a general overview of the entire operation and detailed in many areas, but the time allocated to the briefing was limited. The areas not covered in detail were left to the responsibility of the officers to pass to the rest of their crew members who were not at the special briefings held prior to or immediately after the main briefing.

An item covered at this briefing that was quite a change from normal tactics – guns would be manned but not test-fired at any time; gunners will not fire at any airplane at any time unless being attacked. Also covered – bombing on primary targets will be carried out within time limits prescribed, otherwise secondary or last resort targets will be bombed; no second bomb runs will be made on the primary targets; and take-offs will be accomplished according to schedule, regardless.

The briefing was always concluded by comments from the Group Commander and a prayer by our chaplains. Individual chaplains of each faith were available for those who needed them. There was a lot of loud discussion after this particular briefing because we finally knew the day of reckoning was upon us. This was 'D-Day'. We were all very excited to be a participant in this great operation.

We next drew our personal equipment, parachutes, oxygen masks, escape kits, etc. The gunners and flight engineer headed for the airplane – the gunners to install the guns; the flight engineer to work with the aircraft crew chief to make sure the airplane was fuelled and ready to fly the mission. The officers next arrived at the aircraft and performed their pre-flight then we all made our last nervous call of nature at the rear of the aircraft. We had a short crew briefing by our pilot concerning the crew procedures and importance of this mission. We then boarded our aircraft and settled into our positions for engine start. As I remember, engine start was 0215.

It was still pretty cloudy, a bit foggy and damp and chilly. We got all engines started and then waited for the flare to start taxiing towards the active runway. The flare was fired and we started to taxi. We were to launch a total of 42 aircraft so the line of airplanes on the taxiways was impressive to see. We had 18 aircraft in the 'A' Group, which we were in, 18 in the 'B' Group and furnished 6 additional aircraft for a Composite Group consisting of aircraft from the 96th Bomb Group and the 452nd Bomb Group, which were also members of our 45th Combat Wing. The green flare was fired and the first aircraft started its take-off roll. We were number 16 to take off so we did not have too long to wait on the taxiway. All aircraft were off the ground by 0254 hours – a very impressive display of the results of many ground personnel who made ready these aircraft for this very important mission.

Our 'A' Group was the Lead Group on this mission – first in line of the entire 8th Air Force! The 'A' Group Command Pilot was Lt Col Chester Cox, the Vice Commander of our Group. The Deputy Leader was Lt Col Henry Henggeler. The Lead Pilot with Lt Col Chester Cox was 1st Lt Campbell, and the Lead Navigator was 1st Lt Carraway. We led an element of three in the Low Squadron of the Lead Group.

The Assembly of the Group was made more complicated when the Buncher Beacon, which was our radio aid for assembly, went out of commission. Additionally, visibility was extremely poor and the fact that it was still very dark did not help the operation.

Formation was effected and we departed on time for the coast-out point. It was much easier for our Group since we were the Leader and the rest of the bomber stream had to form on us and then follow us into the Target Area. Each Group had its own flare color to identify the unit and aid assembly. The sky was filled with colored flares – it looked like the Fourth of July. En route, our Group Commander made the decision to bomb using Pathfinder Force (PFF) Methods (radar bombing) since the visibility was very poor.

However, the visibility was not too poor for me to see the immense flotilla there in the English Channel holding all our troops heading into that terrible battle that was to consume so many lives. I was very glad to be a part of the operation and very glad that I was in an aircraft and not down on one of those ships or boats. We saw C-47 aircraft towing gliders and many other types of aircraft in the sky as we headed in on our bomb run. It was an awesome sight, which I will never forget. We could see some shells bursting near the shoreline of France, but there was so much smoke and haze it made it hard to make out much detail on the ground.

About that time, we re-formed into squadrons line abreast and bombing was done by groups. As I mentioned previously, our Group was the first to drop bombs in support of the invasion on this day. Bombs were away at 0656 hours from 15,050ft for the 'A' Group, and 0703 hours from 13,850ft for the 'B' Group. The composite group did not attack and returned with their bombs.

No flak or enemy aircraft were seen. We all returned to base safely and all were on the ground by 1043 hours. That was mission No. 1. Our Group was to fly three missions this day, and we were alerted upon landing to prepare to fly mission No. 3.

We left all our equipment at the aircraft while it was being refuelled and loaded with bombs for our next mission. The crew chief had to change some spark plugs, but there was minimum maintenance required for the second mission. The take-off time for the second mission was set for approximately 1700 hours. That gave us time for a bit of rest and time to get some food into our systems. We accomplished that in a highly professional manner.

At 1230 hours, the navigator and I attended the mission-planning and target-study briefing for our second mission while the rest of the crew made sure the aircraft was properly prepared. We could not get any definitive information concerning how the landing phase of the invasion was going – everything was hush-hush. Some said they had heard we were doing OK, but that we had suffered many casualties – so we all said a few prayers for our valiant attack force. The target for our second mission was the coastal defences at Pont-L'Eveque, France.

The weather had moderated, at least at our base, and we even saw a few rays of sun. It was a bit warmer so we thought our second mission would go pretty well as briefed. We assembled at 1420 hours for the second briefing. We were told that the invasion was going very well and that made us all feel a bit better. One of our crews, 1st Lt. Gabler's, was to carry Sgt. Saul Levitt, Yank (a weekly magazine published by the Army) staff correspondent. At 1500 hours, the mission was scrubbed. We all milled around talking and then started to disperse back to our quarters.

About 1620 hours, we had loaded on the truck for transportation to our airplanes so we could pick up our personal gear to close down the day's activity when they came running out of the briefing room telling us that the mission was back on. The trucks immediately took us to our airplanes as take-off was scheduled for no later than 1730 hours, leaving little time to loiter. We hustled aboard our aircraft and got ready for engine start.

We were scheduled to put up two Groups of twelve aircraft – each led by a Pathfinder crew. One group, our 'A' Group that we were again scheduled with, was to fly the high position in the 45th 'A' Combat Wing and the 'B' Group was to fly the high position in the 45th 'B' Combat Wing. The 45th Combat Wing led the 3rd Air Division. Our primary target assigned was Pont-L'Eveque, aiming at German troop concentrations. Colonel David, our Group Commander, flew in the Lead Aircraft of the 'A' Group as Command Pilot with 1st Lt Gabler as Deputy Lead and 1st Lt Campbell as the Lead Pilot (PFF). Major Forrest was the Command Pilot of the 'B' Group, with 1st Lt Prendergast as Deputy Lead and 1st Lt Kneemeyer as the Lead Pilot (PFF).

Twelve aircraft of the 'A' Group were all airborne by 1722 hours, and the twelve aircraft of the 'B' Group were all airborne by 1744. Assembly was effected as briefed and no aircraft aborted. We proceeded to the coast-out point of the White Cliffs of Dover and encountered considerable cloud coverage en route. The visibility was getting very poor, less than a ¼ of a mile. This made it difficult for the formations to stay in visual contact with one another.

Our Group, the 'A' Group, could not attack the primary target as it was obscured by clouds. We had been briefed to only attack the targets under visual conditions to make certain that we would not release bombs on our own troops. We then proceeded to look for a target of opportunity and ended up hitting a railroad choke point at Flers about 40 miles south of Caen, France. Bombs were away at 2022 hours from 22,000 feet. Strike photos showed a loose pattern on the railroad choke point and a road intersection. One crew reported at crew debriefing that they saw a large explosion.

The 'B' Group attacked the primary target as briefed. No enemy flak or aircraft were encountered. Both Groups re-joined and turned back toward England. The weather conditions continued to deteriorate and the decision was made to break up in elements of three aircraft and to descend to a lower altitude in hopes the visibility would improve. We were the leader of three aircraft and as we approached the White Cliffs of Dover an English destroyer fired about ten rounds of flak at us, but fortunately they missed us.

We were two or three thousand feet over England heading toward our home base when we lost sight of our two wingmen. Johnnie, our pilot, pulled up a bit and suddenly right at the 12 o'clock aircraft position, nose on was another B-17! Johnnie reacted immediately and dropped our left wing. We missed that other airplane by no more than a foot. I had a wonderful view of the entire operation as I was sitting in my bombardier's nose position. There was no time for any comment during the encounter, but we in the front end of our B-17 were a bit excited and very grateful for the fine reaction and coordination of our pilot. He saved our lives.

However, that manoeuvre left us all alone and lost over England. It was very foggy and black as it could get at night. Radio silence was always maintained as much as possible, but we decided to utilize the lost procedure, which we all called 'DARKY'. We transmitted on a secure frequency and the ground control, DARKY, finally gave us a 'DF (direction-finding) steer' toward an RAF (Royal Air Force) field, Tuddenham, about twenty miles WSW of Knettishall. By then we were really in a world of hurts as we were about out of fuel. We saw the lights of the RAF field and started our approach. We had an 8th Air Force Staff Officer, a Major, aboard as a passenger and he started firing flares out of the flare port between the pilots on the top of the fuselage. He was trying to alert the ground personnel that we were in an emergency condition and might crash. Some of the flares he fired were colored RED-RED and these were supposed to be fired only if there were wounded aboard.

We were high on approach and Johnnie knew that he could not risk a missed approach or go-around approach since we were so short on fuel. We touched down about halfway down the runway and Johnnie saw that we would run out of runway before we could get stopped so he tried to deliberately ground loop the plane but it would not cooperate. The tail wheel was still locked in the landing position and would not allow the aircraft to turn enough to effect a ground loop. It also had a shear pin that was supposed to break if side pressure was applied to the tail wheel to allow a ground loop, but this one did not shear as it was designed to do.

He and Russ Weekes, the co-pilot, had the brakes on the rudder pedals as far down as they would go. We had a screeching beast sliding down the runway. We hit the gravel over-run end of the runway and finally slid to a stop. It was a heart-stopping moment. It took a few moments for us all to compose ourselves before we could even talk. We looked out of the airplane and, although we had no wounded aboard, the British had two or three ambulances there waiting for us. We finally managed to taxi in and park, being directed by the RAF ground personnel. Two of our four engines ran out of fuel and quit while we were taxiing into the parking area. It was now 0025 hours on the 7th of June. The British were a little unhappy with us over the RED-RED flares, which caused them to dispatch the ambulances, but soon forgot all about that as we talked about our mission and the invasion. They transported us to an area where we gave a short mission debrief and then they took us to the Mess Hall where we all had some fresh eggs and a good breakfast.

We were so beat that we kept falling asleep on the ride to our billets. We had been up and on duty since 2200 hours on the 5th of June, had flown two missions for a total of fourteen hours and ten minutes, and here it was the 7th of June. It was indeed the Longest Day for us. Since we were so tired, none of us thought to call our home base and tell them we were at RAF Tuddenham and on the ground safely. The next day the weather improved so we refueled our airplane and flew back to Knettishall. After landing, parking, and unloading we were debriefed and found out that since we had not reported in after landing safely at Tuddenham, we were listed as MIA (Missing In Action).

The weather turned bad later on so no missions were scheduled. We finally got some well-deserved rest and recuperation.

Perhaps fatigue played a part in the omission to tell Knettishall of their safe diversion to Tuddenham; perhaps inexperience. It is also a reminder that these were young men and the lapse in communication was akin in civilian terms to forgetting to tell your parents where you were the night before. The dawning realization of the 'Missing in Action' report must have been a sobering thought as, given normal circumstances when a plane fails to return, it is the phrase that eventually is used to inform relatives at home. It is fully understandable given the action and significance of the day both in the crew's history and world history that some lapse of concentration happened. There is, however, a quiet omission in the account as to what was said to them as they would have faced some searching questions. On the other hand, such was the intensity of the days ahead, all sorts of issues that in peacetime flying would have been addressed with some vigour were let go – this was war. As a postscript to the incident, Johnnie recalls that he had the opportunity to apologize to his commander, Major Goodman, at a reunion for failing to inform Knettishall of their safe landing. There was a little delay; the reunion was in 1999.

Whilst the Colburn crew sheltered at Tuddenham, Dong Ong and crew were heading out for their first combat mission of their war on 7 June. The task was to bomb a railway bridge and marshalling yards at Nantes in France. Nantes is some distance from the invasion beaches to the south and west and would not, at first glance, seem like an important target. However, success in Normandy depended on Hitler not being able to deploy reinforcements to the area in time to halt an advance. Normandy had already been kept a secret and all efforts had gone into trying to fool the Germans that the hammer would fall much further north. The Ong crew's despatch to Nantes illustrates the keenness of the Allied command to restrict Hitler's options in drawing in forces, particularly Panzer divisions, from the south of France. Targets including the railways in this region had not yet received the attention necessary to prevent such a movement of men and tanks. One of the reasons for this was that the Allied command had no wish to tip off the Germans as to their intentions for Normandy.

The attack that day was rated as a success with more than one target being hit. Dong Ong doesn't record how he felt, but records show he had flown his first mission with another crew on 6 June attacking railways near Flers. This was normal practice to enable a new pilot to gain a sliver of combat experience before leading his own crew. It was the same raid the Colburn crew flew on and with the poor weather in England pushing the Colburn crew to land away from their home field, it was after midnight before Dong made Knettishall. He must have had little sleep as planning was under way for the Nantes mission later that day. No doubt the adrenalin of this 22-year-old kicked in as he led his own crew on their first mission.

This was a double initiation for the Ong and Colburn crews. In normal combat flying they would be joining the bomber streams and targeted to factories, oil installations and other strategic targets. Over the period of the Normandy landings, the 388th was tasked to fly against targets to support their ground troops, something no one had yet done.

Chapter 3

Through the Keyhole

I've never looked through a keyhole without finding someone was looking back.

– Judy Garland

I didn't doubt that despite fine words and good intentions, the task I had set myself was going to be a challenge. How do you go about finding the families of, at best, old men and most probably men who had passed away? My initial source was an engraving done seventy years ago but now, only possible in the last few years, I had the internet and a wealth of information. I had to accept that when it came to names, the internet probably listed every name and initial possible, so it was not just a matter of finding a name, it was a deeper investigative enterprise. Add to this conundrum the fact that I'm a Brit living thousands of miles away and in a different time zone. They were far from forgotten but in the internet age the older generation does not use email or social media as much as younger people. Even the children of the crew – if they had children – were likely to be in their sixties and I might have to rely on a third generation of their family to follow the tracing task through.

My first conversation, with Terry Ong, was encouraging. There were a couple of silences and pauses for thought, but Terry told me his son, Justin, would help get things together as he had a keen interest in such things. I wondered if I had just dropped lucky with my first attempt at a contact. Perhaps it was best I had a first positive experience because if a series of dead ends had presented itself I would probably have lost heart. I was assured though that the records of the 388th Association and database would provide a rock upon which to build a house.

Another pressing and disturbing thought pervaded my thinking: would the relatives be interested? I have to pick this thought apart and divide it into two categories. The first seems obvious: if your father had been in the Second World War and served in an often talked about and written about field, it is safe to assume that close relatives would be interested, even enthusiastic. This was a comforting thought. I wasn't trying to sell anything, not a concept or a dry intellectual history, but I wanted to talk about their father, uncle or cousin. It was the second category of 'disinterest' that troubled me most. Just because a relative served in an honourable role it is not safe to assume they were nice people. Wars can make nice people terrible and terrible people even worse. Stories abound of returning veterans not being able to cope, of drinking, violence and abuse. Without delving too deeply into psychology, the simple truth might be that certain characters don't cope well with life, war or no wars. Phoning a complete stranger and asking about their father may be a disturbing, even traumatic, experience; I could be the blunt instrument of bad memories swung above their heads. The old Yorkshire saying 'there's nowt so queer as folk' has an enduring ring to me – an old saying that uses 'queer' and 'folk' in a different way to our latest colloquialisms. I knew I was going to unearth some strange situations and in writing a book I was going to have to edit pieces out of certain stories for the sake of comfort and reputation of the families.

Fear is another factor I had to overcome. I don't like buying drinks at a bar or asking questions in shops, unless they are 'man' shops that sell bits for cars or other similar stuff. The number of times Trish has said, 'Why don't you ask,' and I say, 'I don't want to,' cannot be counted in our marriage due to their great number. Of course, when I'm lost I never ask anyone, at least when I'm in a car. Strangely, if I was walking I probably would because walking takes time and effort – and I can't abide wasting either on wandering. One other silly discomfort falls into this category; I don't like American ring tones. I don't know why, I can't imagine it makes any difference, but somehow when the telephone makes a longer ringing sound than the British tones, it sets off an anxiety. Perhaps now is a good time to stop listing my peculiarities. Suffice to say, the task in hand would be demanding.

My September 1944 crew pilot was Johnnie W. Colburn and the first thing I noticed was that Johnnie was spelled 'Jonnie' on the trophy. I trusted the 388th website database more and it told me Johnnie's birth date in 1919, and that he was originally from Texas. His 'W' was Wilmer – a good mixture of names with which to try a search. It was so good that his name popped up almost immediately and I saw his wife, Beatrice, had passed away in 2009. Two children were listed in her obituary and one, a daughter, also had quite a distinctive name pattern. I won't give all the details here and I'll just use one of her names, Darlene. I trawled through other obituaries and grave websites but there was no mention of Johnnie – could he still be with us aged 95? I could also see his daughter, Darlene, had popped up on Facebook. Indeed, it seemed only one person on the planet shared her names. Up came photos and entries and, suddenly, a picture of her with an old man under a B-17 bomber. Another photograph posted in February 2014 showed Johnnie – it was another exciting moment! Trish was already propped up in bed reading when I appeared waving my laptop to show her the picture.

The last few days had seen a pattern of late nights put into this search. I sent a message to Darlene on Facebook, but with no reply; I suppose I tend to ignore complete strangers, too. How frustrating. Perhaps the dire warnings about how exposed our identities are on the internet need to be heeded. Before long, like an internet stalker, I knew much of Darlene's immediate family, where she worked, that a daughter had married recently and much about her private and working life. Eventually, I sent an invite via another social media website and got the reply:

'Hello David,
How do I know you?
Have a great day.
Darlene'

My reply had a phrase that was to be a recurring one in future days, 'You don't know me yet, but … ' and I told her the story of finding the trophy.

The email reply said it all and was headed 'THAT'S MY DAD!'

A good many emails began to flow to and fro and I started asking questions, which Darlene put to Johnnie. Just as we started this transatlantic communication, Johnnie became a little unwell and this meant patience as he needed rest; after all, at 95 he should be allowed the luxury of taking it easy.

Each night towards the end of May and into June seemed to get later and some nights I would spend hours looking though names and sources to try to find families. One tradition in America really helped me and that was the naming of first sons after their father, very often with the same middle name, to create a 'Jr'. This was also a British tradition, perhaps spanning the world too, but the British have gradually begun to skip a generation or two. Invariably the names return into the family but in the grandchildren, as in the case of our two daughters who have the first names of both my grandmothers.

I was hoping that key elements of the lives of these airmen would not be lost in the detail. What was their favourite food, what movies did they like and what hobbies did they pursue all feature in building a rounded picture. To quote (possibly misquote!), Martin Luther King Jr, 'What is man?' I've read many books about aviation and military history, and perhaps the striking thing is that many authors cannot describe the individuals of whom they write because, of course, they have not met them. They can write about what they did, even why they did it, but when it comes to daily life they can only guess at what colour socks they preferred.

My early idea was to write this book almost as a diary, an 'as it happened' venture, but so much happened with so much information coming in that I found myself writing in the past tense. As I wrote, it was 5 June 2014, right on the seventieth anniversary of the eve of D-Day and the start of Dong Ong and Johnnie Colburn's missions, the flying that earned them a place on the trophy. The appearance of the trophy came right on cue; after nearly seventy years of disappearance the timing, at least to me, was remarkable.

I had thought initially that I would be even-handed in my research, find one name in one crew and then try another in the next crew. It didn't work out that way. The presence of Johnnie, even thousands of miles away in Texas, spurred me on and one by one his crew appeared. Only Johnnie remains with us out of his crew; finding and talking to the other families was still the big challenge.

With the anniversary of D-Day nearly upon us, Darlene told me that Johnnie had to go into hospital with pneumonia; he had been troubled the past few days with a chest infection, it seemed. I had primed Darlene with a load of questions but now was a really bad time to seek answers. I had to trust that the obvious longevity he had enjoyed meant he was capable of getting well again. Still, it was a blow but I had to examine my motives. Johnnie's health was really all that mattered. Darlene gave me an important contact though, the son of Robert 'Bob' Simmon, Colburn's bombardier. Simmon was also a key figure in the 388th Association for many years and had written about some of the experiences he had with the Colburn crew. He passed away in 2009 but his son, also Rob, seemed to have a lot of records and information.

By the significant 6 June anniversary I had talked in person to two other Colburn crew relatives, Ann Kragle, wife of radio operator George Kragle, and Blanche Nutt, the daughter-in-law of rear gunner Frank Nutt. Ann sounded a little confused when I spoke to her and I began to wonder whether calling people out of blue was such a wise move. At the end of the day though, I knew I had to start somewhere and the quickest form of contact is the telephone. I had sent her son Jim a message on Facebook and I hadn't heard back. Of all the Kragles on Facebook, Jim had posted the Colburn crew photo, which of course had his dad in it, on 28 May, within days of me beginning to look.

My conversation with Ann therefore sounded a bit strange. It went something like:

'I've left a message with your son, Jim, today.'
'You've spoken to Jim today! Where?'
'Oh, not on the phone, on Facebook. On the internet.'
'Where is he?'
'I don't know, it didn't tell me.'
'Oh, 'cos I sure don't know where he is ... .'

Thankfully, despite my inconsistent start, I got in contact with another son, George Kragle, and I had a firm contact with yet another name. The vagaries of the internet are somewhat difficult to explain and as useful a tool as it now is, it brings its own set of related problems. I had also tracked down two other families of trophy names and called and left messages for the Neiman (navigator) and Heslam (Mickey operator – see later) relatives.

As 6 June drew to a close on the British side of the Atlantic, Rob Simmon Jr responded by email and, through a series of emails over the next few days, information and photographs began to flow. As I've mentioned, his father Bob Simmon was Colburn's bombardier and, of all the men whose name might have appeared on the trophy, Bob later became a shining light in the 388th Association and built up an early database of contacts and information, in the days of card files. It was clear that all the crew kept in contact through the 388th Association, but one by one, as they passed away, contact was lost. I realized what I was doing was trying to trace and join families together that had never related. Their father's had but the next generation had lost their key element in the story. This is a natural process but, with my experience of

First World War research, I realized it was the second and third generations who were now fascinated by their grandfather's or great uncle's involvement.

The definition of the crew is also interesting; all the textbooks will tell you that a B-17 had a ten-man crew but the trophy only lists nine. In the case of the Colburn crew, there are ten on their well-sourced crew photo, but Heslam, who is named on the trophy, is not there. The answer lies in the changing roles within a B-17 crew and also the seniority and experience of pilots such as Colburn. The waist gunners seem to have been dispensed with in certain cases and the lower ball turret on lead aeroplanes had the radar bombing equipment stowed in it instead. This equipment, the role of which is often referred to as PFF, Pathfinder Force, was called Mickey and the operator gained the identity. Richard Heslam was a specialist who came along later, did not train at the start with the Colburn crew and changed crews as necessary to operate the Mickey equipment.

As an aside, it's worth noting that the Pathfinder Force in the US Air Force, and I'm aware that the correct term at this time should be the US Army Air Force, differed in character and role from the British Pathfinders. The British, bombing mostly at night, chose to put their blind bombing devices Gee, Oboe and H2S radar on to separate aircraft in a specialist squadron outside the main bomber force. As the war progressed, the Pathfinders were equipped with a variety of aircraft as well as the heavy bomber. Typically these were the lightweight, fast and very manoeuvrable de Havilland Mosquito. The aim was to fly just ahead of a main force and, once the target was identified, drop coloured flare markers on to the area in advance of the bombing force. In the American system, the role and equipment remained with lead aircraft that were part of the regular squadrons and not an entirely separate unit – at least in the case of the 388th Group. Something else was happening in the defence of the daylight US bomber and that was the role of the fighter cover flying with them. Gunners, so essential at the beginning, were being removed in the case of lead aircraft to make way for the new bomb aiming technology – and its operator. There was a recognition that, slowly but surely, substantive air superiority was being gained. The most obvious change was in colour scheme as the B-17 and B-24 bombers moved out of their original brown and drab green colours to polished aluminium. Brightly coloured tail insignia and nose art emphasized that there was a new air of confidence about the force. No longer was it assumed that hostile fighters were above them looking down, it was assumed that fighters were climbing trying to reach them.

There is an assumption that all the crews stayed together as one unit and there are plenty of instances where crews flew all their missions together with little change. In the cast of the Colburn and Ong crews, this is only partly the case as changes seemed to have been made mid-tour for some. As explained, perhaps some of this was due to the introduction of new technology, but there seems to be a margin of crew change through injury and operational rigours.

Justin Ong, Dong's grandson, took a keen interest in the search for information and sent me a fascinating selection of papers regarding his grandfather's career – a career that extended well beyond the Second World War – and I realized that, in the telling of the story, a whole web of additional facts and personalities begin to emerge. Like any good Shakespearian play, the main actors are accompanied by numerous other speaking parts and the temptation to move sideways and start investigating them as well is a daily challenge. How much time and how big would this book get? Having decided that I would stick to the names on the trophy, it was now clear that not to mention some other notable names would do them a massive injustice. Other recognized and established crew names were not on the trophy and I conclude it is only a snapshot in time and perhaps only refers to a mission or two that was outstanding enough to merit an award. Ong's navigator, Edmund 'Goldy' Goldstein, appears in the 'team photo' along with the trophy as 'one of theirs' but had stopped flying with the Ong crew in July.

Darlene had given me Rob Simmon Jr's phone number and, rather than just calling it, I took some time to line a time up with Rob via email. This, I decided, was far more sensible as my late nights were really catching up with me. My day job is a builder and, although it would be nice to report that I have a large staff who work efficiently to my command, I had decided many years before to devote my life to a simpler pattern; which means I do most of the work myself. After plastering a ceiling or installing new windows I was getting home and, after a meal, starting the process that would lead to the late-night phone calls. Even calls to America at midnight might only translate to late afternoon or evening for my recipients with the time zone differences. The other problem was that I was thinking – thinking all the time some days about information coming to me, what it meant and how to write it down. It was a good job that many of my work tasks were familiar to me as the body was doing one thing while the mind wandered off.

So, my call to Rob Simmon was planned and my day ordered around it. We talked for more than an hour and it was a good start. What I really wanted was the real men behind the engraved names and fading photos – the problem with so many histories is that the men or women fade into a flat image based around what they did and not who they were. It's very apparent that in this story what they did moulded who they were for the rest of their lives. Seeing Johnnie Colburn's recent photos, he still sports a leather jacket with large badges, including the 388th Bomb Group motif. Those months in 1944 not only defined them as young men, in their survival – and many did not survive – it transformed who they would be in the future and, just as importantly, who their society recognized them to be. In middle age they would become respected and employable, in old age revered and doted on. I asked Rob some questions about his father that he couldn't answer; the question had not arisen or been answered during his father's life and now, here was this strange Brit coming along and raking the garden. They were some simple enough questions but my quest for detail aside from the main facts seemed more of a challenge – they had never talked about it. This is very common and in my research on the First World War, relatives who remember their forbears in affection and detail will often say, 'But he never talked about it.' Some of this phenomenon in relation to witnessing the horrors of war is understandable but some of it happens by accident. My father was an Anglican clergyman and recalls talking to an old man about his time on a battleship at the Battle of Jutland. Fortunately, my dad is interested in all things military too and I can see where the roots of my inquisitions come from. The old man talked freely and in detail of his experiences, and after a while said: 'I've never told anyone this before.'

'Why?' my dad asked. 'Did you not tell your family?'

'Well, they never asked – they didn't seem interested,' the man replied.

My conversation with Rob promised many things but, obviously, I had found a channel for many of my questions and someone to bounce ideas off. I thanked him for the conversation by email later and said that, 'We seem to have much in common and absolutely nothing at the same time!'

A couple of days after my talk with Rob, I phoned Darlene for the first time and asked after her father Johnnie. He was recovering slowly from the pneumonia and the plan was for him to move from his sheltered housing to a nursing facility. Darlene was charming and helpful, and what I had expected with her Texas accent coming through. This journey was a road trip into American culture for me too and to understand where these men came from and who they were to become, I was going to have to embrace more than historical facts. Darlene wanted to ask her dad some of the questions I had queued up, but I really didn't want to push this too much. However, Johnnie was my last chance saloon on some details – only he would know. I should add, by now I had realized that Johnnie was the last of his crew still with us. Of all the names on the September 1944 list, it was he, the pilot, who was last man standing. Of Ong's crew, I had only just started research but the likelihood of finding a living name seemed slim indeed.

With all my attention on the Colburn crew, I was beginning to feel a little guilty about not progressing the August Crew of Dong Ong. I picked a name from the trophy and decided to look at Carl N. Lindorf, the tail gunner. I noticed on the website that his full name was Carl Nels Oscar Lindorf, the researcher's dream; a name of individuality. My first search found him straight away and, linking through to a family history site, I found his daughter had posted the crew photo on a site asking for information. It was from five years earlier, so I wondered whether answering on the forum was worthwhile, but I gave it a go and sent a message to Penny. Her reply came later that day and, although she was travelling at that present time, she told me that she had lots of information to share and that she was very excited.

With this kind of research in the relatively new world of social media, I realized that at the end (if there were ever going to be a true end) I would probably have forty new friends; social media 'friends' at least. It seemed in this brave new internet world it would be an exemplary exercise, as the new friends would be previously unknown strangers and the meeting would mostly be virtual.

After seventy years it was time, albeit on a very small scale, to announce the trophy's existence to a wider audience. I had posted the story of finding it and the start of the book writing to my friends on Facebook. One friend worked at our local radio station and I got a call from a producer on BBC Radio Cumbria who liked the story and wondered if I would do a breakfast show phone interview. It was conducted on the same morning of *Antiques Roadshow*, a BBC TV show that moved around the country filming for the day at a location where the public would bring their precious items to be scrutinized by experts.

So, after the interview I set off the twenty miles down the road to Lowther Castle near Penrith with Ellen, my youngest daughter in tow. The historic family seat of the Earls of Lonsdale, Lowther Castle is now a ruin after the estate was driven to the edge of bankruptcy by the 5th Earl of Lonsdale in the early 1930s. His love of cars, horses and gambling were hallmarks of his legendary extravagance which effectively wiped out centuries of accumulated wealth. The weather, for Britain, was great with lots of warm sunshine, which promptly toasted Ellen's shoulders a rosy red colour. Being 16 though, she is old enough to look after herself, so I was not subjected to the 'neglectful father' talk by Trish when I got home. Indeed, the occasion when I lost her on a beach in Margate to find her splashing about in a rubber ring with another unconnected family is told and retold at dinner parties – but she was only 3 at the time. Today, we had to queue for hours to get a spot next to an expert at a small umbrella-shaded table.

I had to smile to myself that of approximately 35,000 items viewed that day, it was the trophy that had got a radio slot. However, our visit did not get filmed, which was a pity. I had hoped vaguely that if it were featured it would jog someone's memory of seeing it in a home in Edinburgh and perhaps start to answer the mystery of how it got north of the border. Nevertheless, we did get the opinion of two experts and the interest in the story behind the trophy was marked. We learned a few interesting facts that answered some questions about the trophy's origin. Firstly, I had wondered if it had been purchased and shipped from the States. The answer was that it was English, made of copper with silver plating and, surprisingly, was late Victorian, circa 1880. Clearly, it had been an existing piece, perhaps picked out from a jeweller's shop to be engraved. It was ornate enough to have been in a large house or even a hotel. This answered, or partly answered, one of my first questions to 388th historian Dick Henggeler: were there any other monthly crew trophies? Dick did not know of any and he was making enquiries. It would seem that the silverware, at least for August and September, was a special purchase and not part of a job lot. Perhaps there were other engraved objects for other months? Only time would tell. I did not realize when I first contacted Dick that he was part of the bigger story as well. His father, Francis, led a squadron as deputy or commander on twenty-seven missions – indeed, he had flown with Johnnie Colburn.

I had a little more to do to determine the origin of the trophy. It was not valuable in itself and perhaps its availability and reasonable price might have been an attraction in picking it. I had two other theories, one that it had been donated, possibly by a local family or hotel, and the second was that it had been 'liberated' from a hotel or possibly an RAF Officer's mess during a bout of revelry. However, the 'theft' theory looked less likely as, although no doubt there were some bar room cowboys, there were also principled and honest men who would take exception to dishonestly gained goods. It seemed a wild shot, but I decided to try to find established jewellers in the towns of Thetford or Diss near the Knettishall airfield that might, just might, have purchase records dating back that long ago.

Mid-June in England can be a very pleasant time. The sun can be warm and spring is at its finest in many places. That year, 2014, we went down to Whitstable on the North Kent coast for a holiday and took Trish's octogenarian parents with us. It had been a while since we went away with them. Fortunately, they live close to us at home, although we know that given age, life and diaries perhaps only a few opportunities remain for us to get together. Lizzie, our eldest, married last year so there was one fewer person on the trip and it was all a bit different. I was born in Dover but I don't remember it as our family moved when I was only 18 months old. Through getting to know a number of friends in Kent, we began to visit on holidays as well as frequently passing through the port to catch a ferry to France. Generally, we love to go to France but often the mid-year budget won't stretch that far, so we like to find places to stay where we can see France and the Channel. Our favourite haunt is a rental property perched high on the White Cliffs of Dover with a large picture window overlooking the Channel. This location is so near the cliff edge that a sleep walk of fewer than fifty yards would mean a 200ft 'free fall' at the end of the garden. It is as dramatic as any property in the region and filled with history of its own. Built just before the First World War, the structure was a control office for gun batteries defending the Kent coast. There was an arms race on with Germany and this had focused sharply on naval power, which meant conversely that coastal gun defences needed to be improved and expanded. Nobody could have imagined that only some thirty years later, and after a war of immense carnage in Europe, the coast would be threatened with invasion. Gun control rooms were built underground for this war and the watch office continued as a look-out station. Of the staff watching the Channel, one young private in the British Army was of Russian, German, Polish and Jewish aristocratic birth, a certain Peter Ustinov. Ustinov had seemingly decided firmly where his loyalties lay and served in the army that his father, as a German officer in the First World War, had fought against. Despite the cold damp night, watches on the cliffs, Ustinov must have loved this place. He bought it from the War Office at the end of the war and converted it into a holiday retreat. Whenever we visit, we can understand why, despite being an actor of huge repute, he enjoyed the simplicity of sitting on a cliff top.

Through all the years of our visits, I had never imagined that it would hold a place in this latest story. As a forward observation position, the men there would have watched the daylight raids on the French coast. The men of the 388th Bombardment Group in their formations would pass overhead and binoculars would scan upwards from the soldiers below. At times it was just to catch a glimpse of the contrails on the high-flying B-17s through broken cloud. By this time though, Ustinov's theatrical career had already commenced and as batman (effectively an officer's servant) to the actor David Niven, his rapid promotion to film and celebrity was a recognition of his obvious abilities. He was no longer on the cliffs watching for a German invasion.

This year though the property was fully booked and so we found a seafront residence in Whitstable instead. This place has a wealth of history of its own and would also have seen the passage of the swathes of bombers heading over the English Channel from their bases and assembly points. When I took time out to write, from my upstairs room I could look out north over the sea with the Isle of Sheppey ahead and, over the horizon, the flat lands of Essex, Suffolk and Norfolk, the cradle of bomber country. As the story of the trophy crews takes place in 1944, it is worth casting an eye back a little further to gain some perspective of the country and war they joined. To the airmen who were plotting their courses, Whitstable lay in the well-defined nose of Kent jutting out from the Thames Estuary ahead of them. At the base of this nose were the famous White Cliffs of Dover immortalised by Vera Lynn in the song written just before America entered the war. As an aside, the American writers Walter Kent and Nat Burton didn't realize that Britain did not have any bluebirds but in the poetic rhyming of the song, one feels sparrows, or even swallows, would not have had the same evocative ring. This was, after all, one of the most successful international songs and, for returning Allied airmen, the White Cliffs represented an immense feeling of safety. However, there was always the chance of being fired on from the coastal defences and even shipping, as Colburn's crew discovered on returning from their second mission of D-Day. Perhaps the destroyer involved was feeling a bit twitchy given the enormity of the day but, still, there must have been some red faces among the Jolly Jack Tars when they realized their error.

Kent is also Spitfire country as the Battle of Britain was fought above it; I should also mention Hurricanes too for historical accuracy – there were, in fact, more Hurricanes than Spitfires in the battle through those weeks of summer 1940. As if to emphasize the nostalgia of the region, a Spitfire flew over Whitstable as we returned from Canterbury a few miles down the road. I was, therefore, sitting in the midst of the theatre where once played our actors. The Battle of Britain was the first substantial tactical battle fought between fighter and bomber of the Second World War. The Spanish Civil War had some aggressive air fighting in which German intervention lacked technical superiority over the Russian-made Rata fighters until the introduction of the Messerschmitt Bf 109 in late 1936. The Germans had gained the all-important knowledge of what was required in a fighter that could take on and destroy bombers; speed, agility, power and an armament capable of inflicting serious damage in a single pass. In the Spitfire and Hurricane the RAF had sufficient technical ability to take on the waves of bombers and fighters launched against London and the home counties but lacked both numbers and, just as important, fire power. Even eight .303 machine guns proved less effective against the Bf 109's 20mm cannon. Despite fighter cover that was technically very able, German bombers suffered substantial losses in their raids. Such was the rate of attrition that the Germans were forced eventually to abandon their daylight attacks in favour of night operations. This was the first setback in the rise of the new Luftwaffe because in its previous areas of operation air superiority had been more easily gained. Then its bombers could range freely in their formations and strike targets at will. The days of radar-directed anti-aircraft guns were still absent and gunners on England's defensive batteries relied on a mixture of simple radar plots, sound detection and the eyes and ears of a special force designed to recognize and plot aircraft, the Observer Corps.

The attacks on London described so ably in the term 'blitz' became a considerable misery for the city, with nearly 20,000 dead and the Luftwaffe returning for fifty-seven consecutive nights from September 1940. Other cities were attacked in force and the total deaths rose to 43,000. The lack of adequate night fighter defence was an enormous problem and anti-aircraft guns, although placed in considerable numbers with searchlights, did not make many inroads on the raids. Perhaps Hitler would have considered his tactics of civilian area bombing in Britain with a little more circumspection had he realized the tiger he was going to unleash. It is perhaps a mark of his obtuse self-belief that he paid no serious attention to the possibilities of British bomber attacks on his own cities. By the time America entered the war, Britain had established its plans to demolish German targets and this included strikes on cities. More importantly, manufacturing was geared up to produce a strike force of heavy bombers beyond the imagination of the Luftwaffe.

Into the frame of this enormous struggle walked the airmen of the 388th Bombardment Group. Largely forgotten now, they were individuals among thousands. The trophy had made eighteen names important to me but as, I researched them, the story became like a child's kaleidoscope. The more I looked into the 388th and its missions, the more names and events came to the fore. Many inter-connected, so members of one crew flew with another. Sometimes airmen left the crew for a while and appeared some weeks or even months later with another crew. There were many questions to be answered.

Chapter 4

The Swede

There is nothing stable in the world; uproar's your only music.
— John Keats

Dong Ong was one of eight children born to Lin and Fong Shee Ong in San Francisco, California. Dong's parents were Chinese and were first generation settlers in the United States. In later life, Dong preferred the name 'Don' and this shortened name was how he was known to many of his family. However, throughout the war his comrades knew him as Dong. On his enlistment he was still regarded as a Chinese citizen and was possibly the first to serve in the USAAF as a pilot. Dong's childhood was a friendly competition with his siblings. He had six brothers and perhaps this bred the tenacity that would be frequently called upon through his later flying career. After completing high school, Dong began his working career as a woodworker but he had already cultivated an interest in flying and it was clear how he would spend some of his earnings.

Dong described his early aviation experiences with some humour in an extract from his recollections of this time:

As a boy I had an intense interest in aviation. I studied the few available aviation books at the local library. When I finished High School, I started flying lessons at a small airport at Walnut Creek, California. I became 'air sick' almost every flight, but managed to solo a Piper Cub. Later, during the first 40 flights of flight training, I became air sick at times so bad that I vomited. However, flying in the rear seat of an open cockpit aircraft, I managed to clear the aircraft. Of course, no one was aware of this since this was cause for elimination. At any rate, I managed to pilot the aircraft with sufficient proficiency to be selected to represent my small group in competition with others.

For some reason the instructor always selected me on Monday mornings to 'wring' the airplane out. On this date, we performed many aerobatic manoeuvres. I became so sick that I wanted to jump out of the airplane. I signalled him to land and after landing the instructor became aware of my sickness. He passed it off by patting me on the shoulder and saying, 'It's probably something you ate.' Strangely, after that episode, I rarely became air sick again.

With the war in Europe raging, young men such as Dong read the papers and listened to the radio with increasing curiosity as speculation about whether the US would be drawn into the war abounded. Winston Churchill, who in Britain would epitomize the spirit of resistance to Nazi ambitions, led a country that was now alone in Western Europe. France, Belgium and the Netherlands had been overrun and had capitulated. For Churchill, who had not enjoyed universal popularity before the war, it was a time of grim determination, yet it was his finest hour. After the threat of German invasion had subsided in autumn 1940, Britain faced the bitter prospect of fighting alone. Churchill's lobbying of the United States during this period was relentless but it was becoming clear that America would not be drawn into the war simply through moral arguments. There were some tangible signs of success in holding and then driving back the German advance in North Africa and the loss of Germany's capital ship *Bismarck* was a great boost to British moral, albeit with the loss of HMS *Hood* and 1,415 of its crew. Such were the tides of war, that the British were now desperate for any sign of success over what had seemed an almost unstoppable Axis advance.

Although the attack on Pearl Harbor propelled America into the war, already by May 1941 there were attacks on US merchant ships and the sinking of the SS *Robin Moor* by U-boat *U-69* was received with much surprise and indignation. President Roosevelt announced 'an unlimited national emergency' and it seemed the march into conflict was an inevitable road, just as it had prior to 1917. America had already committed to supply Britain with large quantities of arms and materials, including many ships and aircraft. It is perhaps no surprise that Germany considered the transportation of transatlantic goods as a viable and essential target. Hitler was playing on American reticence to become directly involved and obviously believed that the odd sinking would deter America from believing that the lend-lease arrangement with the British would not be painless. By September 1941, the US Naval Command described orders to attack any Axis vessels found in American waters as 'all-out war'.

When war was declared in America, Dong Ong, among many others, decided that it was better to enlist than wait to be drafted. The risk in waiting was that when the draft came, it might be harder to negotiate where you would serve and Dong wanted to fly. With a passion for aviation, here was an opportunity for a young man to fly something far more advanced than anything otherwise available in the civilian world. Dong had already soloed in a private aircraft in 1941, so 9 June 1942 found him standing in a short queue at the army enlistment office. Listed as a 'semi-skilled' worker and with the nationality 'Chinese', Dong's sign up registration was under the name 'Ronald'. Whether this is a copying error in the records is hard to tell but it seems likely. His name is correct in all other records.

Having signed up, Dong was not called forward for aviation cadet training until November. He remained in California at Dos Palos during his initial flying training stages, flying the Ryan PT-22 Recruit, a two-seat, open cockpit, monoplane aircraft. It was at this time he had his most acute experiences of air sickness, as he recounted earlier. The PT-22 carried its trainee pilots in the rear cockpit and, as Dong says, would allow for the results of air sickness to be unobserved and undetected as the rear cockpit was also clear of the wing. All air forces at the time used fairly basic training aircraft at this stage of a trainee pilot's career. They had more in common with a First World War model than their modern cousins. Most functions were directly mechanical; the joystick fed control cables and pulleys, while other functions would see knobs and handles employed. The undercarriage was fixed and robust – it had to be given the student pilot's tendency to land too hard, too fast or even at completely the wrong angle. From the earliest days of aviation the saying was that the 'third bounce would kill you' and a landing capable of producing such unwelcome upward motion was not at all uncommon. An instructor would generally take control if a pilot got everything out of shape close to landing as, for reasons of self-preservation, he had a latent desire to return home that evening. Problems often arose when a pilot went solo and there were instances of the most severe of accidents happening during this first instance. There is little doubt that flying and flying training in particular was a hazardous process at best compared to today's sanitized world. Even the robust training machines could be pushed beyond their design limits and most accidents occurred due to pilot error.

Dong seemed to do well in this primary stage of flying and seems to have enjoyed the confidence of his instructors. So much of the skill of the new pilot is down to the combination of mastering airmanship and being able to maintain confidence, even when things go wrong. This is a fine balance, as another old saying goes:

There are old pilots and bold pilots, but not many old bold pilots.

Overconfidence probably killed more pilots in the Second World War than nervous pilots. Being in command of larger aircraft also requires a consciousness and a consideration of your crew. Fighter pilots had a reputation for being party animals on the ground but a singular breed in the air. After the war, when jet fighters carried navigators increasingly, certain humorous phrases were used for the rear navigator's station, amongst them the baggage compartment. As a broad generalisation, and there are notable exceptions, it is the fighter pilot who is more likely to tell his ground crew when a problem occurs but not be particularly interested in the technical efforts to fix it. Even at the basic training stage, instructors will begin to form an opinion about who is most likely suited in temperament to fly bombers or fighters. As a boy from a big family, Dong most likely had a grounding in understanding others that would stand him in good stead for leading a team.

The second stage of Dong's training was still in California, at Lemore on the more sophisticated Vultee BT-13 Valiant. This aircraft was deemed to be a basic trainer but had all the features necessary to prepare a pilot for the rigours of more powerful and complicated aircraft. It had an enclosed rotary engine, retractable undercarriage and a 'greenhouse' enclosed cockpit with sliding covers. Apart from not being blown about in the wind, the student would notice immediately the surfeit of power available to him. His pre-flight checklist was longer and, once in flight, there was far more to take in and make sure everything was functioning correctly. With all the extra workload, it was not uncommon to forget important details and many a student pilot had a flare fired to warn him that he had forgotten to lower the undercarriage on approach to landing. The Valiant was nicknamed the Vibrator and, although opinion differs as to how it got the name and which vibration it was noted for, one thing remains clear, it vibrated. It was at the end of this stage of training that final decisions were made about who would make fighters and who would be selected for bombers. Although the fighter pilot was still the sought-after position for many young men (and it was a popular profession for those wishing to impress the ladies), one does wonder whether in many cases certain individuals could not be entrusted to fly anything bigger. Some pilots demonstrated a reckless lack of consideration for their own safety that confounded any effort to make them responsible for any other crewmen. Given an equal playing field through a flying course, sometimes the decision was based on operational demands and not purely on the merits of the individual.

That Dong was selected to fly bombers is self-apparent and he doesn't record what his feelings are about this decision. He moved out of state for the first time to go to Marfa, Texas, to fly the twin-engined Cessna AT-17 Bobcat. The move from single-engined aircraft to twin or multiple-engined flight has a significance of its own; there was no turning back and to flunk this course would probably mean a discharge from flying duties. The Bobcat looked quite similar to the British Avro Anson and served the same role, although the Anson also had a bombing role early in the war and was later used in a variety of functions in addition to training. In October 1943, Dong was promoted to 2nd lieutenant and with it moved into a different social strata within the army, an officer. In the desire to ensure that captured airmen were treated well, the Air Force made all aircrew up to sergeants with the pilots being made officers.

A subsequent move to Roswell, New Mexico, brought Dong face to face with the B-17; the aircraft that would shape his future and, of all the aircraft he had flown to date, by far the most iconic. He was chosen to command a B-17, a huge responsibility for a young man of 21 years old. Learning to fly the B-17 was only half the story as operational requirements on how to fly in formation, how to bomb, and understand navigational and meteorological information, all came into play. He moved on again to his last training position at Ellsworth, South Dakota, for his operational training stage, which finished in May 1944. Within weeks he would be at 'the front' flying bombing raids in Europe from a very different landscape, with very different weather conditions and, most dramatically of all, against an enemy who would try their best to kill you at any opportunity. He had also gained a group of young men around him, his crew. Each had undertaken their long journey from 'home boy' to bomber crew member. The youngest was 19 and really still only a boy.

In the way the military often works, the officers around Dong Ong were allocated accommodation by alphabetical order. So it was that 'Ong' found himself lodging with Odstrom, O'Hare, Puckett, Patten and Petersen. In stature the others towered over Dong and with his characteristic sense of humour he made light of the situation by jesting that he too was 'Swedish' in build. Thus the nickname 'The Swede' stuck – a lifelong reference to the irony of the alphabetic selection procedure. Petersen and Patten seemed particularly close to Dong and remained buddies into their old age.

By the time Dong's crew gathered around their aircraft on the morning of 7 June 1944, the cat was well and truly out of the bag. The long expected invasion had arrived. Ironically, the crew probably had more certainty of the invasion than Hitler who, having procrastinated into the late afternoon of 6 June, had finally been persuaded to commit his Panzer divisions. Dong had flown his first mission as co-pilot as part of Andrecheck's crew on D-Day itself, part of the common practice of easing in a pilot as a 'buddy' on a flight. It wasn't that much experience but gave the pilot a little head start on a potentially nervous crew waiting for their first combat experience. Dong flew on the third raid of D-Day in which the 388th went to Pont-L'Eveque and, very neatly for the purposes of the trophy story, Johnnie Colburn's crew flew in the formation just behind Andrecheck's on only their third mission.

It was an early start and one of many to come for Ong's crew. That said, even finding the right aircraft in the right dispersal area could be a game on a dark Suffolk night. Dong's crew's first mission was to fly 160 miles south of the invasion beaches to hit the rail marshalling yards in Nantes. Key tasks of both British and American bombing groups were to prevent the Germans from reinforcing the area of the beachhead. As well as troops, mechanized German units, particularly Panzers, were of great danger and the quickest method of transportation was by rail. The mission went well although Dong's crew, flying B-17 *Miss Fortune,* encountered one of their greatest foes for the first time during the mission – flak. Described in official records as 'moderate' and 'accurate' that day, it must have left the crew in no doubt that these puffs of black smoke were not birthday firecrackers. Everyone who had taken off landed home safely and this, first mission or no first mission, was always something to be relieved about.

The term flak was a relatively new word which was devised in the 1930s as a shortened form of *fliegerabwehrkanone*, literally 'aviator-defence gun'. Most guns were the German 88mm, which could fire a shell accurately to 25,000ft and beyond. The idea was not to hit the aircraft directly with the shell, as this was considered too difficult given the target was moving, although many were hit directly. The shell had a fuse cap that could be altered so it would explode at the desired set altitude. The exploding shell had a casing that would then disintegrate into hundreds of shards, almost as a shotgun effect on the passing planes. Once the gunnery was set into batteries, it was possible to provide a curtain of flak of many hundreds, even thousands, of shells. To the crews, the first black smudges would appear before them and before long turn into a series of miniature black clouds. Where flak was far enough away it could not be heard inside the plane, although many testified to hearing its effect beating against the skin of the aircraft. Some likened it to the sound of gravel being thrown against the plane. Where it was close it could be heard and the explosive effects could pitch a B-17 up and down. Small holes could appear suddenly in the skin of the aircraft and vicious pieces of metal could rip through the fuselage, damaging equipment and severing control cables.

One of the many German units receiving orders to move on 7 June was a Panzer Group noted for its battle experience. The 2nd SS Panzer Division Das Reich was based in the southern French town of Mountauban, near Toulouse. It had fought through 1943 on the Eastern Front before the move south to re-equip with fresh equipment and men. There can be no doubting its toughness, but also its ability to act brutally in suppression of enemy soldiers and civilians alike. Through its actions in Russia it had every reason to be hated and it would come to be known and despised in France, too. On 6 June 1944, D-Day, the order was passed to Das Reich to 'come to march readiness'. From its 400-mile distance from Normandy, it was clear early on that, whether the invasion in Normandy was a feint or not, Das Reich was needed further north. The bombing raids on northern French railway hubs had, of course, been anticipated by the German command. One of the reasons for stationing this key fighting element so far south was to allow it time to re-equip and train without being threatened from the air. In a well-orchestrated plan of attack, both sides knew that the denial of rail transport to a Panzer division was an opening gambit in trying to stop any reinforcement of the defences around the invasion zone. Even while Ong's attack on the railway at Nantes was in progress, Das Reich was in a high state of readiness and by the morning of 8 June it was on the move northwards.

In tactical terms, the denial of first railways and then road bridges, river crossings and even the roads themselves was an essential part of containing the threat to the Allied beachhead. We see in the missions both the Ong and Colburn crews flew in these first days after D-Day this emphasis on disrupting transport hubs. Part of the Allied plan of disruption was to try to hold up Das Reich in its journey north. Key to this was the actions of the French Resistance, the Maquis, who had been mobilized to begin both direct attacks and acts of sabotage on the route. In 1940, with European countries quickly toppling to the German armies, the British formed the Special Operations Executive (SOE) which, with its later championing by Churchill, led to the equipping and training of guerrilla fighters in numerous countries. The path to unified resistance in France was complicated by the differing political leanings of partisan groups and periods of deep suspicion between groups was exacerbated by German success in breaking them. Betrayal seemed commonplace and even today theories abound on how far each group was supported and protected or not by the SOE.

In the case of the delaying tactics to Das Reich, there was much success and commentators note that, while some elements reached their intended positions by mid-June, others were delayed by up to fifteen days. On 9 June, an SS battalion commander, Helmut Kämpfe, was captured by the Maquis and subsequently executed. In an act of retribution, another SS battalion entered the small town of Oradour-sur-Glane on 10 June and murdered 642 men, women and children in cold blood. Burning the town followed in an attempt, however feeble, to cover the evidence. The debate as to why Oradour-sur-Glane was singled out includes some reports that another nearby Oradour might have been implicated in partisan activity. What is certain is that the town had no military value and was defenceless against such a brutal onslaught. Even in this early stage of the battle for Normandy, the effect of the strategic denial of transport links was causing frustration among key German units.

The next day, 11 June, was a very early start for Dong Ong's and Johnnie Colburn's crews. They were tasked to bomb a railway bridge at Pontaubault, some sixty miles south of the Normandy beaches. With take-off planned for shortly after 0400 hours, at around midnight it was difficult for crews to work out whether their next meal was breakfast or an extension of the day before. Coffee was a solution for some and, as night merged into morning, the general buzz of getting on with the job was enough to banish thoughts of sleep. This was only Ong's second mission but for Colburn it was already his sixth in fewer than eight days. The last few days had been an intense flurry of activity with most missions focused on targets around the invasion beaches. Reports detail 'little flak and no fighter activity'. In relation to this story and the trophy, this is the first time both Ong and Colburn crews flew on the same mission, with Colburn in the lead squadron and Ong in the 'low' squadron. Ong flew *Skipper and the Kids*; it was his first and only mission with her. In the history of the 388th, perhaps *Skipper*'s is one of the most poignant as she was lost in December 1944 on the Isle of Arran in Scotland in a pre-Christmas flying accident. Detailed as a 'training flight', the presence of a mixed group of officers and medics illustrates this trip was very likely, as rumoured, a whisky trip for the officers' mess. The reason for the trip is perhaps not as flippant as it may sound; the numbers of officers at Knettishall and their ability to drink spirits cannot be underestimated. The supply of all food and drink was a large operation and with Christmas approaching it was probably felt that obtaining this luxury item could not be left to the normal supply chain. The weather in the United Kingdom can never be counted on as fair in December. Some days are fine and clear but during the flight of more than 300 miles north from Knettishall it must have been very apparent that the conditions were not good. Although spotted by the Observer Corps on the coast of Scotland not too far from Prestwick, the aircraft was noted but not positively identified as it passed by. The cloud was low and visibility was poor by official accounts, and *Skipper and the Kids* disappeared mysteriously and was presumed lost at sea. It was not until March 1945 that her wreck was found high in the hills of Arran. All had perished in a loss perhaps as keenly felt as any other loss in combat.

The weather was also an issue on 11 June and, as the aircraft took off and began the process of assembling into their formations, the weather was clear and the crews hoped that, despite a forecast of haze over their target, they would have a clear run in. Colburn was flying *GI Jane*, an aircraft that seemed a regular mount in those early days. Dong Ong's bombardier, George West, gazed out through the best view in town; the B-17's large transparent nose. From his position, he had the grandstand view; a seat resembling a simple office chair with the Norden bombsight between his legs. Of all the crew, the bombardier can see the most and his job includes taking control of the aircraft via the autopilot and linked bombsight on the final run in to target. This can take anything from five to ten minutes and is perhaps the most jittery part for any crew, flying straight and level without any deviations. George West flew fifteen missions of Ong's first thirty-two and was replaced by Morris Gumpel, whose name made it on to the engraved trophy.

The crews' route took them well north of London and they tracked across the heart of England with the patchwork of green fields and small towns and villages. To describe an English spring and its verdant greenery is sometimes lost on those outside the country. It has to be experienced, but this June the weather was making the green into grey as swathes of cloud and rain swept in. As they flew south the weather grew progressively worse with grey storm clouds and rain beginning to hamper the formation. As they flew out from the Hampshire coast it became clear they would have to climb to try to get clear of the clouds. By the time they approached their target the clouds were as high as 21,000ft – far higher than briefed – and made for a bombing run 8,000ft higher than planned. Unknown to them, the clouds had already claimed a B-17 from another bomb group, the 96th. She collided with another B-17, seemingly from a completely different sortie, and in the twisting confusion of her death dive only one man escaped.

At 0831, with the target still totally obscured, they released their bombs. They relied on PFF, Pathfinder Force, the blind bombing guidance system in the specially equipped lead aircraft. How accurate this particular raid was is hard to say but it was one of a number on Pontaubault in that week. Bombing accuracy was improving steadily but to hit a single target still required a quantity of bombers to drop a carpet of bombs on the area.

The future of bombing accuracy was taking a leap forward as, two days earlier, RAF Lancaster bombers of 617 Squadron had dropped enormous 12,000lb Tallboy bombs on the Saumur rail tunnel with impressive accuracy. Saumur was farther south in the wine-rich Loire Valley and was perhaps not the most obvious target. However, its position on the south–north rail line made it an important hub and the lasting way to create disruption was to strike the tunnels and not solely the rail tracks, which could be repaired more easily. It is interesting to note that earlier raids on what are now considered 'diversionary' targets on the Pas-de-Calais did not use the new weapons, even though their effectiveness on deep fortifications was not to be doubted. D-Day was to provide not only a strategic advantage but, in modern jingoism, was to be an attack of 'shock and awe'. For the 388th, there was no chance of using the new massive bombs as the design and payload of the B-17 would not permit it, but the role of the B-17 as a strategic daylight bomber was undimmed.

All the aircraft of the 388th had returned from the Pontaubault raid by 11.14 am. Within hours, detailed photographs of the raid, indeed every raid, were being checked and distributed. Some photos would be obtained usually from the raid itself but in this case, due to the complete cloud undercast, there would be no point in taking any. The real workhorses of these information gathering sorties were Spitfires mounted with cameras and stripped of guns and any extra weight to give more range. They were dispatched to record post-attack targets and provide the eyes of the raid planners. The job required skill and fortitude as these were lone sorties without an escort in a fast in-out fly-by. A new version of the Spitfire, the Griffon-engined Mark XIX, entered service in May 1944. These blue-painted spies became the masters of the air reconnaissance war after D-Day. They had pressurized cockpits, which enabled them to fly higher than the war-weary German aircraft, and had substantial speed benefits at low level. The RAF provided much of this work, but by then the USAAF was also using Spitfires. The imagery captured used two cameras and from these it was possible to produce what was, in effect, a 3D image when viewed through special but uncomplicated optical devices. This enabled photo interpreters to see buildings, chimneys and aerials and judge the effects of a raid more accurately.

On this particular Pontaubault raid, the railway bridge must have been a very difficult target to hit. The nearby road bridge, which is a prominent feature of the town as the name suggests, did not sustain damage and played a vital role as General Patton's Third Army stormed across it on 31 July in the significant break-out from Normandy into Brittany.

For the crews, there was little time for rest and reflection. Both would fly the next day to Amiens, another town in northern France. The attack, again through clouds, was an airfield and, again, it was an attempt to disrupt the defenders of the French coast. For the period after the invasion, the mission tally mounted for both crews and resembled a tourist map of northern France. Berck-sur-Mer, Amiens, Caen and Saint-Lô were all the subject of missions in the denial of transport links to the invasion area.

Germany was a lower priority target for the first weeks of June but as airstrips were established for aircraft such as the Hawker Typhoon in liberated France, the day of the heavy bomber as support for ground troops shifted. The eyes of Bomber Command once again began to look deep into occupied Europe and Germany. The strategy now was to destroy the Luftwaffe and, more importantly, destroy the fuel supplies to mechanized units attempting to halt the Allied advance. Germany did not have its own oil and produced synthetic oil via coal. It was these plants that became primary targets.

At the early morning briefings, a curtain was pulled back to reveal the map of Europe with the day's target marked and ribbons displaying the route in and out. As Dong Ong and co-pilot Earl 'Corky' Lippert were to discover, Germany would be their most difficult journeys. On the morning of 18 June, the curtain revealed the city of Bremen and the Ong crew's first taste of a mission to Germany. Here were defences that were far better established than targets in France and, as the crews learned to their cost, ones that were capable of cutting their planes to ribbons.

Chapter 5

Walking in Other Men's Shoes

*'So new to him,' she muttered, 'so old to me; so strange to him, so familiar to
me; so melancholy to both of us!'*
                                        – Charles Dickens, *Great Expectations*

Over the past fifteen or so years I have developed a particular style
of learning and relating to history. I'm a bit like a method actor or
a jury called out of the courtroom in a crime case; I like to walk
the ground, see the view and imagine the scenes before me. This all came
about through my first visit to the First World War battlefields in France
and Belgium. The spurring force was not what I did on that trip, but what
I could not do. It was a standard bus trip organized by our local newspaper
and visited key sites over a four-day period. My father-in-law came with me
and, although there was a generation gap, we both had grandfathers who had
fought. It was late October and after a long trip we soon found that nearly all
the places we visited were shrouded in a dense autumn fog. It was cold, quite
atmospheric, but hopeless as a field trip of any sort really. We stopped and
the guide, good as he was, could only muster the basics of the history before
pointing into the fog and saying things like: 'Over there, about 100 yards
away, was the German front line and the British and Canadians advanced
across ….'

We all stared into the fog, sometimes no more than 20 yards of visibility
and even with the most vivid of imaginations, we couldn't quite grasp the
scene. Indeed, the amount of concentration expelled should have burnt
off the fog, but there we were, wrapped up like children waiting to build
a snowman – there was nothing that could be done. We viewed the famous
Cloth Hall of Ypres across the town square but even its tower was fading
quickly into the fog. We were happy to have been there, but we weren't quite
sure where we had been.

Not to be defeated, it occurred to me that I could muster this sort of trip
on my own using my car. The next April, my father-in-law and I headed

off for what has now become a regular excursion. This time the weather was clear and, after visiting the tourist trail for a while, we went 'off-piste', which, particularly in France, means following agricultural paths and into ploughed fields. Our eyes were invariably fixed downwards into the turned earth and we would find bullets, shrapnel and sometimes even buckles and buttons emerging for the first time in many years. As well as the enjoyment in finding items, the geography of the trenches and fixed strongholds could be found. One such topographical feature is the Butte de Warlencourt, an ancient man-made mound, which, for reasons of a view over an otherwise unremarkable landscape, was fought over on many occasions. The fields around this mound are filled with lead balls – shrapnel. We found that the intensity of action could be measured by the field finds and by walking what is now a normal field, well cultivated and ploughed regularly, it was still possible to see where the trenches ran and imagine the scene.

Airfields are quite a different story and a disused one is more akin to an old factory than a battlefield. In Britain we built airfields at an incredible rate during the Second World War and there is now such a surfeit of disused and abandoned runways that, with the exception of London City Airport in the old docklands area, it hasn't been necessary to build an all-new airport for the last seventy years. Many are slowly disappearing back into agricultural land, many are industrial sites and in Cumbria, my home area, Great Orton became the site of the burial of thousands of animal carcasses during the foot and mouth epidemic of 2001.

To tell the story of the trophy I knew I was going to have to pack my walking shoes and travel around to some of the airfields to which the crews flew. I didn't have to, I could read about them, look them up on the internet and probably write a breezy account as if I had been there. However, there is a set of values that compels the reporter to stand in the spot, breathe the air and write what it feels like. This said, in layman's terms, there's nothing much to see on an old airfield, other than it's flat and windy with some old buildings. To the enthusiast, however, it is a theme park of the imagination. Hangars, now used for storing all sorts of industrial goods, become the backdrop with technicians working inside on stripped down aircraft. Taxiways, known as peri tracks, are filled with coughing aircraft engines and dispersals, the round defensive positions used for parking aircraft, are alive with crews climbing in and starting up. The runways are ready to be walked down as the chorus of skylarks above are drowned by the rhythmic beat of engines in full song, propellers beating the air. For some crews, these yards of concrete or tarmac are the last pieces of earth they experienced and felt before their ultimate mission – many never landed again, some are missing still.

I started to make a list of key sites that would help me in this task and I realized that some key areas were already in my travel plans. It wasn't just the airfields that were important, I realized that some of the routes in and out of the targets would be good to visit, too. Two elements of our present lives were going to help me. The first was that we loved visiting France on holiday, normally the Loire Valley which is in mid to southern France and doesn't really feature much on my two crews 'shopping list' of missions. This year was different though, we had only one week and we had decided to go to the beaches of Normandy. I could enjoy showing Trish some D-Day beaches, but also just enjoy the coast and being in France. The beaches today are good holiday beaches with the normal influx of tourists sporting swimwear and blow-up life rings. On a good day you will find hundreds of people doing what is best done on a beach, swimming, lying in the sun and playing games where once obstacles and landmines filled the sand. I used to head off to such parts with some of my male friends, the 'old contemptibles', to the First World War battlefields, D-Day beaches and Arnhem in Holland. In the last few years, Trish has realized that perhaps a bit of history here and there doesn't hurt, and also that I seemed to be having far too good a time wining and dining out on field trips. As long as I keep my enthusiasm for military themes under control, all is happy in the Price household.

My list of visits for the trophy story now included the White Cliffs of Dover, Cap Gris Nez when we travelled into France a month later and the beaches of D-Day. Airfields included RAF Hawkinge, which is now a housing estate near Folkestone and is where B-17 *Mary's Sister*, flown once by Ong, met her end; RAF Knettishall, of course, in Suffolk, and RAF Tuddenham, where Colburn ended his D-Day missions with screeching tyres at the end of the runway. I didn't know when I could visit Suffolk but, as the research continued, I felt sure it was inevitable and needed to be in the summer. One place I decided not to visit was Prestwick in Scotland where many crews had first touched down on British soil after their transtlantic flights. This was because Prestwick is now a commercial airport and the operators would take no pleasure in me trying to walk the runway! Prestwick continued to fulfil a military transport role and even saw Elvis Presley transit through in 1960 on his way back from Germany. Not all crews flew the Atlantic and many braved the ocean through the threat of U-boats in all weathers. There were other places I'm sure would pop up in the research so a travel budget would need to be in place. Anyone who knows us well will know that the phrase 'budget' implies some form of financial organization – we are very much a 'see how it goes' family.

On this day we began the sloping walk up a track covered with flints and dead leaves that lead to cliffs. Unlike the images the mind creates at the word 'cliffs', the south coast of England near Dover has fields and grass stretching to the very edge of the sheer drops of the cliffs. Popular with walkers, it is tempting to get too close to the edge and it is wise to stick to the well-worn paths. As in most recreational pastimes, the walkers you meet are invariably friendly and, although not many people stop to talk, one has the feeling that given a moment and the right inclination, you would learn much about your fellow walkers in five minutes.

The sun was breaking out from what had been a rather sullen morning with grey clouds forming a carpet above us. Now everything was bright and beginning to glint with the warmth, and even the breeze was gentle. Ahead across the Channel was France, twenty-two miles away, and as the visibility cleared we could see the coast quite clearly and the ever present shipping in its prescribed lanes passing through the Straits of Dover, the narrowest part of the Channel. Due to the volume it is necessary for shipping to adhere to a directional course and lane; southbound closer to the English coast, northbound to the French side. Across this constant lateral movement of merchantmen, ferries dash across between the two coasts, timing the gaps of their passage to avoid other ships. With the opening of the Channel Tunnel it was believed that the traditional ferry crossing would die out. Perhaps the lure of the sea still plays a role in the enjoyment of crossing and the ferries continue to ply their trade.

I had come with the intention of getting some photographs of Cap Gris Nez, the opposing promontory of rock to the White Cliffs that juts out into the Channel on the French side west of Calais. It was on this promontory that the first bombing raids of my story were launched by the Colburn crew two days before D-Day. Through my long lens I could see the shape of the cliffs and some aerials perched on top. During the Second World War, the Straits of Dover and the towns of Dover and Calais were in the front line of a shooting war. Large guns placed in concrete casements by the Germans made a nuisance of themselves by bombarding the English coast constantly. The guns were a danger to shipping too and were a constant reminder that, despite bombing raids and artillery duels, the Germans were far closer to English shores than was comfortable. To counter the guns and also to try to fend off a German sea-borne landing, the south coast and White Cliffs in particular were heavily fortified. Large gun emplacements were built just behind the headland containing guns with a variety of calibres. Nicknames for the guns such as *Winnie, Pooh, Clem* (in tribute to Churchill's wife) and *Jane* humanized an otherwise deadly shooting match. Two hundred and sixteen of Dover's residents died and more than 10,000 buildings were damaged during this period.

Air raids were commonplace and the Battle of Britain was fought overhead in 1940. Through 1943 and into 1944 the tide and direction of the battle turned with Allied bombers flying over en route to targets in northern France. With the D-Day invasion taking place much farther down the French coast, residents might have thought that quieter days lay ahead. A new menace appeared almost as soon as the invasion had begun, the V-1. These pulse-engined pilotless flying bombs were launched in their hundreds towards London from launch ramps on the Pas-de-Calais and the Channel once again became a battleground of interception aircraft and banks of anti-aircraft guns. By August 1944, eighty per cent were being destroyed before reaching their targets but they were a considerable thorn in the side of the Allies. Finally, in September 1944, the Allied advance had pushed north and overran the launching sites. At last the south coast could enjoy relative peace.

For targets in northern France and west, the south coast was more than a nice geographical feature for bomber crews. It represented safety. It's hard to imagine the scenes of seventy years ago walking on the cliffs today. Nature, in its abundance, has overgrown and covered nearly all the defensive positions. Buildings and bunkers have been pulled down or buried, and the history seeker must stray a little off the paths to find relics of this sprawling fortress. Most tourists now have no idea of the history; all is now green and bright – at least today. Perhaps with the subconscious radar I operate on any battlefield, my eyes tend to scan the paths and soil around. I'm not thinking about it, it's just a habit. I came across rusty grenade springs and bits of barbed wire. It's obvious that parts of the cliff were used for training and rusting shards of grenade are not uncommon on these paths. I've found them before in this area and, with the constant wear of tourist boots, a fresh trove surfaces each year.

We walked past the pretty and now preserved South Foreland Lighthouse on our return and, taking an upper road towards St Margaret's Bay, we were walking on bare chalk. A thin dark green line on the path caught my eye. Could it be? A second glance confirmed my find, a bullet buried lengthways in the path as it had fallen during the Second World War. Stooping down I picked it out and, running my finger across the smooth copper jacket, I could see the rifle marks left by the barrel. Other than this, it was in perfect condition, a .303 bullet. Many thousands were fired in this area and above it. Machine guns were scattered all over the cliffs, most pointing skywards to try to catch low-flying enemy aircraft. Battle of Britain fighters fired millions of rounds during the conflict; most would fall to the ground or into the sea without hitting a target. This was one such fallen bullet. I decided to take it home in the hope that perhaps one day I'd find a friendly ballistics expert who could tell me what kind of gun barrel it came from. There was a vague chance it was German, but it looked very much like many other British .303s I have found over the years on old firing ranges and battlefields. I had to be cautious though because such small items end up being tucked into bag pockets and camera cases, and the problems I could cause myself at an airport through such 'forgotten' items is a sobering thought.

I'm reminded that on a previous visit to The Coastguard, a seafront pub in nearby St Margaret's Bay, I read a small story posted on the wall about local divers finding the wreck of a B-17 bomber. I would need to call in and check the identity of the aircraft; well, that's what I would tell Trish, although she is far from averse to the charms of wayside hostelry in any event. My memory is correct and details about 42-97883 *Miss Lollipop* are on the wall. Her remains were found by divers less than a mile from the shore and her career lasted only three weeks in combat service, and three months after construction. Hit by flak over the French coast on 12 June 1944, she was on the way back from the target of Rosieres, near Dunkirk. She was part of the 100th Bomb Group based at Thorpe Abbotts in Norfolk, only fourteen miles from Knettishall. Sadly, only two of *Miss Lollipop*'s crew survived, which proves that even a 'milk run' could be deadly.

Another B-17 crash-landed across the headland near St Margaret's on 8 January 1945 on its return from Frankfurt. The aircraft, 43-39068, was part of the 487th Bomb Group based at Lavenham, Suffolk, and was badly damaged, necessitating a crash-landing at the earliest opportunity after landfall. Happily, all the crew were saved although the B-17 was cut up rather ignominiously where she lay three days later – but this was the practicality of war.

With my White Cliffs walk complete, I decided to drive the short distance through Dover to the site of the Battle of Britain airfield of Hawkinge. I knew before I went there that Hawkinge had had houses built on it, but the sight of it was even more depressing than I could have imagined. As a historian, I am saddened by the complete lack of grace and recognition for the site; it's a typical cock-up of a development that, it seems, only British planners would allow on an historical site of such merit. Perhaps doubly distressing is that we are reminded of its former glory as a grass airstrip in the 1969 film *The Battle of Britain*, which starred Michael Caine. Although other airfields such as Biggin Hill and North Weald played a large part in the battle, the loss of such an historic site is extremely short-sighted.

My real purpose for going was to see if any of the runway track could be traced. On 5 January 1945, B-17 42-97528 *Mary's Sister* was returning from Hanau with the Reuther crew and made what is listed as a 'landing' at Hawkinge, but the subsequent crash claimed all but two of the crew, who were listed as wounded. *Mary's Sister* was the closest I had yet come to an aircraft of either Ong's or Colburn's crews; Ong took her to Munich in July 1944. By the time of her final mission she had completed seventy operations and was a seasoned old-timer. Perhaps the sands of time had to run out for her, certainly the statistical probability of amassing so many sorties made her grisly end more than probable. *Mary's Sister* may have led a relatively charmed life but not without incident. On 16 November 1944, Gerald Holt flew in her to Germany and on the return leg diverted to RAF Colerne due to bad weather. It was Holt's first mission and, coincidentally in this story, it was Johnnie Colburn's last, completing his tour of duty. Details are sketchy but it appears *Mary's Sister* was involved in a taxiing accident that put her out of service for nearly a month. Holt went on to complete thirty-five missions, so the incident did not seem to hurt his flying career.

As I looked around the housing estate that was the former RAF Hawkinge, a lesson on research was about to be sprung on me. I left convinced that, as little as I could see, I had been in the right area to commemorate *Mary's Sister*. It was not until the next day that I remembered that I had posted an information request on an aviation site – I had not checked back for weeks.

Once back on the forum I realized my mistake. Just as I had hoped, an eyewitness account had been posted, and I had been in the wrong location. Although the writer was not certain exactly when the incident had taken place, his identifier of 1944 or 1945 and the location makes the account very likely given the photograph of the destroyed aircraft taken at the time.

Peter Verney writes:

As a child I can remember watching a damaged Fortress circling Hawkinge firing off Verey lights. We were at Elham about 3 miles away and saw it descend below the trees and the resultant column of black smoke. We jumped on our bikes and located the crash site at Paddlesworth. It had landed on top of the inland cliff which overlooks the Channel Tunnel terminal at Folkestone. It had gone over the edge leaving the tail at the top while the rest of the aircraft looked just like a rubbish tip down the cliff. An ambulance was in attendance and there were numerous used and unused little glass morphine phials scattered about. I think one casualty was recovered. My memory of the exact location is not clear but we were on the road which runs at the top of the cliff.

The B-17 had not made a landing at Hawkinge, or at least not a successful one. This site is less than a mile away and, following a straight line from the 'runway' at Hawkinge, (a grass strip and not concrete) and given the eyewitness account of the direction of the fuselage and final resting place, it looks likely that the B-17 either attempted to land or overflew the runway before a crash-landing. I decided to locate the correct area this time and it only took a few minutes on a map to see the location – or at least within a few hundred yards. This time I took my father-in-law with me and at a very healthy 84 years old he was useful as another pair of eyes. We found the fields and cliff edge quite easily after a climb up a high-sided Kent road, which at times resembled a tunnel as the trees on either side arched over. What we hoped to find was a long shot, a piece of debris in a path or verge side that would confirm the location. The crops were in the field so we looked down the steep slope that led from our cliff edge road down towards the huge Channel Tunnel terminal bustling with trains and traffic below. This area was not built on during the war so the view we have today is modern. That said, our patch of countryside was almost completely unchanged, so unlike the airfield at Hawkinge, and it took only a small amount of imagination to picture the scene. A handmade poppy had recently been attached to a gatepost leading to another part of the lower footpath. We were not alone in our act of remembrance – others too felt it was important.

Of the field in which *Mary's Sister* attempted to land, it was an open space but quite unsuitable in many ways. It sloped quite steeply towards the inland cliff, most likely a sea-formed cliff in ancient times when the sea level was higher. The precipitous drop must have presented the pilot with a terrible choice of an early touchdown in the sloping field; he didn't make it and *Mary's Sister* seems to have landed very heavily and too late to avoid the cliff edge. We found no trace of the aircraft but, given the time of year with an abundance of growth everywhere, it was not surprising. I made a mental note to go back the next time I was in the area, preferably when the soil was empty in the main field. It started to rain and the time was right to get back in the car, but it had been a satisfying mini-expedition.

Our week in Whitstable was over, the England soccer team were once again on the verge of an ignominious exit from the World Cup and we had a long drive north once again. Carlisle is only six miles or so from the Scottish border at its northern edge and is sometimes mistaken for a province of Scotland. Despite its proximity, it is very definitely English. Sometimes the drive from Kent to Carlisle can whistle by but today was Friday. Everyone had decided to drive somewhere and it was a long, tedious start-stop journey. It gave me lots of time to think over all the details and matters arising over the trophy story. I was encouraged though because for every dead end in searching for the families, there was a wide open road on the next turn of a page. I wondered what further surprises lay in store.

Chapter 6

Fickle Fannie

He who has conquered his own coward spirit has conquered the whole outward world.

— Thomas Hughes, *Tom Brown's Schooldays*

Affection and friendship can at first be hard to find, as the experience of many new arrivals at an operational bomber squadron can testify. The pain of losing friends can be acute and in a world where the mind of the individual is already grappling with a mixture of fatigue, homesickness and terror, often in equal measures, defensive behaviours are commonplace to protect oneself from further hurt.

The term 'new boy' is a reminder of what each airman was when he first arrived. The term is really more at home in an English public school but these new arrivals were truly boys in many cases and, although in popular clichés we like to term them 'men' after their experiences, they were still boys. Some found the enthusiasm of the new arrivals annoying, others deliberately avoided closer contact until they were more experienced. Culturally, there were marked differences between the men, not only in ethnic backgrounds, but region and state played an important part. Some were louder spoken than others and sometimes in that simple transaction were mistaken for brash kids. Each time an aircraft failed to return and a crew's beds were empty, it was a stark reminder that you could be next.

When Johnnie Colburn, together with co-pilot Russ Weekes and the other officers of the crew, including Bombardier Bob Simmon, arrived at Knettishall in May 1944, they were shown to their quarters. The curved tin roofed buildings were not unlike other quarters at other camps, but their hut in the 562nd Squadron area was strangely quiet. They found they had the room to themselves as they realized the other occupants of their accommodation had 'failed to return'. Of the 562nd crews lost in May, it is possible the missing spaces belonged to members of Lou Heying's crew, who were shot down near Cherbourg on 8 May. Some, including Heying, were taken prisoner, but a number died. The B-17 formation was both the testing ground of a new crew and the ladder to acceptance. Flying in the lowest right-hand corner of the formation was often referred to as 'Purple Heart Corner' after the medal awarded following injury in combat. Although there is no evidence to suggest that new crews were assigned to more risky parts of the formation as a test, it is true that, with experience, seniority was established and this led to greater responsibilities – becoming lead crews. Senior officers quite quickly had to mark out the men out who were capable of leading. There was never any guarantee that a chosen crew would be around long enough to exploit their skills fully.

Johnnie Colburn had signed up as an aviation cadet in June 1942 and was called for training on 12 November 1942 at 29 Palms, California. He undertook elementary flying training in a Boeing Stearman, a rugged biplane with fixed undercarriage that was used widely throughout the Second World War. Progression in flying training led to postings to Lancaster, California, for basic training and on to Fort Sumner, New Mexico. Assigned to fly B-17s, Johnnie met the four-engined wonder for the first time at Hobbs, New Mexico, and was also promoted to 2nd lieutenant. After flying much smaller aircraft, most new pilots were somewhat overwhelmed at the size and complexity of the B-17 – until they flew it. It seems the universal experience was that of delight at how easy it was to fly, how well it handled and how forgiving it could be in the hands of new pilots. Once his flying of the type was well established, Johnnie was transferred to Salt Lake City, Utah, where he was allocated a crew of nine. Many compared Salt Lake City to a blast furnace and living conditions were not considered advanced, even by wartime standards. The formation of the crew was a very important time and, in Johnnie's case, was the establishment of some lifetime friends. Bob Simmon, writing in 1999 about his Air Force career, described Johnnie Colburn as 'my best friend to this day'.

The new crew then made a further move, to Dyersburg, Tennessee, for combat training. During this time radio operator George Kragle was having problems with air sickness. Johnnie decided a kill or cure approach was called for:

We were to make high altitude practice bombing missions, and as we approached 20,000ft. George would get airsick every time and we would have to descend. This happened about three times and it appeared that I would have to have him replaced, but I wanted to keep him and George wanted very much to stay on the crew. We were assigned the altitude mission once again, and I told George that we were going on up to 30,000 whether it killed him or not. We went on up and I don't remember whether or not he got airsick, but he never got airsick again.

Interestingly, Johnnie recalls this period being cut short. Events and plans for the D-Day invasion had obviously necessitated the calling forward of all available and suitably trained crews. Dong Ong and crew, although not training at the same bases as the Colburn crew, were also called and arrived in Britain more or less at the same time. The Colburn crew flew the Atlantic in a new B-17, whereas the Ong crew were dispatched by sea. The Colburn crew flew from Kearney, Nebraska, to Grenier, New Hampshire, then to Goose Bay, Labrador, on to Meeks Field, Iceland, and finally Prestwick, Scotland, landing there in late April 1944. The normal procedure for an arriving crew was to hand over the new aircraft before heading for a crew clearance camp. Bob Simmon recalls:

We then proceeded to Bovingdon, England, which was a Combat Crew Training School for the 8th Air Force, where we learned the crew procedures in place at that time. This was essentially ground school training covering formation procedures, communications, bombing and navigation procedures, aircraft recognition, gunnery procedures and information concerning differences in relationships with the English population. I remember it lasting about a week. At the completion of this training phase we finally received our assignment – to the 388th Bombardment Group (H), 3rd Air Division, 45th Combat Wing located at Station 136, Knettishall, England.

The make-up of every crew was distinct, but with young men it takes only a few short years to differentiate between a carefree singleton and a married man with responsibilities. Johnnie Colburn came to the crew as a 25-year-old married man, which, to someone aged 19 such as engineer William Tobias, must have seemed a generation above him. To add to the drama of his impending operational role, Johnnie received a communication from his wife's father that his son, Johnnie Jr, had been born on 12 May. The Colburn crew did have a slightly older balance of ages with the co-pilot, Russ Weekes, aged 25, and Navigator Morris Neiman, aged 27.

While the minds of most young men were engaged in avoiding death, the pursuit of female companionship came a close second. Opportunities to fraternize on base were limited, with the attentions of the girls who served as part of the Red Cross in short supply. Some made efforts to meet local girls and attended local dances. Some forged new friendships and were invited to parents' houses for meals. Trips to London were the regular way to let off steam when passes permitted. Drinking and dancing were favourite occupations but, while some took the opportunity to extend the boundaries of their experience, others had wives or steady girlfriends back home and chose more wholesome ways of enjoying themselves.

Bombardier Bob Simmon was also relatively newly married to Katie. They had married while he was an aviation cadet on 25 September 1943 at Deming, New Mexico. Simmon completed his elementary flying training as a pilot but did not complete his later training due to getting sick and missing the end of his intake course. In the conveyor belt of pilot training he was moved on and into bombardier training at Deming. Later in life he expressed a little regret that he did not pursue the option to drop back into another pilot course. Time off meant the opportunity to hit London. While many crews confessed to their fair share of carousing, it was also clear that many airmen took advantage of the more sensible opportunities that a big city offered. Simmon had his picture taken at a respected photographers in Oxford Street to send home to his wife. Photographers Mindel & Faraday had an exclusive clientele and, in the honeypot of Oxford Street in the war, were assured a good living. Michael Mindel went on to found one of Britain's leading photography and electronics chains, Dixons.

There was nothing new in warfare about scepticism for newly arriving soldiers to a front. In the First World War the life expectancy of the British front line infantryman was counted in days rather than months. One young soldier sent into the front for the first time was particularly impressed at the care and attention he received from his sergeant. It seemed this kindly soul would check on him very frequently, ask him if he was OK and give him helpful advice. The young soldier mentioned this to another comrade only to find that the sergeants had bets on that he would be killed early.

Thankfully, many lessons from the First World War had been heeded twenty-one years later. In respect of servicemen facing danger and seeing death first-hand in intense circumstances, it was recognized that the mental pressure could not be sustained for a long period. Aircrews differed in their role and their exposure to danger but, in the case of bomber crews based in Britain and flying missions into occupied territory, more strict limits were set. The Royal Air Force's Bomber Command structured its crews into 'tours' of duty. The heavy bombers flew mostly but not exclusively at night and by 1944 could be found alongside their American compatriots in large daylight raids. By 1941, the RAF stipulated that a bomber crew's first tour of duty was to be twenty-five missions, (the term 'sorties' was more in use by the RAF than mission). With a loss rate of three to five per cent per raid, the chances of surviving a tour seemed mathematically improbable. Nevertheless, thirty-five per cent did and were placed into training roles for a six-month break. The number of sorties expected in a first tour increased to thirty in 1943, although it is clear that some completed as many as forty. It was not uncommon, and indeed was expected, that a crew would return to combat flying and a further twenty missions would be carried out on a second tour. Despite the dangers, many had lobbied hard to return, finding training too boring.

The losses were every bit as bad as front line troops in the First World War. Statistics vary a little, but it would seem in RAF bomber operations that of every 100 who joined the force, forty-five would be killed, six seriously wounded and eight would become prisoners of war. The RAF drew from all around the Commonwealth with a significant percentage of casualties being Canadian and Australian. By the time America entered the war and the first bomber groups arrived in Britain in 1942, the pattern of limiting the number of missions was well established. The USAAF adopted the twenty-five mission limit and, after the dawning realization that their bombers were more vulnerable than anticipated without constant fighter cover, even this figure looked optimistic. Nevertheless, as the war progressed and the all-important milestone was reached of fighter cover for the whole mission, the limit had increased to thirty. This was the golden figure for the new Colburn and Ong crews as they began their hectic career.

The springboard of their mission target was D-Day and the preamble to it. The mission-to-month ratio was increased greatly; indeed, the mission-to-day ratio was outstanding. Many 388th crews took five weeks to complete their first ten missions in late 1943. In Johnnie Colburn's case, he flew his first ten in just over two weeks and Dong Ong in three weeks. The Ong crew carried on to finish their tour in fewer than three months, finishing in August 1944, instead of the average five to six months. For them, it was a short sharp exchange and perhaps this influenced Dong to return for a second tour. It is a clue too to them being named 'Crew of the Month' for August. Johnnie's crew flew on into November, so their tenure at Knettishall was far less rushed but not necessarily less intense.

For now though, they were 'the new boys'. It is important to note that the crews were in different squadrons at Knettishall, Colburn's was with the 562nd and Ong's with the 560th, and this meant in practical terms that they might fly on different missions on different days. The 388th Bombardment Group was part of the 8th Air Force and, in the chain of command, served as part of the 3rd Bombardment Division in the 45th Bombardment Wing. As with many bomb groups, the structure meant that it operated its own base and had four squadrons of B-17s on site, the 560th, 561st, 562nd and 563rd. Even though the unity of the 388th was important, each squadron still retained its own identity and even the living quarters were separated out into squadron areas. Colburn's 562nd area was quite close to the runways and located next to the group's headquarters. Ong's 560th was a little way down the hill and much closer to the village of Coney Weston. The bike was an important commodity if one was to avoid walking miles – and often the business of the day did not allow time to loiter. For 'official' business, such as transporting crews to the flight lines, there was always transport available. However, Knettishall was a rural area and for a young man away from home, his thoughts were about exploring – and not too far away in his mind there was the lingering hope that a young lady might be found in the locality.

The formation and strength of the Colburn crew seems self-apparent; it had been a successful match. Early photographs of the crew in training seem to show enthusiasm but also fun as they get into the challenges ahead. At some point, and it's not clear when, the crew adopt the identity 'Fickle Fannie'. Whether Fannie was a real person linked to the crew is unclear. The reference may be from the film *Las Vegas Nights* (1941), which featured Tommy Dorsey's band and was the first brief screen appearance for a singer called Frank Sinatra. Fickle Fannie seems to be the name of one of the clubs in the film – and maybe was a real life club. This might relate to the crew's time at Salt Lake City and the more than probable trip down to Nellis Air Force Base and Las Vegas. Whether the in-joke was about the loss of money or partying, it seems a common strand that kept the crew amused.

The early missions of Colburn's crew must have been perplexing at times, if not frustrating. The first eight were into France and were probably considered 'milk runs'. There was little or no fighter opposition and flak tended to be light and inaccurate. So far so good, but June 1944 saw some of the worst weather in Europe for many years. Not only did the bombardiers not get to see their targets visually, all too often it was hard to see the ground at all for much of the trip. Worsening weather conditions also threatened to disperse the force for landing and getting back 'home' could be delayed. The raid to the Cognac region on 19 June resulted in no bombs being dropped with clouds stretching ominously up to 29,000ft. There must have been times in these early days when some of the new crews wondered whether the weather was ever going to clear for them. Their training in the States had taken place in clear blue skies with arid landscapes below them, particularly around Salt Lake City. Here, in a not unusually unsettled European summer, it seemed to rain constantly and taking off and descending through cloud seemed an endless toil of nerves. The results in terms of bombing accuracy during the extended period of these cloud blankets were not outstanding.

All crews knew that Germany was the tough nut to crack; this was where the opposition was strong and where the odds stacked up more keenly than over northern France. Going to Germany, or more accurately coming back successfully, was the start of the progressive ladder from new boy to old boy. These were the raids most feared but also the raids that would distinguish you as an outstanding crew or a ragged crew lacking in composure. The majority came to Europe hoping the war would still be on by the time they got there. This cocksure spirit quickly disappeared, sometimes after only one flight across a flak-filled sky. Many confessed to feeling a wave of fear and hopelessness, with their waking hours filled with the nagging uncertainty of their survival. Nevertheless, most kept their nerves in check and did not talk openly about their fears.

The Ong crew had to wait a little less time than the Colburn crew to see Germany as they were dispatched to Bremen on 18 June. They were positioned at the back of the 388th's B lead group that day with another rookie crew off to their right led by Ken Snedeker. Between these two crews was an old hand. George Little was sitting on twenty-four missions and a tough mix of operations at that, eight to Germany with three to the hardest of them all, Berlin. No aircraft were lost on this mission but the official record says that 'flak over the target was accurate'. If the Ong crew had any romantic notions of their war, Bremen probably taught them what it was about and, more soberingly, what it may be like in future. It is likely they counted the holes in their B-17 when they returned.

Bremen, a northern city with a major port and link to the North Sea via the River Weser, was no stranger to bombing raids. This was the twentieth significant raid since 1940 and, with its mixture of port, refineries and U-boat shelters, it was bound to attract Allied attacks. They were well prepared and practised in terms of flak batteries; Bremen lay on the potential aerial thoroughfare to Berlin. However, for the residents of Bremen, there had been a lull from the RAF night raids of 1942 and the daylight raids of late 1943. The devastation had already taken a major toll of lives and buildings in Bremen, and June 1942 had also seen a 1,000 plane raid that had knocked out the Focke-Wulf factory and flattened much of the city. For six months a false peace held over Bremen during the first part of 1944. Then, a raid on 18 June signalled the beginning of another pattern that continued until 30 March 1945. According to German records, the daylight raid of 18 June saw 762 explosive devices dropped on the city resulting in twenty-one deaths and four other serious injuries.

One date is significant for the Colburn and Ong crews: 21 June 1944, the day both crews flew to the Berlin area. Dong Ong's aircraft was one of only three 388th planes flying with a much larger section of the 96th Bomb Group. It was their first taste of deep penetration into Germany with all the rigours and perils of a Berlin raid. Apart from the need for sufficient numbers of aircraft to furnish the raid, the decision to send Ong's crew among only two others seems to point to a desire to give the crew experience. The Colburn crew also flew to an area just south of Berlin, the Ruhland, to attack synthetic oil refineries. Twenty-nine aircraft were tasked to go but the mission had one major difference from any other mission of the 388th. They were to fly on to the Soviet Union and land there at a specially prepared base. Not only would the mission be an eye-opener for the crews, it would prove to be so dramatic that no member would ever forget it and no historian would omit to mention the name Poltava in relation to the 388th Bombardment Group. Johnnie Colburn and crew were about to experience a defining moment, not only in terms of memories, but in terms of their very survival.

Chapter 7

The Homecoming

Never say goodbye because goodbye means going away and going away means forgetting.

– J.M. Barrie, *Peter Pan*

U p until now, all my contacts with crew family members had been via telephone or email; nothing had been face to face. It was now mid-July 2014 and it had been just over two months since the trophy shook my life about, but so far it had been a great trip. I'd had direct, meaningful contact with five families and another four with whom I'd had some contact but I was yet to get to the nitty-gritty of gathering information.

I was working during the day, thinking a lot and trying to follow up contacts at night. Some nights it had been hard to sleep as, with the time lag between the States and here, it was often quite late by the time I got something new. Rob Simmon, the son of Johnnie Colburn's bombardier, had been very helpful and was sending me new photos and insights regularly. I had been talking to Dong's co-pilot's family, the Lipperts, and discovered they had a scrapbook and possibly even some early cine film of the crew training in South Dakota.

To coin a phrase, I had the bones now; it was time for some flesh on the bones. That flesh was meeting real people, not that those communicating by electronic means were any less human, but we've all had that moment when we have met people for the first time and thought, 'I never imagined you looked like that.' There's something rather significant, too, about physical meeting; it's the point you touch history rather than just talk about it. I'd already concluded that my research and book was ten years too late but there was, I believed, a reason for it and that was more about the generations that followed and our future perception of the Second World War.

Mid-July is a significant time in the history of the 388th Bombardment Group. It arrived en masse on 10 June 1943 and its first combat mission was on 17 July. This year, Dick Henggeler, the 388th historian, was coming over to the Knettishall area for a few days and was bringing the son of a 388th bombardier with him. Dick was no stranger to Knettishall and had visited many times. He's been my first point of call for information but also, just as importantly, our meeting would be my closest contact to date with a relative. I might have been grasping at distant straws, but Dick's dad, Francis 'Hank' Henggeler, was commanding officer of the 563rd Squadron. My two crews were in the 560th and 562nd, but Hank flew with Johnnie Colburn as mission commander to Dusseldorf on 9 September 1944. Johnnie was lead pilot and Bob Simmon lead bombardier. It might have only been one mission, but Hank was sitting alongside Johnnie for that trip and that was enough contact to make him a part of this story. It was also a significant raid in the picture of Colburn's crew being named crew of the month in September.

After some to-ing and fro-ing of text messages, we agreed to meet at an air show at Duxford in Cambridgeshire – an annual pilgrimage for all things warbird for the enthusiast. I'd not been for years but it was a prime opportunity to refresh my memory of the sights and sounds of the historic aircraft and is one of the places you can see *Sally B*, the UK's only airworthy B-17, flying. It was a warm day and I set off early to try to beat the crowds. Crossing the Pennines (a stretch of moors and low mountains) across to the east of England is not my favourite journey. One of Britain's first main trunk roads, the A1, is always a challenge as it has long stretches of its original two-lane configuration. It was a four-and-a-half hour trip and I had time to mull over what I wanted to see and what I wanted to experience. Duxford is always impressive, it also houses the Imperial War Museum collection of aircraft; it's a unique experience. I had agreed to meet Dick and friends outside the huge glass-fronted American Air Museum during the afternoon. As in all good spy movies, I described by text what I was wearing: 'Pink T-shirt and khaki shorts.'

'Green shirt and khaki pants,' came the very American reply.

The air show was in full swing when I walked up to the agreed place. Two Piper Cub aircraft were displaying and they are fairly small and quite quiet, so it was not a bad time to meet up. However, due to it being a warm day and the front of the building being in shade, there were a couple of hundred people sitting or milling around. I stood at one end and kept watch but it took a few minutes to spot the bright green shirt and a man pacing up and down looking into the crowd:

'David?' said Dick, holding out a hand. I resisted the urge to reply, 'Doctor Livingstone I presume,' and shook Dick's hand. Sometimes one has to remember that, although the British and Americans share the same language, or at least in part, not all cultural references would be understood. I now needed to find out whether Americans knew about David Livingstone.

Our meeting place had a symbolism that I failed to grasp until a few days afterwards. Behind the huge glass wall of Duxford's American Air Museum and just feet away from where we stood was B-17 *Mary Alice,* a true veteran of the air conflict that more than seventy years later was the reason for our meeting.

Dick introduced me to Andrew and Corinne Kaufman, who had come in the footsteps of Andrew's father, who had passed away the year before aged 90. They were from Long Island and Corinne assured me in a friendly way that my shirt was more 'salmon' than pink – she was an interior designer, so I didn't argue. Andrew's father, Paul Kaufman, had flown only five missions in September 1944 before being shot down by flak on his sixth raid, which was to Merseburg. I hadn't heard of Merseburg at this point, but it was a synthetic oil refinery and one of the most heavily defended targets of the war. The crew survived and became prisoners of war in Stalagluft 1. Their flying career had lasted barely eighteen days in September 1944 – after two years of training it must have been a bitter pill to swallow but their luck had held in surviving. Looking through the records later, I saw that in the six aircraft they flew, three of them had been flown in the past by Ong or Colburn, including *Betty Anne,* the Ong crew's sweetheart aircraft. So there were a couple of tenuous links to the trophy story. In many ways, the story of the Kaufmans follows a common thread. When fathers and mothers are alive there is the natural acceptance that any newsworthy stories from their lives would be told to their offspring but, unless opportunity arrives or is created, this is not always the case. Corinne Kaufman tells me how she interviewed her father-in-law knowing that the stories he held might be otherwise lost.

Air shows are perhaps not the best place to meet for a first time and have a meaningful conversation. We had a stab at it but by the time some of the noisier acts were turning up it was time to sit and watch. *Sally B* flew her slot with precision and a P-51 Mustang flying alongside was a poignant moment. Although I had seen *Sally B* some years earlier, it was the recollection and the refreshing of memory about the sound of her engines that stuck with me. For the uninitiated, each aircraft has its own sound and a radial engine has a certain deeper tone that is heard not just with the ears, but really hits your chest as well. Put four of them together on one aircraft and you have a very special sound. We all decided to make an early start for the exits and agreed to meet up the next day at another American base with a small museum, Thorpe Abotts, home to the 100th Bomb Group, the Bloody Hundredth.

So, alone once more, I made a dash for the car and squeezed myself out of the parking field before the big rush was on. I drove on for a further forty-five minutes away from Cambridge, on into Suffolk and eventually into the country lanes that yielded small knots of English countryside hamlets and villages. Many had well-proportioned churches, thatched houses and narrow roads that testified to a prosperous agricultural past and now enjoyed elements of exclusivity for the discerning country escapee. Soon I was passing through the boundary villages around Knettishall: Barningham, with a sign to Coney Weston, Market Weston and on to Hopton, where my guest house for the night was located. I realized that Hopton was on the boundary with Norfolk and, indeed, my guest house was in that county.

The sun was still warm but it was getting towards mid-evening so, a quick change later, I went back out to find a pub to eat. I had a mind to go to the closest village from the old airfield, Coney Weston, and the pub there, The Swan. The encampment of the 560th Squadron was literally a short hop over a wall into the street of Coney Weston and The Swan was a regular watering hole for curious crews. How Coney Weston, a village at that time of barely 200 people, reacted to the shock of finding nearly 3,000 Americans living on the doorstep is hard to fathom. By all accounts they got on well and relations were very cheery. No doubt the transformation from sleepy country idyll to a town containing thousands of eligible young men wearing uniform was enough to spin the heads of many a young local girl. What the local young men, many of whom were in reserved occupations in farming and unlikely to get into a uniform, thought of this impossible competition is hard to tell.

On this evening though, there was no food in sight at The Swan and, after a brief look around, I concluded that this was a locals' drinking pub – and no harm in that. Perhaps, for historical purposes, it was comforting to know it had changed little. At the time it was described as having bench seats and a single barrel of brown ale to its name. It's a small pub too, so there must have been a way to limit visitors from the base – not that the base was short of places in which to buy a beer. So, with a little chagrin, I withdrew to the next village and enjoyed a very agreeable meal washed down by that most British of beers – Stella Artois; hats off to the Belgians. I admit I'm not that much of a traditionalist. Having dealt with my hunger, and still with a mildly throbbing head from standing in the hot sun all day, I had one more important appointment to keep. It was just starting to get dark, or as dark as it gets in early summer here. It happens quite slowly and, in the north of England, the light from the setting sun lasts through to daybreak. I was in the south though and I knew that it would get quite dark before too long. My appointment was with Station 136, RAF Knettishall. I had seen on maps that the course of the main runway was now cut by a through road and so I drove up to that point. I was made aware of the locality by the concrete pad boundary roads and former taxiways that sprung off from my left and right. It is worth noting that, as is the case with many of the airfields in these parts, there has been a concerted effort to return them to the fields from which they came. Knettishall has been no exception and the runways and concrete have been removed purposefully to allow for uninterrupted agriculture. For those like me of a misty-eyed, yesteryear disposition, it seems sad that such an historic site should have been the subject of deliberate de-construction. The reality is though that East Anglia alone hosted 111 established airfields and by the time temporary and diversionary flying fields are accounted for, the figure is considerably higher. As a rough rule of thumb, there was an airfield every five miles in any direction and Knettishall had six others within pea-shooter distance. Not all were American bases and the RAF also stationed its heavy bombers there, too.

My route took me past the small corner of trees that shelters the 388th Bombardment Group memorial, a trio of black granite slabs containing the names of those who never returned to Knettishall – or anywhere else for that matter. Theirs was the sad privilege of giving up their lives for our modern world. As the light was beginning to fade, I decided not to stop but to come back the next day for a better look. I found my trans-runway spot and pulled the car on to the remaining slabs of concrete. The line of the main runway was preserved by a box of trees spanning both sides of the road. They were quite well established and fitting, given the other two runways have now completely gone, and they mark the lines of the runway well. The two open spaces left at the side of the road are crumbling away and used by farmers for storing strong smelling, animal-derived fertilizer – that is my poetic description! Nevertheless, I got out and took a walk into the deafening silence of the evening. A breeze was building, a refreshingly cool breeze given the humidity and heat earlier.

I used my surroundings to imagine carefully the thundering activity of this runway, the large rubber tyres of the B-17s scooting along this surface, either trying to get airborne or landing with the whine of propellers and spluttering of engines with closed throttles. My imagination was helped by the noise of the B-17 I had heard a few short hours earlier. I had set myself up well for this visit. Of course, if it had been down solely to me I probably could not have co-joined as many components so successfully. There was that sense I was a tiny observer of a huge picture and a definite sense of purpose – a purpose designed by the great architect. I had begun to think of those who had left this runway, the last piece of safe earth they knew, each one knowing the risks they ran in the undertaking. The clouds on the horizon were building into a leaden grey and God gave me the sound effects for my thoughts. Lightning flashed on the horizon and thunder rumbled over the otherwise still Suffolk countryside. I was caught in a Steven Spielberg moment, in a movie script of improbable timing, alone in the breeze of a Second World War airfield that was now a sleeping giant under the fields.

Despite the approaching thunder, there was no risk of immediate rain and in the fading light I took a photo on my phone to post on Facebook. In the back of my car was a cardboard box with the trophy in it, safely wrapped in a blanket. As far as I knew, this was the first time it had come back for nearly seventy years. I regret not taking it out and placing it on the old runway for a photo, but it's something I will do at some point in future. After all is said and done, the trophy is a bit of old silver plate with some names engraved on it, important names in history, but it's still an inanimate object. With a glad heart, I drove back down the gentle incline to Coney Weston. I had imagined that all East Anglian airfields were as flat as the proverbial pancake but I was surprised to find more ridges and trees than I imagined. Knettishall Heath, the land on which the airfield was built, rolls quite a bit around the villages and the airfield almost sits on a crown of flat land above them. My sleep that night was very solid, I think more akin to losing consciousness than a normal sleep. I was bushed.

The next morning, my hosts at the guest house nearly killed me with their full English breakfast. It would have been rude to leave any and it set me up for the day in kingly fashion. I waddled out to my car burping my appreciation and hoped that I could still breathe properly when sitting down to drive. My meet-up with my American friends was booked but there was time to call up to Knettishall again to take in more of the old airfield site.

I took some time to examine and photograph the war memorial this time and, in the sea of more than 500 names, I suddenly spotted my own, David Price. It jumped out so clearly that it took me by surprise and, looking away and back again, I was fascinated how my eyes and mind found that name again in a split second. My namesake had suffered a sad misfortune even though he was part of the ground crew and not a combat crew. It was one of these unexpected incidents of war:

On the foggy morning of May 20, 1944, some three hours after the last plane had taken off for the day's mission to Brussels, M/Sgt. Price was relaxing in his line tent near the runway with fellow crew chiefs Allen Gregory and Clove Wells, unaware that a troubled plane was coming in for an emergency landing. Aircraft 42-97352 had aborted the mission when its #1 engine failed, along with the electric and hydraulic systems. At 9:50 a.m., with the plane's wheels cranked manually into position, the pilot was making his third landing attempt when engine #1 burst into flame. The pilot brought the plane down abruptly and at high speed, missing the runway. The plane then sped across the grass, ploughing through the crew chiefs' tent. Sgt. Price and M/Sgt. Gregory were killed instantly; M/Sgt. Wells was injured but recovered. In addition to M/Sgt. Gregory and Sgt. Price, R. W. Young was killed in this accident.

388th Bomb Group Database

It appears that not only did the B-17 overshoot the runway and hit the tents, it also carried on to demolish a Nissen hut, causing the death of R.W. Young. The pilot, August Schneider, was on his tenth mission and the third in this particular aircraft. Despite this terrible incident, Schneider and crew carried on to notch up an impressive thirty-five mission total and returned safely to the States, although '352 never flew again. Of my two crews, both were probably on pre-mission training at Knettishall and what they made of this accident as newcomers leaves plenty to think about.

Having examined the war memorial, I made my way up the incline to the runways once again, as I had done the night before. It was far more of a normal day with cars and people passing regularly; you can't have special experiences every time. I made my way along the field track, which is what remains of a much larger section of runway. At the bottom, where two runways used to intersect, there is a rather battered tin hangar. It's a far more modern addition but, with a windsock and a piece of mown grass strip, clearly flying still happens occasionally at Knettishall – fitting indeed for this otherwise deserted field.

As I walked examining the abundant fields of growing crops, a low-flying jet slowly rumbled through the cloud above me. At first I couldn't see it but, as it broke through a gap, I could see a US Air Force KC-135, the military equivalent of the old Boeing 707 airliner. It began a wide circle flying a few miles around the boundary of Knettishall. Only a few miles away lie the large US air bases of Mildenhall and Lakenheath, the former being the source of my Sunday morning flyer. I laughed to myself that while I was reminiscing about one old airfield and the influx of American airmen now long departed, there's a real sense that they came seventy years ago and never left. The KC-135 crew had no idea that they were part of this story too and how it all interlaced together. Robert Simmon Jnr, the son of Colburn's bombardier, had told me that he visited Knettishall with his father years earlier and stood at the war memorial. Rob had also served with the US Air Force and, to make telling the story easier, he served on KC-135s.

Looking at the time, I realized it was time to go and drive the fifteen miles to Thorpe Abbotts, the home of the 100th Bomb Group. The day was warm again, but this time heavy showers were a feature and I had to drive through large puddles and surface water as the heavens opened. The small museum at Thorpe Abbotts centres around the preserved control tower and I found Dick, Andrew and Corinne already engrossed in the many photos and mementos displayed. They looked a little surprised when I appeared with a wet raincoat after unsuccessfully dodging the latest heavy shower. 'Is it raining?' they asked and, being British and used to getting wet without warning, it seemed a funny question at the time.

Like the 388th, the 100th Group flew B-17s and there was a lot of crossover of missions, and also a lot of common threads in the activity of the base and how it functioned. From the top of the tower, or watch office as they were known, one could make out the lines of the old runways, but, like Knettishall, the demands of agriculture had taken much away. Nevertheless, it did not take much imagination to picture the way the base functioned. A large model of the airfield helped tune our senses to where everything had been and, looking down on what little remained, the complexity of the base was surprising.

In another outbuilding, some pieces of B-17 were mounted on a wall. One was full of shrapnel holes and a stark reminder of the dangers of flying in a war of ever increasing sophistication. Reading histories and accounts of those who flew B-17s is one thing, but seeing the effects of the much feared flak was another. It seemed little wonder that so many crews experienced damage to their aircraft, some of it quite extreme. For many, it seemed nearly every mission brought its harvest of holes; sometimes one or two, at other times literally hundreds of holes blasted through the thin metal skin. Statistically, the majority were near misses and, although they caused surface damage, did not impair flying seriously. When internal damage occurred, it could be almost anywhere and might affect control cables, fuel tanks, engines or instrumentation. Such damage was like a spinning coin; heads you won, tails you lost. Many returned successfully with knocked out engines and shot wheels and brakes, others experienced the terror of the slow fall from formation, controlled or not. Leaving formation was always a perilous journey as Luftwaffe fighters were prowling, waiting for the lame ducks to fall behind. All too often the kill was swift and merciless, with multiple attack passes knocking the aircraft down in minutes. The other aircraft in formation could only look on helplessly and hope accompanying fighters could rescue the damaged B-17.

Perhaps what remained with me after the visit was the story of the brewery run carried out almost constantly throughout the operation of the base. One returning veteran had recounted how his job was to drive a six-wheeler GMC truck to the Midlands and transport kegs of beer back to the base. The journey there took a whole day, such were the roads then, and after resting overnight he would return with the beer. It would be a constant task to keep the base supplied; 3,000 men with a thirst was something to be organized. It demonstrated to me the vast array of jobs necessary to get bombers into the air and keep the base functioning; no easy task given the restraints of war.

It was time to play 'show and tell' with the trophy and I brought it out of my car to show my new friends. Some of the volunteer staff of the 100th museum joined us around a small table, fascinated by how this silver object had evaded attention for so long. Hopefully, it was an encouragement for them too that historical objects could pop out of obscurity after decades. One of those mini-moments happened when Dick took hold of the handles to look at the trophy. He was the first relative to touch it and I wish I'd taken a photo.

The next part of my trip was back to Knettishall and up to a farm not far from the old airfield, which is the location of the 388th Bomb Group Museum. This is a small collection housed around one of the old Nissen huts that used to pepper the base. Nearly every one has been moved away from its original site, but they can still be seen on many farms in the area. Dave Sarson, owner of the farm and a keen member of the small group that runs the museum, greeted us and soon others were arriving to meet us. Their warmth and enthusiasm was infectious and we were quickly engrossed in different stories of the base and airmen. The museum had all kinds of memorabilia, uniforms, models, papers and personal objects. We were joined by Percy Prentice, who, as a young lad, became the 'mascot' of the 388th. He spent much time on the base over the two years it operated and confesses to missing a lot of school. The airmen had a uniform made for him and one photo in the museum shows him meeting General Doolittle, the acclaimed airman and leader who commanded the 8th Air Force. It was clear immediately that those two years changed Percy's life – for where else would a lad from a small country village in England suddenly have a new culture and experience so unreservedly encompass him? Percy, who looks after the war memorial, is now an old man. I hope he doesn't mind me describing him as that but, despite his check shirt and baseball cap, I'm reminded that I'm looking at one of the older generation that won't be with us forever. Here lies the generation that experienced the events and is now, ever so gently, slipping away from us.

Percy was my first contact with someone who was a participant in the events of 1943–1945 at Knettishall. He remembers the Americans coming and he remembers their going. The men of the 388th were his friends and he and his family experienced the joys and grief of knowing them. Percy's mother would take in laundry, particularly shirts for the airmen, and when washing was not collected, it meant something had happened. Percy had not seen the trophy before, but it represented yet another link in the story. He remembered Dong Ong clearly and his numerous missions and yet again testified, as others had, how much everyone liked him. Perhaps Johnnie Colburn was less assuming for it seemed, at least in the company of the historians, his name was not well known.

My time was running out, it was Sunday afternoon and work beckoned me the next day. It was time for me to leave and, after getting photos of everyone in various groups around the trophy, I started back on the six-hour trip home. There was plenty of time to think, but also muse on how East Anglia, the area that hosted so many bomber bases, was still without a motorway. The country lanes were largely unchanged in the last seventy years and, despite the march of change in modern society, you did not have to squint your eyes too much to imagine life in these parts during the war. In terms of history, the lodging of the 388th, and indeed every American unit in the United Kingdom, was but a blink of the eye, fewer than two years in many cases. The war is still hugely significant in the eyes of our society because we are, in the timeline of world history, so very close to it. I was born eighteen years after the end and my parents lived through it. As short as our lives are, this means that it will still take a little while for the memory of the war to flicker. What seems certain is that both world wars will merge into one twentieth century conflict because the protagonists will seem the same. Tonight though, as the sun sets in my eyes, I weave my way northwards and eventually, as the sun dips below the horizon in that orange hue that clear summer evenings in this part of the world produce, cross the Pennines to home. In my car I carry a little extra weight: some small lumps of broken concrete from one of the runways at Knettishall and some memories and impressions to last a lifetime.

Chapter 8

Dropping Bombs

If you prick us, do we not bleed? If you tickle us, do we not laugh? If you poison us, do we not die? And if you wrong us, shall we not revenge?
— William Shakespeare, *The Merchant of Venice*

'I suppose you think that I'm a murderer.' The words of the former Lancaster bomber tail gunner took Aileen aback. The man, at that time in his late 80s and living in a residential home, had agreed to a recorded interview for the archives of Solway Aviation Museum in Carlisle. Aileen, one of the museum volunteers, was putting together a schools educational programme and getting some living memories was an important task. Although Aileen assured him that this was not the case and, indeed, his family were very proud of him, it showed that, even in this latter part of his life, he was still dealing with the memories and contradictions of morality that took place in a brutal war.

Much has been written and debated about the Allied bombing campaign of the Second World War. I, as an aviation enthusiast, have a distinct predisposition towards the men who flew the missions and I accept I could be accused of a bias towards the acceptance that the strategic decisions made to area bomb the cities of Germany were correct. The origins of doubt about the Allied bombing campaign emerged as soon as troops entered the cities of Germany. Stories of the terrible conditions and suffering abounded, whole cities appeared wiped out with nearly every building damaged — surely we had overreacted?

The concept of precision bombing, that is attacks on specific targets that have some military advantage, is taken as read. These targets can include anything from columns of advancing infantry to small rural factories producing the nails for wooden ammunition boxes. The reality of war is that the enemy must be stopped, pushed back and finally made to capitulate — and people are going to die in this process. Area bombing is a step further where the civilian population of any age and disposition become targets in the effort to break the will of their government. At its heart is not necessarily the numbers of those killed or displaced, but the breaking of their courage to resist and halt the supply of even the most basic of commodities to the army they serve. At the start of the Second World War, the idea of shattering a community to the point that it became impossible to govern was a well-propounded theory, but a theory nonetheless.

The origins of the strategy can be linked back to a number of respected military theorists, Lieutenant Colonel Giulio Douhet from Italy being notable. His observations of the First World War led him to the conclusion that air power was a key factor in breaking the deadlock of trench warfare. He was not alone in his energetic support for any weapon or strategy that would prevent the industrialized carnage of troops in mud and water-soaked trenches. The eyes of a whole generation had witnessed at first hand the terrors of war, the damage, the death and stench. On every side, potential protagonists looked at ways of winning wars more decisively, with greater movement and speed. Both Hitler and Churchill had fought in the trenches, and nearly every seasoned military commander of the 1930s had experiences of the stalemate and pointlessness of static warfare. Where Douhet expanded his theory of offensive air warfare was in the area of the strategic attack of any entity that could benefit an enemy's war effort. As a direct result of this thinking, the civilian population became accessories to their army's efforts. His book *The Command of the Air* (1921) detailed the mechanical destruction of civilian centres behind the enemy line using waves of bombers dropping different kinds of explosive and incendiary devices. He is quite emphatic on the desired effect:

A complete breakdown of the social structure cannot but take place in a country subjected to this kind of merciless pounding from the air.

Although Douhet's thinking undoubtedly inspired bombing strategy in both Allied and Axis powers, fortunately, his vision of the final wave of bombers carrying poison gas never became a reality.

However, Douhet was not the sole architect of area bombing; during the First World War the Germans were the first to step over the boundaries of civilian and military life in aerial warfare. Using large airships, the Zeppelins, fifty-one bombing raids were carried out over England from early 1915. Although there were some attempts to hit targets of military importance, the real emphasis was on undermining public confidence – in short, to spread fear. Alfred von Tirpitz, Secretary of State of the Imperial Naval Office, wrote that:

> *The measure of the success will lie not only in the injury which will be caused to the enemy, but also in the significant effect it will have in diminishing the enemy's determination to prosecute the war.*

The British public were left in no doubt that the Germans were a people prepared to go to any lengths to win the war. The casualty lists were much smaller than the Second World War, but still a substantial number, with 557 killed and 1,358 injured. Further attacks by aircraft resulted in the loss of a further 835 killed and 2,508 injured. Some attacks were particularly monstrous in the public perception, and on the morning of 13 June 1917 a German bomb exploded in an infants' school class at upper North Street School, Poplar, in east London, killing eighteen children.

British bombing raids into Germany also began in response to the gathering air war, although their targets tended to be the rail yards and munitions factories in towns such as Mannheim and Mainz. This said, it is improbable that most raids were particularly accurate and civilian casualties must have ensued.

Even before Orville and Wilbur Wright had completed their first powered flight at Kitty Hawk, North Carolina, in December 1903 the international community had begun to voice concerns over the possible effects of aerial warfare. The first Hague International Conference in 1899 prohibited the dropping of any kind of projectile or bomb from a flying machine. The slip in standards manifested itself rapidly once the military potential of the new flying machines were realized. By 1907, a subsequent conference had diluted the wording to forbid the bombing of 'undefended localities'.

Aerial warfare in the First World War expanded dramatically during the conflict. The earliest encounters between aircraft were somewhat of a friendly affair with hearty waving and friendly exchanges. This stopped quite rapidly as it was realized that these spotter planes were now gathering information that was of significant military use, not least in artillery direction. The use of balloons for such purposes was well established and it was realized that aircraft could be used to attack the balloons as well as other aircraft. The first efforts involved pilots firing small arms at their adversaries and before long an observer was armed with a machine gun. In turn, the machine guns were mounted forward on fighters with the biggest step forward being the propeller synchronizing gear designed by Dutch designer Antony Fokker. This allowed the gun to fire between the spinning propeller blades. Meanwhile, early bombing was a crude affair with bags of flour being dropped by the pilot or observer on to a target to practise accuracy. Using small hand-dropped bombs was more of a nuisance factor than a strategic weapon and experiments with steel darts, known as *flechettes*, were less than conclusive, although widely used over the trenches. There are accounts of casualties inflicted with these basic arrows, but it was obvious that no strategic advantage could be made by such simple means. Once wing-mounted bombs and bomb racks were developed, it gave the aircraft the ability, depending on range, to launch effective attacks and create substantial damage. The bomber as a type of aircraft was born and developed rapidly in range and effectiveness.

The end of the war saw many of these larger machines used for all manner of cargo and passenger services and they instilled a good deal of excitement for the future and the possibilities of unhindered aerial exploration. In Britain and America, the large stocks of airworthy, but unwanted, aircraft after the war led many to venture into entrepreneurial schemes, some for the carriage of goods such as post and newspapers, others to feed the gathering demand for aviation entertainment. Aviation was brought to the masses by larger than life characters such as Alan Cobham in Britain and Charles Lindbergh in the United States. Pioneering flights and expansive passenger services seemed to be the order of the day. Sadly, the new era of optimism was short-lived and, as the Great Depression broke, once again strategists were steering development of aircraft for military purposes as quickly as for civilian purposes.

By the 1930s, the bomber was tipped as a weapon of mass destruction that everyone feared. The damage it could inflict was well recorded in the First World War, but now its potential was hard to measure and lurid speculation began to circulate about its destructive power. Some of this speculation came down to an increased public appetite for science fiction and writers such as H.G. Wells fuelled the morbid belief that any future war would decimate the populous cities. The 1936 film *Things to Come* had a screenplay written by Wells and depicts a global war dominated by air power that lasts into the 1960s. As well as feeding the public's curiosity about future weapons, there is a real sense that politicians believed earnestly, and indeed expected, any future conflagration to involve civilians as war targets.

There is a sense that the power of the bomber and the weapons it carried became overstated in the 1930s. This was highly insightful, for the development of nuclear weapons capable of fulfilling the nightmare was only just around the corner. The Spanish Civil War in Europe and the Second Sino-Japanese War both had instances of intense bombing raids. The bombing of Guernica in Spain in 1937 by the German Condor Legion provoked an international outcry, as did the intense bombing of Nanking and Canton, also in that year. What was apparent was that too little development work had been put into anti-aircraft measures and that the fighter and bomber threat was considerable to countries that could not maintain air superiority. Given that Britain was an advanced technical nation, perhaps it was all the more surprising that air defence and the development of effective fighter aircraft was woefully inadequate. Up to 1937, Britain was still exclusively using biplanes in front line fighter squadrons, even when in Spain the first Me 109 was tearing into the opposition. The introduction to the RAF of the Hurricane and then the Spitfire in 1937 and 1938 respectively was just in time, although by the outbreak of hostilities in 1939 there was a significant lack of numbers. What saved Britain from the protracted Luftwaffe onslaught of 1940 to 1941 was the chain of air defence radar; the network of observers and organized control rooms linked by telephone. In America too, the all-metal monoplane fighter was slow out of the starting gate, although the lessons of Europe were followed keenly. It was apparent that the USAAF would need substantially more advanced aircraft and in the global arms race that preceded the Second World War, the Curtiss P-40, Lockheed P-38 and Grumman F4F all took shape prior to 1940.

Another element of the structure of bombing was that bombers travelled in formation. There was an understanding that with accuracy being difficult to achieve with a small number, a formation was much more likely to inflict the sort of damage desired. This 'cloud' of aircraft idea was born directly out of experience in the First World War, but also featured in the subconscious imagination of the strategists. The concept of an aerial armada might have been seen as an obvious practicality, but its roots lay with the history of seafaring and the great sea battles that had shaped nations such as Britain. The 1920s and '30s had also spawned the theatrical idea of terror; to truly frighten a civilian population required huge armadas of aircraft. In science fiction films, including *Flash Gordon*, destructive spaceships travelled in large numbers for dramatic effect. The Nazis understood the power of propaganda and terror more concisely than their enemies. In their development of the Junkers Ju 87, the Stuka dive-bomber, in 1935, they built sirens into the undercarriage legs that howled as the aircraft dived on to its target. This distinctive noise became the hallmark of blitzkrieg, or lightning war.

In practical terms, there were significant drawbacks to the bomber formation. There was the necessity that they flew together and accurately, that bombing must be synchronized and that the target must be recognizable. The biggest problem the bomber had, no matter how big, was that the weight of bombs made it slower than its fighter adversaries. This slowness made it an easier target for anti-aircraft guns and a formation made for even more hazardous flying when being fired at. Part of the perceived answer was to fly at greater and greater heights, but this too brought problems of reducing the accuracy of bombing and, for the crews, the freezing conditions and lack of natural oxygen were an incredible challenge.

By the outbreak of the Second World War most of the civilian population in urban conurbations assumed that bombing would not only destroy them as a community, but could possibly destroy the very fabric of civilization. The fear was not without grounds because testing such a devastating weapon had been limited. A generation had returned from the First World War with first-hand experiences of the effects of intensive shelling. Front line towns such as Ypres in Belgium had felt the full force of every kind of bombardment; very little remained of it apart from its cellars. The British soldier had used his characteristic sense of humour and irony to make a terrible situation lighter, with jokes and stories about 'Wipers' abounding. The battlefields had been reduced to a barren, featureless lunar landscape with a stench of death and decay adding to a misery of four years of terror. Even here, in the network of trenches and defensive earthworks, 'road' signs emerged with creative names often featuring the names of home towns. Other more colourful references such as Happy Valley, Caterpillar Valley and Hellfire Corner appeared. Even in the worst of situations, the human spirit emerged to make light of seemingly impossible odds. Perhaps it was this aspect of human survival and ingenuity that escaped the attentions of the pre-war strategists. Social disorder and collapse was not something easily attained by an enemy, even using the most sophisticated weapons at their disposal.

When the Germans invaded Poland on 1 September 1939, Britain and France were drawn into war, but even before then civil defence had become a priority with gas masks issued in Britain to all the population. The use of poison gas on the First World War battlefields had been extensive and now, with the new understanding that the civilian population were as much at risk as the military, preparations were extensive for the forthcoming conflict. Tens of thousands of children were evacuated from major towns and cities in Britain. Some found the idyll of the countryside an amazing adventure, particularly when they were lodged with caring 'foster' parents. Others found it very distressing and miserable, with numerous stories of heartless carers making life even harder. Bomb shelters were being built everywhere and, in true British style, the personal family shelter became very popular in small back yards and gardens. Space did not always allow for shelters to be very far from houses, but it seemed the mass shelter was something less appealing. The Anderson Shelter was the most popular version and consisted of curved tin sheets that could be partially buried to give an underground space. Some families equipped these with chairs, table and bunks to make an outdoor home from home. These do-it-yourself defences came to epitomize the British grit in enduring what was to be termed the Blitz. The effectiveness of these structures is very dubious but, in the context of bombing breaking public morale, they were valuable in allowing individual families to plan their own shelter.

Elsewhere, fire defences and pumps were being assembled and teams of volunteers were being trained as air raid wardens to help watch for fires and supervise preventative measures. Heavy blackout curtains were mandatory, with fines handed out for persistent showing of light, and windows were taped with crosses to limit glass shatter. Schools, hospitals and churches, indeed most public buildings, were equipped with emergency sand buckets to throw over incendiary devices. A thin, hand-operated pump was issued, the stirrup pump, of which many can still be found in the cupboards of village halls around Britain. These precautions would be of very little use in the event of a serious attack, but, in the course of war, it made the general public believe they could do something.

Although the rest of Poland had fallen relatively rapidly, Warsaw was besieged and was the subject of intensive aerial bombing by the Luftwaffe. As the city was pounded, Europe held its breath as, so far, the dire warnings of aerial might had seemed to have come to fruition. As bad as the bombing of Warsaw was, it came in the light of the Polish army withdrawing into it rather than an attempt to bomb civilians indiscriminately. However, with the fall of Warsaw, it suited the German taste for propaganda to exploit the terror effect of the bombing. The next incident of heavy destructive and strategic bombing of a city came in May 1940. The Germans invaded France through Belgium and they stretched north to take the Netherlands. In an unstoppable move, they swept through the lowlands. The Netherlands accepted its fate within only a few days and began tentative surrender negotiations. On 14 May 1940, only four days after the invasion started, German bombers attacked part of Rotterdam and virtually destroyed the medieval town, killing nearly 900 people and making 30,000 homeless. As in the case of Warsaw, the bombing was seen as a strategic attack on military targets. With the threat that Utrecht might be next, the Dutch government surrendered in haste, although even before the Rotterdam attack negotiations for the surrender of the Netherlands were well advanced. Here, before the eyes of all in Europe, was the nightmare that most feared; the apparently indiscriminate bombing, near complete destruction and a resulting strategic surrender. The role of the bomber as a war winner seemed greatly enhanced. Even in the case of Rotterdam, where the bombing seemed well orchestrated in order to pressure a surrender, it appears that part of the bombing was not fully in line with German policy as some Luftwaffe elements attacked after an order to hold back; an order not received by the bombers in time.

The hard grind of static trench warfare, men fighting for weeks, months or even years for pointless gains, had been replaced with fast movement, air superiority and the spectre of killing enough civilians to make a nation surrender. Paris fell without destruction; no one could bring themselves to destroy this jewel of Europe, or even allow the possibility of partial destruction. Even when Hitler ordered the destruction of Paris by ground forces at the German retreat in 1944, the order was disobeyed.

Another important element had taken place in these early months of the Second World War. The allied perception of Nazi Germany as an amoral aggressor was firmly established by the bombing of cities and civilian deaths; it had appeared to have become a tool of choice for the Axis. However, even Hitler was against the concept of wholesale attacks on civilians, with the caveat that it would be a last resort. It fixed in the Allies' minds the need to strike back, to damage enemy war production, but also to destroy the morale and will of their enemy's civilian population. The die had been cast and the opening moves of the war almost guaranteed the future destruction of German towns and cities.

In some more modern views of history, the Allies were wrong to pursue a mass bombing campaign against Germany. It was the Nazis that were the problem, not the German people. In this simplistic view, it is difficult to address the proportion and scale of Nazism and the line drawn between the hard line uniformed party members and those whose views broadly embraced Nazi sympathies. The Nazi system was widespread and infused the thinking of a whole population, so it was impossible to attack those of Nazi persuasion in singularity. It would not be possible to bomb a factory and only kill or injure those signed up to the Nazi ideal. The level and calibre of German brutality against its neighbours and sub-sections of their communities, such as the Jews, ensured there would be no political will among the Allies to withhold their hand from German cities. In some quarters of the Allies it was believed it was possible to force Germany to surrender by aerial destruction alone. At least this was the initial theory. Politicians and military strategists alike talked of the 'knock-out blow' and some believed a short, sharp attack on London would leave 150,000 dead and millions homeless. Like boxers in a ring, each side speculated how quickly they could knock the other out. As the war progressed, it became more apparent that Germany was too large and well structured to buckle under the weight of bombing alone. Berlin, one of the most modern cities in the world in 1939, was reduced to heaps of rubble by 1945, precipitated by Hitler's maniacal refusal to contemplate surrender of any sort. Meanwhile, an unstoppable conveyor belt of heavy bombers hit Germany night and day.

In 1939 and into 1940 the Anglo-German aerial slogging match was yet to materialize. There were bombing raids, but these were small affairs compared with later phases of the war. Britain had realized that, with no prospect of closer airfields, long range bombers would be necessary to hit its enemy. Most pre-war designs were inadequate to take the war effectively to the Germans. The equation of bomb load verses range proved a difficult balancing act. Added to this was the need to defend the bombers from attack and this meant adding guns and crew to operate them. Two bombers, the Handley Page Hampden and the Vickers Wellington, formed the vanguard of this approach, although from the outset the Hampden was cramped and uncomfortable for the crews. The Wellington was a different affair with much more room, an ingeniously strong, metal framed fuselage and the flying characteristics of a thoroughbred. Both these aircraft had two engines, but hot on their heels were the larger, faster four-engined bomber designs.

The Luftwaffe had introduced lighter and shorter ranged aircraft that suited the blitzkrieg model. As they operated from forward airfields in occupied countries, fighter escort was always available. Armament was lighter and less developed than the Allied bombers and, in most respects, the aircraft performed admirably in the task given them. The Germans made two developmental errors that affected their future attacking and defensive capabilities. The first was to fail to comprehend and develop the jet engine earlier in the war. The second was the development and building in numbers of a long range bomber force. Hermann Goering, the effusing self-absorbed head of the Luftwaffe, understood the fighting and tactics of the First World War – he had been an accomplished fighter pilot. However, rising through the ranks of the Nazi party had stripped him of much of his fighting and strategic skill. In the refusal of the Nazis to believe anything other than Hitler's view of total domination, a set of strategic imperatives were overlooked, a scenario of German retreat from occupied countries that would make longer ranged bombers important. As the U-boat war in the Atlantic raged, the opportunity to bomb convoys far from the protection of fighter cover was lost. Equally, as ground was lost in Russia, the ability to strike deep raids from Germany into the Soviet Union was an opportunity that could not be seized.

Britain was next to feel the force of an attempted blitzkrieg and as the Battle of Britain was fought in the summer of 1940, towns and cities experienced a bombing campaign at the hands of the Germans every bit as devastating as forecasters had warned. The Battle of Britain and the failure to gain air superiority forced the Germans to begin night bombing and, although key areas such as London and Liverpool docks were bombed, the scale and variety of targets set before the Luftwaffe proved too extensive for the force it had at its disposal. As the German daylight raids had proved too costly to its bomber strength, so too the RAF considered daylight too hazardous for its bombing raids.

For RAF Bomber Command, a number of pre-war problems led to its effectiveness being limited. Navigation devices, and particularly bomb sights capable of producing accurate results, were underdeveloped. While German night bombers followed radio beams that transected their proposed targets, the guidance of RAF bombers was still at an experimental stage.

Such was the inaccuracy of British bombing in the early part of the war that sometimes the Germans were unable to identify where the intended target had been. Some statistics show fewer than three per cent of bombs made it to their targets. Ironically, this led to widespread disruption over a large area as those, even in rural locations, headed for air raid shelters.

The Americans were about to enter into this perilous strategic melting pot. They had decided on a strategy of bomber design before the outbreak of war in Europe that had dangerous, untested assumptions about the ability of a bomber to operate in daylight. Their solution was to design long range bombers that could fly long and high as part of an armoured formation capable of defending itself. The concept of a 'Flying Fortress' was born and the fruit of this concept was the Boeing B-17, which first flew in 1935 and was christened with the name of the concept. It seemed, on paper, a good option that combined attacking prowess with strong defensive attributes. The RAF had suffered unsustainable losses in daylight raiding, but they were not aircraft bristling with guns. Could the B-17 and stablemates such as the B-24 Liberator really succeed where the British and German air forces had failed?

The development of the gyro-assisted Norden bomb sight by America was an area in which it had the lead. When combined with British designed radar developments, it made accurate bombing a possibility, given the right conditions. The entry of America into the war had expanded the possibilities of mass producing the armaments necessary to vanquish the Axis powers. The additional manpower was another essential component, but alongside both of these capabilities was a continued arms race that saw technological breakthroughs in many areas. Soon, the development of electronic devices were providing some of the answers in navigation and bombing aids that would turn a rather inaccurate practice into a more sophisticated science. New names, often in code, appeared, among them Gee, H2S, Fishpond, Darky, Moonshine and Oboe, and many other radar and radio devices. The race for technological supremacy saw both sides reaching in similar directions and, as the jet age was reached, so too research into the atomic bomb promised a weapon that could at last deliver 'the knock-out blow'. In one area the Germans were far more advanced: research and testing missiles, particularly the rockets that were to become the V-2. It is not surprising that at the war's end Wernher von Braun, the architect of the V-2, and his team were spirited away to America.

By the time the 8th Air Force B-17 bombers began arriving in Britain in numbers in 1943, the Royal Air Force had established a highly effective command and control structure. The RAF also had some of the best bombers of the time and were producing them in numbers, principally the Handley Page Halifax and the Avro Lancaster. Both packed a punch in speed, endurance and bomb load, with the Lancaster able to carry more than three times the bomb load of a B-17 at a higher cruise speed.

The seeds for bombing cities had been sown early and, as Britain struggled on alone in Europe against Hitler, bombing raids into Germany by the RAF became a key morale-boosting exercise. Hitler was infuriated by what, due to inaccuracy, appeared to be indiscriminate bombing. On 4 September 1940 after a raid on Berlin, Hitler declared in a public speech one of the founding keystones in the future conflict against cities:

The other night the English had bombed Berlin. So be it. But this is a game at which two can play. When the British Air Force drops 2,000 or 3,000 or 4,000kg of bombs, then we will drop 150,000, 180,000, 230,000, 300,000, 400,000kg on a single night. When they declare they will attack our cities in great measure, we will eradicate their cities.

The hour will come when one of us will break – and it will not be National Socialist Germany!

In the coming months, the Luftwaffe attacked Britain's major cities in waves of intense attacks – the Blitz. London, Birmingham, Coventry, Liverpool, Manchester and Glasgow were among the targets and by the time the intensive raids ended in May 1941, more than 40,000 had been killed and up to a further 139,000 injured. On 31 December 1941, only a few short weeks after the attack on Pearl Harbor, Winston Churchill addressed the Canadian parliament and, in specific references to the 'Cockney' Londoner and his fighting spirit, made his feelings known:

We shall never descend to the German or Japanese level, but if anybody likes to play rough, we can play rough too. Hitler and his Nazi gang have sown the wind; let them reap the whirlwind. Neither the length of the struggle nor any form of severity shall make us weary or shall make us quit.

By early 1942, a serious re-assessment had been made of the RAF's capability and organization and saw new leadership under Air Marshal Arthur Harris. Unlike some of the disparate attacks of 1941, raids were conducted far more in the German model of intensity. Lubeck was attacked in March 1942, a raid that destroyed much of the medieval city, followed by Rostock in the following month. There was no doubt the intensity and damage of the raids shocked Germany and, unlike some of the actions later in the war, it seemed even the Nazi high command were affected. Nazi propaganda minister Joseph Goebbels wrote of the destruction of Lubeck in his diary:

> *The damage is really enormous, I have been shown a newsreel of the destruction. It is horrible. One can well imagine how such a bombardment affects the population.*

What followed were a series of revenge attacks on British towns known as the Baedeker raids. Not only were the towns chosen because they were civilian centres, but the cultural and historical significance of the targets played an important part in the plan. The towns included Exeter, Bath, Norwich and Canterbury – all cathedral towns. Baedeker was a pre-war German tourist guide and formed the basis of the information in terms of historical significance. Raids continued throughout 1942 and 1943 in a pattern of what the Germans saw as vengeance attacks. The boundaries of war against civilians had been moved and, although debate rages about which side was more or less criminal in their actions, the bottom line was that nothing short of the end of war was going to see a cessation of the bombing of towns and cities on both sides.

The entry of America into the war brought with it a vast industrial force that was capable of producing large quantities of weapons and, with it, advanced technology. The British development of radar also gave the bombing forces the ability to bomb blind at night for the RAF and in cloud undercast for the Americans. No one was promising the kind of pinpoint accuracy that has become the expectation of bomber forces in the late twentieth and early twenty-first century. Accuracy was an immense problem for the, but by the time the trophy crews were reaching Knettishall in spring 1944, the first attempts at pinpoint accuracy were taking place – and with some success.

By this point in 1944 the belief that civilian populations could be bombed into complete social breakdown was diminishing. The effect of Nazi propaganda in relation to the bombing onslaught was producing a hatred of the bombers and the men who perpetrated the acts, but the bombing was not inducing German communities to rise against the Nazis in all but a few isolated cases. The chances of bailed-out airmen surviving impromptu civilian mobs were limited and there are many accounts of airmen being rescued by German troops, sometimes firing over the heads of their own countrymen to gain control.

The strategic bombing of factories, power plants and oil refineries was a high priority in Allied targeting. Looking through the missions lists and targets of the 388th Bomb Group, there is always a reason to bomb. There are no indiscriminate targets for, just as fuel and materials were precious to the Axis powers, so too were the resources of the Allies. Air Chief Marshal Arthur 'Bomber' Harris, often portrayed as a champion of indiscriminate civilian bombing, had identified the oil targets as a priority at the Casablanca Conference of 1941. As the Allies pressed on towards the D-Day landings, strategic priorities lay with breaching communications links and destroying defensive positions. A new threat had also emerged from the information gained through spies and radio intercepts. The Germans were building vengeance weapons and the launch ramps and manufacture sites of V-1 flying bombs and V-2 rocket facilities were thrown into the target list. However, the factories and oil refineries were always considered key targets.

It is also possible to reflect that a clearer understanding of how the Nazi regime functioned was in place by 1944. While there were still proponents of large scale city bombing, there was a recognition that targets of importance to the Nazi hierarchy could also yield lasting psychological results on the men pulling the strings.

As the formations of Allied bombers grew in size, there was nothing unusual about a 1,000 plane raid and the giant procession of formations cutting the sky with contrails had a psychological effect on all who witnessed it. For the occupied countries, it was a sign and promise of might and for the Axis powers it was the portent of an unstoppable force. When a raid was in progress, the Germans had to prepare as the bombers advanced. In every town on a possible route air raid precautions had to take place, factories had to cease work, schools were to empty and military units were alerted to try to counteract the threat. Like a huge game of chess, the bomber formations would change direction or weave to mask their final target. Even before a single bomb was dropped, thousands of people had their day interrupted and, in a time when war production was an essential, work had slowed.

The 'knockout blow' may not have been a reality, but in its place the remorseless grinding down of capability meant that, post D-Day, the resilience of any opposing force was weakened. Bitter experience showed that to win the war men would have to occupy every village and town on the way to Berlin. When Glenn Miller came to Knettishall on 25 August 1944 he quipped that, with all the air power he had seen, the Air Force might win the war on its own. It is notable that the officers present were quick to dispel any such talk. Even when the end finally came, there was little dignity left in the business of bombing. When the crews finally had the chance to view the cities of Germany from a much lower altitude, even they were taken back at the damage sustained. The men of the 388th had fought a high altitude war in the freezing cold and on oxygen. Sometimes they never saw the ground over Europe properly for weeks due to poor weather. They had their own bombing strategy, which consisted of their world, the task in hand and the threats arrayed against them. Their principal strategy was to survive.

In the context of the eighteen men of the trophy, it is important to remember that, unlike the men on the ground, they did not see a single German from their vantage point. At more than four miles up it is hard to distinguish buildings and nearly impossible to see a person. The only movement might have been the steam of a train far below or a plume of smoke from a factory chimney. The only Germans they encountered were fast flying fighters that appeared as specks and streaked through their formations in seconds. Sometimes they could see the pilots but, with any adversary, the goal was to destroy their machine before they destroyed yours.

Chapter 9

Going Frantic

Carry fire in one hand and water in the other.
— Russian proverb

The idea was simple, at least on paper. With the strongest anti-aircraft defences located to the north of Germany on the routes to principal strategic targets, an opportunity to attack from a different direction would seriously stretch Axis resources. Progress had been made in the liberation of Italy, but a southern attack route was still hard to establish in terms of having the right materiel in place. Nevertheless, a southern bomber route was established.

The eyes of the strategists strayed eastwards towards their Soviet allies. What if bases were established in the Soviet Union where bombers would fly on to from their targets in Germany? The return leg, or boomerang, would provide a second opportunity to attack and, from a direction that would be much harder to defend. The idea was first formulated by USAAF staff officers soon after the German invasion of Russia in June 1941. Of course, this was before the Japanese attack on Pearl Harbor and the entry of the United States into the war, but it is an indication of the movement towards all-out war that such thinking was encouraged. The prospect of Russian co-operation was virtually non-existent in those early days, although Stalin began to chide Britain to provide him with more resources. His early demands were for thirty British divisions to fight on the Russian front, something completely out of the question given the need to rebuild the British army after Dunkirk. The Russians also wanted Spitfires and Churchill, caught between the need to defend Britain yet stop the Nazi advance in the east, offered to send Hurricanes instead. It was decided to send 200 fighters a month to Russia from October 1941 to June 1942. American P-39s and P-40s were also sent.

The first British-Russian air co-operation involved sending active RAF Squadron personnel to assemble the newly arrived Hurricanes in Russia.

Named Operation Benedict, the aim was to provide air cover for the coast around Murmansk. Pilots were also sent as it was recognized that it was impractical to simply supply aircraft without sufficient mechanical and piloting training on the Hurricane. Secrecy was paramount and by September 1941 the first aircraft were assembled and readied for action. It was not long before the RAF pilots were engaging German aircraft and with a creditable measure of success. The element of surprise was clearly demonstrated as the Luftwaffe ran into aircraft and pilots that were battle tested. By November, the British were returning home after passing on their charges to the Russians. The exercise had shown that it was possible to have operational British squadrons flying alongside their Russian counterparts. Perhaps the big difference with what transpired later was that this early co-operation was still under the direct supervision of a Russian commander.

A series of conferences, known as the Moscow conferences, were held at the highest level to plan Allied strategy. Held every year from 1941 to 1944, they proved to be the main channel of agreement of strategy to defeat the Axis. Through the swirl of ideas and, at times, mutual distrust, Stalin and Churchill formed an unlikely bond. At the 1942 conference held on 12 August, it seemed initially there was much accord, but later sessions proved difficult, due principally to Stalin's bullish behaviour. Stalin was a man who was unpredictable and, arguably, a dictator just as brutal in his methods of keeping ascendancy as his rival, Hitler. Indeed, through the 1930s some 3.3 million people had been deported to the gulags of Siberia. Half of them failed to survive. Churchill, on the other hand, was probably everything Stalin would normally despise; an aristocrat of influence born into a strict class system with an unquestioning loyalty to a monarch.

Stalin had much to complain about. America's entry into the war had resulted in frequent talk about a second front to pressurize the Germans from the west. Stalin believed firm promises had been made that 1942 would bring these actions, but nothing had materialized. It was a series of miscommunications and promises made by the Allies that the author Sir Max Hastings believes were made deliberately to string Stalin along:

They broke almost all their promises about aid deliveries to Russia in between 1941 and 1943 and most importantly they explicitly led Stalin to believe that D-Day on the continent was seriously on the agenda in 1942 when it was not.

The fear was that Stalin would negotiate a peace deal with Hitler in the light of the terrible losses already suffered in Russia. The level of unpreparedness in 1942 for a Western Front invasion was aptly and cruelly demonstrated in the Dieppe raid only seven days later. A total of 5,000 Canadian and 1,000 British infantrymen attempted to storm the French channel port, hold it for a short period and then destroy all they could in their planned withdrawal. The operation was nothing short of a disaster, with the majority of forces pinned down on the beach and sea wall. More than half the Canadian force were either killed or taken captive.

When all looked difficult at the 1942 Moscow Conference, it proved to be a late night and less formal dining session that broke the impasse. A plentiful supply of food and, importantly to Stalin, an endless supply of alcohol, some of the coarsest variety, oiled the wheels of diplomacy. The Permanent Under-Secretary at the British Foreign Office, Sir Alexander Cadogan, was summoned to the Kremlin and wrote of the meeting:

There I found Winston and Stalin, and Molotov who had joined them, sitting with a heavily laden board between them: food of all kinds crowned by a sucking pig, and innumerable bottles. What Stalin made me drink seemed pretty savage: Winston, who by that time was complaining of a slight headache, seemed wisely to be confining himself to a comparatively innocuous effervescent Caucasian red wine.

It would be wrong to suggest that an evening drinking together had wooed the Russians and British into trusting each other, for trust, in this environment, was challenged constantly by the positioning and posturing that evolved into the Cold War.

By 1943, the Americans had joined the party and the Moscow Conference in October gave US staff officers the chance to pitch their ideas about operational Allied bomber bases on the Eastern Front. Again, there was no invasion of France to tell of, but landings in Sicily had been successful in August and the Allies had landed on mainland Italy at Salerno in September. There was definitely a feeling that the tide had turned; after all the promises, something was happening. The Germans were not defeated fully in the Soviet Union, but the battle of Kursk had dealt yet another substantial blow to any ambition to subdue Russia.

The American delegation pitched its idea to Commissar Vyacheslav Molotov in October and this was followed by a direct request made by Roosevelt to Stalin at the November Tehran conference. It was a different proposal to earlier ideas as it entailed Allied servicemen serving directly alongside the Soviets in Soviet territory. In February 1944, Stalin approved the plan, but limited the operation to 200 bombers operating out of six bases. In the end, only three were used and enthusiasm for the project within RAF Bomber Command was muted to the point of being dismissive. It was to be an all-American operation as the RAF decided it could not afford to split resources on what it saw as a 'stunt'. There is no denying that the operation had a high political significance, but it was not devoid of military substance. It would allow bombers to strike targets deep in Germany normally considered out of reach. In fairness to the RAF, the operation was too close to D-Day to consider dividing resources in such a way. Its maximum effort would be to support the landings and aftermath. How far eyes were cast to the post-war period is impossible to fully ascertain. Did America see established air bases on the Eastern Front as a way of curbing post-war Soviet territorial ambitions? More to the point, did the wily Stalin suspect America of trying to unbalance him?

The name Frantic was chosen for the operation and, although it was meant to convey a sense of constant activity, history will record it as 'frantic' for reasons not envisioned by the planners. The three airfields selected were at Poltava and Pyriatyn for the B-17s and Myrhorod for the escort fighters, P-51s and P-38s. The first issue encountered with the proposal was that the bases were deep behind enemy lines and much further away from Britain than envisioned originally. The level of sophistication of these flying fields was fairly basic and much below the standards of their western counterparts. Added to the problems of distance and facility levels, the German withdrawal had resulted in the destruction of a good deal of infrastructure. The town of Poltava itself was largely in ruins. Some 1,300 American ground staff were involved in setting up the bases to receive their aircraft and all supplies had to be brought in over huge distances. Some came by ship through Murmansk and by rail, other supplies arrived by air from Iran. Every move and plan had to be monitored by the Soviets, but throughout these difficulties relations between the Americans and Russian servicemen were very good; perhaps too good for the ever suspicious Stalin.

The first 'shuttle' missions were flown on 2, 6 and 11 June 1944. Escorted B-17s struck targets in Hungary and Romania and shuttled back to Italy, proving the viability of this ambitious operation. These operations constituted the first shuttle mission of Frantic.

The second mission was to take place on 21 June and, although there had been losses in mission one, these were not attributed to the location of the Soviet bases. It is here in the story that the 25-year-old Texan Johnnie Colburn and his crew become participants in this bigger picture. They had been flying in combat for fewer than three weeks and they were not quite wet behind the ears, but this mission was a huge challenge. They had been airborne on 19 June to Cognac and as a spare plane on the 20th to Germany, although they turned back as planned as they were not needed. For this second shuttle mission of Operation Frantic, the primary target was to be a synthetic oil plant in Ruhland, a town seventy miles south of Berlin. Even as the crow flies, Ruhland is 560 miles from Knettishall and Poltava a further 900 miles beyond that – a significant distance.

The 388th was tasked to provide twenty-nine aircraft as part of a bigger group that, including other bomb groups, totalled 163, of which 145 made it to their primary target. Statistically, the B-17s had the capability to carry out the raid and carry on to Poltava, but could it be done in practice? The raid against Ruhland seemed to go well with the target 'shacked', in other words there was concentrated bombing into the target area with clear visibility. As the formation carried on flying east, enemy fighters attempted to attack over an area east of Warsaw, Biala Podlaska. The Germans knew by now that the B-17s were not flying back to their home bases. Johnnie Colburn was flying 42-102666 *Wizard of Oz* and, as well as the regular crew, they also carried Oscar Price, who was most likely from ground crew to help supplement the Poltava operation. The scene on the ground at Poltava as the B-17s approached began to get chaotic. By this time, after eleven hours and forty minutes, most aircraft were desperately low on fuel and it became a race to get down on this strange airfield. Some of the signalling was done by flags and as the B-17s flopped down on to the field they were instructed to taxi, sometimes through longer grass than normal and park in rough dispersal points. It was, however, a large airfield, but the B-17s eventually parked up and stopped their engines. The crews scrambled down and stood looking at the sight and the strange flat geography. Their hosts, both the American ground crew and the Soviets, were enthusiastic in their welcome. Most crew were dog tired and glad to be out of the air and on to solid land, for this was their first view and experience of 'Mother Russia'.

Before long they were queuing for hot food and talking in relief about their trip. It was at this time that several of them saw a glint in the sky; an aircraft. In retrospect, it is now believed that this was a German reconnaissance plane that had followed the formation to Poltava and now left the scene unopposed. According to General Doolittle, who was instrumental in planning Frantic, the German plane was an He-177, a plane that, although having only two engines, might have been able to tag along behind the B-17 formations without arousing suspicion.

There are several factors that contribute to Poltava and the other airfields being not as secret as their hosts would have desired. Obviously, to move such numbers of men and material unobserved over the period of preparation was always a risk. Mission one had been a success, but the locations and paths of the bombers must have been noted, at least in part. Were the Germans preparing already for a second wave of bombers? Did they suspect that this time the shuttle might be from England and not Italy? The questions are open for debate and one more crucial factor comes into play that perhaps was not realized by the men, or even some observers since. They had not landed in 'Mother Russia' at all – they had landed in Ukraine. In that the Soviet soldiers who greeted them were likely to have been from all over Russia and clearly Russian was openly spoken, Ukraine, if the newly arrived airmen had even heard of it, probably did not come into their thinking. In the USSR, individual statehood had been sacrificed for the common unity and this 'unity' was enforced brutally. Stalin had dragged off and killed many thousands of dissenters and nationalistic jingoism about individual statehood was not going to surface in a hurry.

There is no doubt there were dissenters and many who were disillusioned with the Soviet model. The tensions between the Slavs and Western Europeans crossed swords in the Ukraine. Poltava itself had been the scene of the 1709 battle between Charles XII of Sweden and the Russians that resulted in a Russian victory under Peter the Great. Perhaps in more recent times the divisions between Russia and the independent Ukraine have become more obvious to the West, particularly with mounting tension and fighting in 2014.

During the German occupation of the Ukraine in 1941, many Ukrainians had supported the Germans believing it a route to their own eventual independence. The German army recruited many hundreds of Ukrainian volunteers, forming a number of Ukrainian battalions in the German army. Many massacres of the Jewish population broke out and, although encouraged by the Nazis, Ukrainian nationalists were the perpetrators. Some of the most savage guards in the Nazi concentration camps were Ukrainian. It is against this backdrop that the choice of Poltava, Pyriatyn and Myrhorod airfields suddenly look a far less secure and safe haven than might have been expected. The arrival of the Americans in setting up theses bases could not have gone unobserved by the local population and the sight of them working alongside Soviet Russians would not have made them popular with those of a nationalist tendency.

Above the political aspirations of its inhabitants, Poltava was also an open wound. Stalin had orchestrated a cataclysmic man-made famine in the region in 1932–33, often referred to as the *Holodomor* – the Hunger. The aim had been to destroy the will of the peasants in the bread basket of the Soviet Union. Harvests of much of the foodstuffs that sustained Ukraine were systematically and deliberately taken out of the region. Famine ensued. Many speculate that Stalin would have deported the whole Ukrainian population of 20 million to the Gulags if he were able. Instead, he chose to starve them. Mortality figures have been impossible to ascertain and estimates vary widely, although one of the lowest figures in a 2008 study suggest 3.4 million deaths. What is clear is that the German invasion of 1941 added yet another layer of catastrophe. The Germans installed a civil government, a *Reichskommissariat*, which functioned until 1944. At its head, Eric Koch, a staunch and high-ranking Nazi, set about improving conditions for the ethnic Germans in Ukraine while supervising the 'recruitment' of 710,000 Ukrainian slave labourers. So many were sent west to work in the Nazi war factories that it was not possible to find enough men to build earthwork defences to try to stop the Soviet counter-attack into the Ukraine later in the war.

The meal at the Poltava airfield was over and Johnnie Colburn and his crew were acclimatizing themselves to their new surroundings – and accommodation. The men were under canvas and this wartime camping expedition to 'Russia' was like nothing they had experienced before. The layout of the tents was in the defined and ordered military fashion that could be expected in the USAAF, but this was foreign soil. Even though they were tired, some crews decided to visit the local town, Poltava, to see what it was like. The experience would have been interesting, but disappointing if they were looking for any form of sophistication. Poltava and the surrounding area had been fought over heavily and many of the buildings were in ruins. As the crews retired to their tents for the night, many would be sure this experience would stay with them for the rest of their lives. Little did they suspect that their tenure of this bleak, flat land was about to be seriously, and in many cases irreparably, damaged.

At 2330 hours, some personnel at Poltava were warned that a force of German bombers had crossed the front lines, but for most of the crews the first indication of trouble came with wailing air raid sirens. It was not a complete surprise; the force commander, Colonel Archie Old, had sought permission to move the B-17s after it was clear the German reconnaissance plane had made a pass. As in many dealings with the Soviets, the chain of command was too weak and slow to respond to such a request. At 0030 hours the Americans were disturbed by the percussion of two large bombs followed by a German pathfinder aircraft dropping a flare over the airfield. Matthew Robb, navigator with the Caffee crew, writing in 1999 recalled:

My pilot, John Caffee, spread his OD blanket out in front of the tent and wearing only his white undershirt and shorts laid down to watch the fireworks. It wasn't long in coming. Almost every kind of German aircraft started flying in dropping incendiary magnesium bombs and what were called butterfly bombs.

The seriousness of the situation quickly began to dawn on the sightseers and soon all hopes of simply watching 'fireworks' were dashed. The Americans headed rapidly for open slit trenches a short distance from their tents. There was no protection from above and as bombs began to drop, some ran and flung themselves in the trenches and on top of their already frightened comrades, but nobody seemed to complain. It must have been a strange and chilling experience to be caught in a role reversal of a bombing raid. Bob Simmon, Johnnie Colburn's bombardier, had flung himself into a trench and recalled how he felt safer when others jumped in on top of him.

The Germans had planned an operation of their own, nicknamed Zaunkonig, (Wren in English). Oberstleutnant Wilhelm Antrup of KG 55 commanded a force of seventy-five bombers flying from Minsk in a bid to destroy the B-17 force. The sky above Poltava was lit brightly both from German flares and the Russian anti-aircraft batteries placed around the airfield. Most of these guns were mounted on trucks and not the heavier calibre that carried altitude-sensitive fuses. The raid was well planned and not a last-minute affair, the Germans knew where to go and what to hit. For two hours the airfield was pounded with incendiary, high explosive and anti-personnel bombs, 'butterflies'. The sound was immense from exploding bombs and the cacophony of the Russian guns; it seemed an unending nightmare for the sheltering American crews. Some decided the bombardment was getting too close to the trenches to handle and ran further to escape. Matthew Robb was one of the escapees:

The explosive bombs seemed to be getting closer and everyone decided to hit the field and get away from those tents. We'd run till the whistle from the falling bombs got close, then slide on to our stomachs and lie flat until it went off, then up and run again. I ended up several miles away under a railroad culvert.

Johnnie Colburn was sharing a tent with co-pilot Russ Weekes and as soon as it became apparent a raid was starting they both made a run for cover. Splitting up with Weekes, Johnnie ran across a potato field and recalled the Americans ran one way and the Russians ran another. Try as he might, he could not find a trench to shelter in and eventually, finding himself far enough away for some modicum of safety, he sat down under a peach tree and watched the drama unfold.

Although the Russians fired 50,000 shells into the night sky, not one German aircraft was brought down. No Russian or American fighters took off to engage the bombers on the orders of the Russian high command. The reasons for this are unclear, but the effectiveness of the fighters was doubtful anyway as there was no radar guidance available.

It was clear from the outset that considerable damage had been done to the B-17s and, as the morning light crept in, the true scale of the devastation became apparent. Moving about was hazardous due to the anti-personnel bombs scattered across the area. Thankfully, due to the distance of the trenches away from the B-17s, American casualties were light with two killed and a number lightly wounded. Of seventy-three B-17s that had landed amid the flag waving furore of a few hours before, forty-seven were destroyed totally and the majority of 'survivors' badly damaged. Only nine were able to fly out three days later. Like many others, Johnnie's *Wizard of Oz* was completely wrecked. She lay collapsed and burned, her wings and engine separated from the fuselage. The forward section and cockpit was smashed and hardly recognizable lying on its side with guns, equipment and fittings strewn all over the site. There was nothing much that could be done and Johnnie and the crew had some pictures taken with the wreck. In them, the sun is shining and Johnnie looks quite smart in his officer's uniform, his hat sits correctly on one side of his head, but nobody is smiling.

The damage to the stockpiled fuel and supplies, so carefully shipped in over thousands of miles, was extensive. It almost spelled the end of the missions when they had barely begun.

The shock of the attack was complete and left hundreds of airmen stranded and misplaced for further action. The 388th had lost eleven of its aircraft outright, the biggest single loss of the bombing group throughout the war. Of the lucky survivors, the aircraft later named *Betty Ann* by Ong and Lippert's crew, 43-37617, was on her first official mission and flown by Tracy Deskin, newly elevated to the first pilot's seat. Deskin was co-pilot to Michael Soldato, who had died on 8 June. Taking the reins of the Soldato crew, Deskin flew on to complete forty missions without a break. '617 was one of the lucky survivors and the official damage assessment made by 388th engineering officer, Max Gillaspy, records her as 'Flyable. Right elevator rib cut.' *Betty Ann* was back and on her next mission from Knettishall five days later. Of the other survivors, *Ol Faithful*, *Miss Bea Haven* and *Wolf Wagon* had breaks in their service career of nearly a month. Some of this time was in battle damage repair, while some possibly took the longer route back via North Africa. Gillaspy assessed twenty-five 388th aircraft after the raid. Only six aircraft were considered flyable (with two listed flyable after forty-eight hours of repairs) and a further nine were listed as destroyed, including Colburn's steed. The damage report was somewhat optimistic in its reporting in the case of 42-97172, flown in by McNichol:

Possibly repairable – 2 months.
Left inner wing panel hit by incendiary.
All tires shot out.
Right inner wing panel hit by incendiary.

Fabric burned off elevator.
Fuselage riddled by machine gun bullets and bomb fragments.
Wiring damaged.
Control cables cut.

'172 was never salvaged, the damage was too great to attempt. The airfield was strewn with bomb craters, wreckage and, more dangerously, many thousands of anti-personnel bombs. Commander Archie Old reported:

There was hardly a square yard of ground in the task force dispersal area that was not hit with some type of bomb. On the next afternoon, there was a hard rain shower and at least a hundred or so butterfly (anti-personnel) bombs were exploded by the rainfall. It sounded like a young war for a few minutes.

Reports vary a little, but it seems that sappers, some of them women, were brought in to help clear the mines and a number of casualties ensued. The Americans were amazed at the Soviet disregard for life and limb in the process. General Doolittle later wrote that:

The Russian sappers had a unique way of destroying anti-personnel bombs. One system was to pick the bomb up and throw it as far as possible and either fall flat on their faces or else run like hell. It worked, but also kept the medical section and coffin builders busy. Considerably more than a hundred Russian men and women were killed and wounded during the raid and the three days following. By the end of the third day, Russian sappers had cleared approximately 9,500 bombs.

Of the stranded crews, the work of evacuation and transportation back to Knettishall began in earnest. C-46 transport aircraft flew them south to Tehran and in hops, along the North African coast before the long and risky flight west of Spain and up through the Bay of Biscay on C-54 Skymasters. In some cases the condition of the C-46s was somewhat suspect and in at least one case the aircraft dropped in on nearly every airfield it could find en route due to mechanical unreliability. There are a number of stories of crews and aircraft 'delaying' their return in favour of the bazaars and sites of North Africa. Out of the way of flak and fighters for a little while, the

Poltava affair had become a short summer break. Johnnie and his crew spend a couple of nights in Casablanca before the trip back to Britain in a B-24. They took a little time to get back and rest, but by 7 July they were climbing into *GI Jane* to go to Bohlen in Germany, an aircraft they have already flown in for five trips. The type of target was getting familiar, a synthetic oil plant, but how different their last sortie over Germany had been. They were now suddenly veterans, survivors; aircrew who had suffered loss yet come back were always a rung higher in the respect ladder.

Clearing the wreckage of Poltava took some time, but strategic decisions happened quickly. Remaining serviceable aircraft were moved deeper into the Soviet Union before flying south to Italy and returning to the UK. Frantic continued that summer, although the strategic objectives were weakened and it was decided to use only fighters in shuttle missions for a while. In all, seven shuttle missions were staged until September 1944. By then the chilly blasts of Soviet suspicion were blowing and Molotov told the US their presence was no longer needed. A good number of other 'unfriendly' factors culminated in the pull-out, not least Soviet gunners' inability to distinguish American aircraft from their foes. It had been a massive undertaking but, at the end of the day, the results hoped for never really materialized. It was clear that the bonhomie at Poltava and the other bases was not shared by Soviet task masters and the risk of Americans winning the affections of their troops was unpalatable.

The betrayals of Poltava came from many sources, but in the movement of war it was also clear that the Americans were capable of 'breaches of trust'. Poltava and Frantic might not have been a success, but in the years after, as Winston Churchill first coined the phrase 'Iron Curtain' to describe the start of the Cold War, America had in its possession a good quantity of reconnaissance photos of the Soviet Union gained through Frantic.

Even though the shuttle missions had been abandoned, Poltava remained active into the spring of 1945. It became a transport and repair centre for damaged aircraft mostly coming out of Poland. Relations between the Soviets and Americans became very poor and boiled over on 28 March 1945 when the commanding officer at Poltava, Major General S.K. Kovalev, forbade all movement of American aircraft from the base. He was acting on instructions from Moscow, which was convinced that America subterfuge and espionage was being carried out in Poland. This move effectively interned 180 American airmen at Poltava. To the infuriation of the Americans, the Soviets also announced that all aircraft now in the country were their 'trophies of war'. The pot had been boiling for some time and a number of incidents propelled the break in the American–Soviet relationship. In February, a B-17 had made an emergency landing in Poland, one of many. The pilot, Lieutenant Myron King flying *Maiden USA*, rested over for a couple of days before being ordered to fly to a Soviet base, Szczuczyn, under escort. When airborne, the crew found that a young Polish man had stowed away and at first they thought he might be an interpreter. The man wanted to get to London where he had an uncle. He wasn't dressed for flying and the crew equipped him with a flying jacket and dubbed him Jack Smith. Sadly, he was discovered almost immediately on landing and the crew were arrested, but were eventually allowed to fly on to Poltava on 18 March. Other incidents followed, including the defection of a Russian engineer on a B-24 whose crew took pity on him when it transpired he had been born in Ohio. After repairs to their aircraft, they flew him to Italy. The fallout from these and similar misinterpreted incidents was huge and reached the highest political levels.

For the men of the 388th, there was still a lot of flying, bombing and surviving to do. They never returned to Poltava although the incident was the stuff of memories; memories to last a lifetime. In discussions with the relatives of the Colburn crew members, Poltava is always mentioned. In the last seventy years, few American servicemen have had the opportunity to visit the Soviet Union as it was then. Frantic is a remarkable episode in history, yet is little heard of outside veterans' circles.

Chapter 10

Betty Ann's Boys

Our names are labels, plainly printed on the bottled essence of our past behaviour.

— Logan Pearsall Smith

By the time I returned from summer holiday, I felt some urgency towards resolving some of the names and contacts that had come my way. I was feeling concerned that, although I had a decent grasp of Johnnie Colburn's crew and had email and voice contact with some key relatives, Dong Ong's crew list was lagging behind. Some contacts were eating away at me, too. I knew who the relatives were, I knew where they lived, I knew their telephone number, but I just got an answer machine when I called. I realized I was the victim of the telesales plague, some strange Englishman calling up and leaving messages was not going to get many places.

Shortly before my holiday, I had an excellent conversation with David Lippert, the son of Earl 'Corky' Lippert, Dong Ong's co-pilot. Earl had died in 2005, but David had provided me with some fascinating information. He told me he believed after crew training in South Dakota, Dong, Earl and the rest of the crew had flown the Atlantic in a B-17. It sounded like the similar route that most of the 388th men made, including the Colburn crew. However, I had my doubts because no other Ong crew relative had mentioned it, but David was correct in that his father did fly a transatlantic crossing – just not with this crew, as it transpired later in my research.

It seems that Dong and crew came over by sea, and Dong refers to this later in a letter. Dong's close friend Gene Peterson placed his remembrances in rhyming poetry and in one extract recounts the crossing:

We were taken to New York City and loaded on a boat;
which joined a large slow convoy of everything afloat.
We zigzagged across the ocean like an unsteady drunken fool.
After thirteen days of crossing we ended up in Liverpool.

It had been assumed that a transatlantic crossing might have been made in a B-17 named after Earl Lippert's new wife, Betty Ann. This was not the case as new aircraft serial 43-37617 was still at Grenier Air Force Base in New Hampshire on 6 June 1944 and assigned to the 388th at Knettishall on the 7th. Serial 43-37617 is prominent in the 388th records and, although the Ong crew flew a number of others, this aircraft became *Betty Ann* and was 'their' aircraft, flying seventeen of their thirty-two listed missions. The records show too that, although they did not fly *Betty Ann* for more than five weeks after their combat missions started, they had her by her fifth listed mission. At what point the crew had the privilege of naming her is not certain. Although a new aircraft at Knettishall, 'permission' to name her might not have been forthcoming until the Dong crew were well established in using her. New crews did not have all the honours and privileges of the older hands. Even when a crew had been marked out publicly, the promise of flying a new aircraft did not always materialize.

Such was the story of Ralph Kittle and crew, who flew and were photographed beside B-17G *City of Savannah* while in Georgia, an aircraft and crew highlighted for publicity as part of a public relations drive. The photos show the nose of the aircraft emblazoned with the text 'City of Savannah 5000th Airplane processed thru Hunter Field Ga 1944'. Kittle's smiling crew were posted in newspapers and bathed in the publicity. The *Savannah Morning News* on 3 December 1944 reported:

> *Lieutenant Ralph W. Kittle, of Ringold, Georgia, pilot of* The City of Savannah, *will be introduced to the guests and will in turn introduce the various members of the plane's crew.*
>
> *Following the ceremony ... Lieutenant Kittle will taxi the giant Flying Fortress to the end of the runway. In full view of the spectators* The City of Savannah *will be lifted into the air and leave Hunter Field to join the thousands of other planes already in combat.*

As romantic as it sounds, the B-17 in question, 43-39049, did not come with Kittle's crew to 563 Sqn at Knettishall. In modern terms, this would be labelled a PR gaffe, but news reporting was then far simpler and more restricted than it is now. Once the photo opportunity was over, the constraints of supply and demand kicked in. The crew began their combat flying on 28 January 1945 and their first mission was in a brand new aircraft, but subsequently they were given all the normal squadron aircraft to fly. In an apparent effort to hold with the story, it appears the 388th named one of its aircraft *City of Savannah*. She was 42-97542 and was flying in April 1944. By the time Kittle arrived she had already flown thirty missions. Curiously, her naming might have been after she was lost by military PR men as Kittle flew her only twice, with the second and last time on a raid to Chemnitz. At 25,000ft on the bomb run the B-17 was hit by flak and lost two engines. Kittle jettisoned his bombs and broke away from the formation, radioing that he was heading for Russia. This was far from the first choice of crews in trouble, but it shows that the problems were very serious. In the end, the crew bailed out and were taken as prisoners of war, except for the tail gunner Robert Warren who is listed as killed in action. Crew member Irwin Boxer wrote of the incident in the 388th Association Newsletter in 2002 and about a news citation that mistakenly reported he bailed out of the second *City of Savannah*:

> *That just goes to show that one should not believe everything that was printed in time of war by military PR men. First of all we were on an old (I might add 'ancient') no name B-17F and not the 'City of Savannah' which was a fairly new B-17G with a chin turret. It was an all-out effort and they were putting up everything (they thought) would fly. Ultimately, it wouldn't!*

Naming aircraft was an important part of morale-boosting efforts, but many aircraft were not named. The identity of the crew and their cohesiveness was the essential element, particularly as battle stress and fatigue set in. When a crew member cracked, the crew as a body carried him and the strength of this unit determined the mental and physical health of the individual. Byron Cook, writing in the *388th Anthology Volume II*, recalls flying a single mission with Dong Ong's crew to Munich on 13 July 1944. In it we get a glimpse into the relationships of the pilot and co-pilot:

> *I had heard that the Air Force usually tried to match up pilot and co-pilot of a plane so that the smoothest running combination would be possible. This was beautifully illustrated in this crew, for Ong was an excellent pilot, but excitable, while the co-pilot was the easy-going steadying influence.*

The fate of the B-17 *Betty Ann* was perhaps statistically predictable. B-17s did not have a set retirement plan, they flew for as long as they were serviceable or until war's end, whichever came first. Some were sent back to the States after being considered surplus after the arrival of newer B-17Gs, but this was not an automatic process. On 17 October 1944, some two months after the Ong crew had completed their tour of duty and returned Stateside, *Betty Ann* was hit badly by flak on her forty-ninth mission, to Cologne. It was a mission where Johnnie Colburn was lead pilot of the formation and other trophy names were involved. Rob Simmon was lead bombardier and Morris (often called Morrie) Neiman was lead navigator on Colburn's plane that day. *Betty Ann* flew behind in the high squadron but, according to eyewitnesses, lost two engines over the target area. Her pilot, James W. Baird, decided to crash-land her at a Belgian airfield, Le Culot, and, according to the 388th database, the crew all returned safely and completed their tour in December, but *Betty Ann* was no more.

There seems to be some confusion in various records regarding this incident. A number of renowned sources believe the crew were taken prisoner or that some might have bailed out prior to the crash-landing. A number of aspects point to a different conclusion. Firstly, Le Culot was liberated by the Allies in September and was being prepared for use as a forward airfield in October. Perhaps most importantly, no Missing Air Crew Report (MACR) was filed, a key element in any incident of this sort where crew were 'lost'.

During my conversation with David Lippert, he mentioned that his father was thoroughly annoyed at the loss of *Betty Ann* and towards the end of his life was quite strong in his criticism of the crew that lost her. Records seem to suggest this criticism might be unfounded, but there may be room to assume that something unusual took place that day. Perhaps there was a feeling that a two-engined landing, even at an unfamiliar airfield, was quite achievable. One thing seemed certain: *Betty Ann* had a special place in the hearts and memories of Dong's crew. Although the crew finished their tour of duty at the end of August, it was not as if that was the last some of them saw of Knettishall and their named B-17.

Dong Ong agreed to return for a second tour as pilot on the condition his crew were not required to return. Their initial tour of duty had been brief, but tough. Earl Lippert also returned as a co-pilot and flew from early December 1944 to the end of hostilities with Loren Johnson's crew. His last official war mission was a food delivery to Amsterdam on 6 May 1945 on a 'Chow Hound' mission, as they were affectionately known. Earl therefore had plenty of opportunity to ask pertinent questions about *Betty Ann* when he returned. More to the point, certainly one of their number had remained at Knettishall, tail gunner Carl Lindorff. Carl had been assigned to ground duties and had not finished his flying tour with Ong's crew, even though he had flown twenty-five missions.

It was obviously a great disappointment to Earl Lippert to find *Betty Ann* was not at Knettishall when he returned. One can only speculate as to whether Earl questioned Baird about the crash. Baird was finishing his tour just as Earl returned, but there was enough overlap and opportunity for contact. At a time when Earl faced the arduous task of another series of flights over a heavily defended Germany, there was no comforting namesake *Betty Ann* to go too.

Dong's return was delayed as much by the bureaucracy of war as anything else. However, he did confess to using this bureaucracy to his benefit and extending his leave by stopping off on his train journeys. Dong even wondered whether he would get back to Europe at all at one point while at the processing centre in Atlantic City. His experiences of the return leg are told in a short recollection published in *388th Anthology Volume I* and recounted later.

Earl 'Corky' Lippert had a head start on Dong of some weeks and in this intervening period, Dong wrote to Betty Ann, a letter now part of her son David's scrapbook. The letter is charming and highly informative, perhaps given the need for operational confidentiality, far too informative for the period. Now with the passage of time, such liberality is welcome in the search for details:

28th October 1944

Dear 'Betty Ann',
    I just passed my physical examination so I guess it won't be long before I get my shipping orders. From the way things look here, we have a good chance of flying across. If we do, I will more than likely beat Corky across. He left from the same port of embarkation that we sailed from the last time.

Dong's hopes of a fast air crossing were not to come to fruition, but as Corky was back on flying duties at Knettishall by 4 December, it seems Betty Ann probably received Dong's letter while Corky was still at sea. Such a lapse of wartime confidentiality would have been frowned on, but Dong seems oblivious. He goes on:

Betty, it won't be so bad over there. We stand pretty high with the group and we will get a good deal when we get there. We probably can pick our missions if we fly again.

It seems that although the 388th was keen to see pilots return for a second tour, statistically few volunteered. The promise of picking missions seemed credible, but Dong found out he was soon swallowed up into the command machine that was working at maximum effort. No luxuries of mission picking were possible, although undoubtedly the offer was made with all good intentions. In the letter, Dong goes on to list every mission and date they had flown. Clearly, Corky had not been able to recount all the details to Betty Ann. Dong had visited the Lipperts during his leave, his letter says as much, and it seems he later had the chance to consult his log. The list is impressive and although not all the spellings of the German targets are correct, the details would have been useful if the letter had fallen into the wrong hands.

Perhaps most telling in this letter and many other wartime letters, is the attempt to reassure friends and relatives of the writer's future safety. Dong attempts to calm Betty Ann's fears by impressing on her Corky's and his own experience:

Don't worry about Corky as I and he will do our best to keep out of trouble. We are pretty good at it also.

Depending on the definition of 'trouble', there is only a certain amount of skill that could carry a crew through. Having skilled and experienced pilots was a good start, but no amount of skill could dictate with any certainty the outcome of an event such as a direct hit by flak in a formation or having the misfortune to be hit by a fighter. Perhaps there is a degree of confidence that a 22-year-old pilot can achieve having flown through thirty gruelling missions. Writing a record for his family of his experiences many years later, Dong recalled:

My crew was experiencing an abnormal amount of battle damage on many of our missions. The damage ranged from knocked out engines and large holes to a few small holes. In one mission we had 300 holes.

Fellow pilot Bob Sherman, who began his combat career at the same time as Dong, recalled in 2001:

> *I have a memory of being over the Channel, on our way home and seeing his plane at about 2 o'clock, low, limping home in distress and thinking, 'Not again! Why do they always catch it? Hope they make it!*
>
> *He had such a buoyant personality, and an infectious grin that seemed to brighten a substantial radius from where he stood.*

Perhaps having a clear head and skill brought Dong's crew home time and again where others might have failed. In the lottery of war we learn the tales of the survivors, some might say the lucky. Dong never turned back from a mission due to technical failure, something of a record in his total of fifty missions. It seems, too, that although they had opportunity to crash-land elsewhere or even bail out, they stayed put and returned successfully.

My return from holiday also coincided with more emails from Carl Lindorff's daughter, Penny Warner. She shared some of the details of letters he sent while at Knettishall. As mentioned previously, Carl served as a waist gunner and flew twenty-five missions before being 'retired' to a ground job. Carl's story is told a little later in this book but, suffice to say, his contribution to the Ong crew was considered very worthwhile.

There were a number of names I needed to find and follow through. One such name was Morris Fleishman, Dong Ong's engineer and a 'whole tour' name, that is, he served on every mission. I pursued my normal web searches and could not find much about Morris. He was nicknamed 'Tex', which, given that his roots were in Texas, was entirely predictable. One thing that occurs again and again in genealogy studies is the fact that many individuals and families tend not to stray far away from their home areas. In our modern world, we tend to think that most people move and become displaced in heritage terms. However, people who move away often return in later life. I was counting on the fact that Morris 'Tex' Fleishman was one of the post-war returnees. Sure enough, I found what I thought looked a pretty good family lead in an area of Texas that looked likely. I decided to call the number and see if I could reach a relative. When the phone was answered, I gave my, by now, well-rehearsed little speech about searching for relatives. There was a slight pause on the line.

'I'm Morris Fleishman,' the man said. 'I served with the 388th Bombardment Group.'

I was a little stunned but, trying to recover, I asked what he remembered about his experiences. He told me that he did not remember much as it was a long time ago. To me, that did not matter, I had spoken to a genuine signed up member of the trophy club. We didn't say too much to one another, but I wrote to Morris shortly after explaining my interest and the trophy search. Now I had two living veterans, one in each crew – I knew Johnnie Colburn was the last survivor of his crew but, seventy years later, could there be even more of Dong Ong's crew still around? Morris Fleishman was born in 1924 and as such was one of the youngest of the crew in 1944. Now, at 90, I was really asking a lot of Morris to recall details of a three-month period of his life in 1944. Of course, there was much I already knew, the life and times of Knettishall are well documented and, being a military establishment, the confines and rules of the base applied to all. Some of the stories in both verbal and written sources about Knettishall related to times when that daily routine was broken. Someone stole a goose, Glenn Miller came and played a concert in one of the hangars and, of course, the various mishaps, accidents and disasters that befell a combat base. There are plenty of commonalities about life at a US air base in Britain and plenty of written accounts of daily life.

I had made a decision early on in the search that I would avoid the numerous paid-for websites that offered all sorts of details from birth and death registers to criminal convictions. Perhaps I was naïve, but my thinking was that if a record was in the public domain and available for free, it was fair to be able to publish the details I found.

I was also concerned that I might miss living members of the crew and there was a real pressure to find out the names and what happened to them. Dong Ong's crew was foremost in my mind in this respect as I already knew that all other members of Johnnie Colburn's crew had passed away. As I worked my way gradually through the names, they became more and more familiar as if my ears and mind were fine tuning the levels of probability. As my list of names and relatives increased, I realized that Morris Fleishman seemed to be the only surviving member of the Ong crew. Some names were holding out, but ever so gradually the question marks on my list of names began to decrease.

With the lists of obituaries and death records mounting, the main problem of those who had passed away was that many were before the 'digital age'. This does not mean they lacked any dignity or the normal records of their passing. As an author seeking to research them, I was looking for their families who, in many cases, were very much part of the digital age. Frustratingly, I was waiting for them to mention their father, grandfather or uncle online before a trace of their forebears could be found. It is perhaps a solemn responsibility we all face to make life easier for our future relatives. I can't help wondering if my great-great grandchildren will unearth some photograph taken of me at a fancy dress party or similar strange social function, which they will display with pride to bewildered guests. I just have to hope I'm not wearing a dress.

The process of digitalizing records does benefit my searches. In particular, US Army enlistment records give a snapshot of the men's lives, their age, weight and, if they were old enough, a profession. The Air Force was the US Army Air Force and the enlistees were therefore part of the army. Another trait common to the human race is the desire to be at, or return to, home. Although many of us are transported to many parts of our respective countries and even the globe, there is a significant proportion who return home eventually and many whose wider family continue to live in a locality they have settled in for many years. The enlistment records are based on local recruiting offices and this gives a snapshot and starting point in the search for extant relatives.

One evening, the penny dropped. I could see birth and death records for all my names. There were indeed only two living crew members. While this made me sad that my search started too late, in other ways it was a relief that the uncertainty was over. My worry had been missing a last chance to interview a crew member. The challenge was still to find the relatives; the sons and daughters may still have a lot of information.

The Colburn Crew

S/Sgt Leonard Granath (waist gunner), T/Sgt William Tobias (engineer), T/Sgt George Kragle (radio op), S/Sgt Frank Nutt (tail gunner).

The officers

1st Lt Johnnie Colburn (pilot), 1st Lt Robert Simmon (bombardier), 1st Lt Charles 'Russ' Weekes (co-pilot), 1st Lt Morris Neiman (navigator).

Above: 1st Lt Richard 'Ted' Heslam (Mickey operator).

Left: Weekes, Simmon and Colburn at Dyersburg, TN on final B-17 training.

Below: Colburn, Neiman, Simmon and Weekes on the ground at Poltava, Ukraine, June 1944.

1944 June, Pilot: Colburn, Nav. Neiman, Bomb. Bob, CP Weekes, Poltava Russia, Shuttle Mission "Frantic"

Poltava, Russia--June 23, 1944.
Operation "Frantic" Shuttle Mission.
Aircraft No. 666 Colburn's Crew's aircraft
Left to Right: Sgt. Frank Nutt-Tail Gunne
1stLt Johnnie W. Colburn-Pilot, S/Sgt Leonard Granath-Waist Gunner

Members of the Colburn crew pose next to their aircraft, now a twisted wreck after being destroyed on the ground at Poltava, Ukraine. 42-102666 *Wizard of Oz*.

Another view of '666' at Poltava.

Poltava, Russia June 23,1944 Operation "Frantic"
Colburn's Crew Aircraft 666
1stLt Morris Neiman-Navigator, 1stLt Johnnie W. Colburn Pilot

Navigator Morris Neiman leaves
42-97760 'K'.

Weekes and Simmon pose next
to a Russian fighter-bomber at
Poltava, Ukraine.

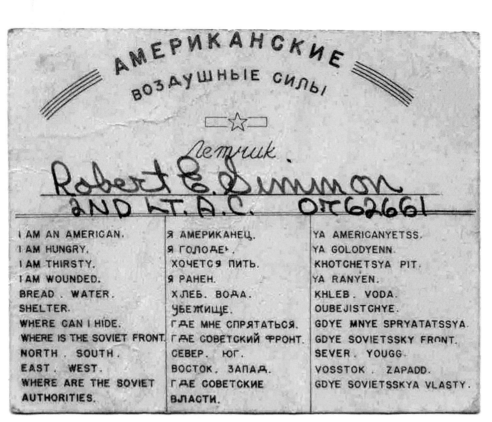

I AM AN AMERICAN.	Я АМЕРИКАНЕЦ.	YA AMERICANYETSS.
I AM HUNGRY.	Я ГОЛОДЕ·.	YA GOLODYENN.
I AM THIRSTY.	ХОЧЕТСЯ ПИТЬ.	KHOTCHETSYA PIT.
I AM WOUNDED.	Я РАНЕН.	YA RANYEN.
BREAD . WATER .	ХЛЕБ. ВОДА.	KHLEB . VODA.
SHELTER.	УБЕЖИЩЕ.	OUBEJISTCHYE.
WHERE CAN I HIDE.	ГДЕ МНЕ СПРЯТАТЬСЯ.	GDYE MNYE SPRYATATSSYA.
WHERE IS THE SOVIET FRONT.	ГДЕ СОВЕТСКИЙ ФРОНТ.	GDYE SOVIETSSKY FRONT.
NORTH . SOUTH .	СЕВЕР. ЮГ.	SEVER . YOUGG.
EAST . WEST.	ВОСТОК. ЗАПАД.	VOSSTOK . ZAPADD.
WHERE ARE THE SOVIET AUTHORITIES.	ГДЕ СОВЕТСКИЕ ВЛАСТИ.	GDYE SOVIETSSKYA VLASTY.

A Russian phrase card issued to the crews for the Poltava mission.

44-6096 *Lady Courageous* burns after being struck on the ground by another B-17 from Fersfield, 29 July 1944.

Time for a smoke. The waist position on return from a raid. Left: Frank Nutt, Leonard Granath. Right: George Kragle, Robert Anderson (Mickey op) – August 1944. Note, the equipment including parachute packs and body armour on the floor.

Pilot Johnnie Colburn poses with 43-37724, *Old Silver*. Johnnie flies her only once in combat, to Mery-sur-Oise on 2 August 1944. She appears to have a cowling removed for maintenance in this shot.

Two views of 43-37520 *GI Jane*; a regular mount for the Colburn crew. She was lost to flak on 28 September 1944 while being flown by the Michael crew, all of whom were taken as prisoners of war.

A serious looking Johnnie Colburn pictured at Snetterton Heath, the headquarters of the 45th Combat Bombardment Wing, on 9 September 1944 after returning earlier that day from a raid on Dusseldorf.

Bob Simmon's 'escape' photo, which would form part of forged papers in the event of being shot down and harboured by the Resistance.

Damage to the ball turret of 42-97328 *Heavens Above* after the collision with the tail and subsequent loss of 44-6123 *Girl of my Dreams*. The aircraft were immediately behind Colburn's over Zeitz, 16 August 1944.

A tail gunner view of a 388th formation.

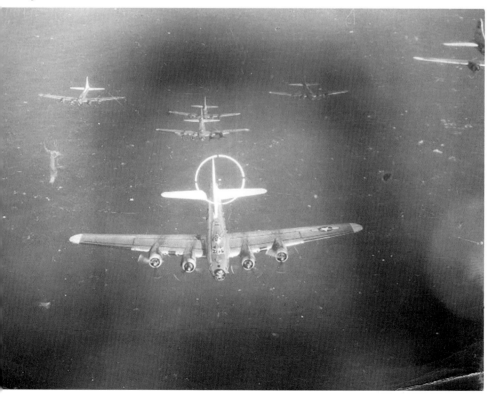

The regular Colburn crew of September 1944, Knettishall as featured on the trophy.

The original ten-man Colburn crew posing with the trophy (bottom of shot) September 1944. Tobias, Ryan, Neiman, Weekes, Granath, Simmon, Schweikert, Kragle, Colburn and Nutt.

Johnnie Colburn and Russ Weekes show off their 'Fickle Fannie' Flying jackets, which seem to show 29 completed bombing missions with one to go. Photo possibly taken before their last mission on 16 November 1944 to Aachen. The B-17 on that occasion was 44-8223 *Miss Karen K.*

Bombs away, a 388th aircraft lets loose a salvo.

The Colburn crew at a reunion in St Louis, 1992. Simmon, Colburn, Neiman, Ryan, (Unknown).

Johnnie Colburn re-acquaints himself with an old friend and flies once again in a B-17.

Johnnie's still proud of his flying jacket, although his original wore out. The badges were recreated by Bob Simmon.

The Ong Crew

Dong Ong in early training.

Dong Ong (far right end) in training at Santa Ana. Also highlighted is Dong's friend, Paul Patten.

A lighter moment at Santa Ana and Dong Ong has already gained the nickname 'Swede'.

1st Lt Dong Ong as the accomplished B-17 pilot.

1st Lt Earl 'Corky' Lippert – co-pilot.

S. Sgt Carl Lindorff – waist gunner. Pictured here in engineering training as most gunners had dual roles.

A large flak hole punched through the vertical stabiliser of 42-39842 *Miss Lace* flown by the Ong crew. Pictured on return from Amiens 12 June 1944.

42-97286, *Skipper and the Kids* flown by the Ong crew on their second mission on 11 June 1944. She was lost in December of that year in a flying accident on the Isle of Arran with the loss of ten men.

42-30851 *Little Boy Blue*. The Ong crew flew her on their first mission to Berlin on 21 June 1944. She was lost in a mid-air collision barely a month later while assembling in a formation.

Operation Union II team the morning after their parachute drop in the French Alps, 1 August 1944 led by Maj. P Ortiz (2nd from left). Sgt John Brunner (4th from left) dropped from Dong Ong's plane.

Dong Ong receives a record of a Coca-Cola radio programme, which featured an interview with him. London, August 1944.

The tangled remains of 42-97528 *Mary's Sister* after her aborted effort to land at RAF Hawkinge, Kent on 5 January 1945. Dong Ong had previously flown her to Munich on 31 July 1944.

The picture that started the search for the trophy names. The Ong crew holding the trophy under what is probably 43-37617 *Betty Ann*.

Left to Right:

Back row: Carl Lindorf (waist gunner), Kenneth Gardner (radio op), Arvid Estrom (?) (ball turret), Daniel Visconti (?) (tail gunner), Morris 'Tex' Fleishman (engineer).

Front row: Earl 'Corky' Lippert (co-pilot), Dong Ong (pilot), Ed Goldstein (navigator).

The Ong Crew as inscribed on the trophy, August 1944.

Here is the list that you asked for.

Mission
1. June 6 — Railways in France
2. " 7 — Bridges at Nantes, France.
3. " 11 — Railway Bridges, France.
4. " 12 — Airfields, Amiens, France
5. " 14 — Socony Vacuum Oil Plant, Bremen, Germany
6. " 18 — Airfields, France.
7. " 21 — B.M.W. Engine Plant, Berlin
8. " 29 — Factory near Leipzig, Germany
9. July 6 — No Ball Target. Crecy, France (Crecy)
10. " 7 — Synthetic Oil Refinery, Leipzig, Germany
11. " 11 — Munich, Germany
12. " 12 — "
13. " 13 — "
14. " 15 — "
15. " 18 — Kiel, Germany
16. " 19 — Ball Bearing works, Schweinfurt, Germany
17. " 20 — Leica Plant, Wetzler, Germany.
18. " 24 — St. Lo, France
19. " 25 — "
20. " 29 — Oil Plant, Leipzig, Germany
21. " 31 — Jet Propellion Plant, Munich, Germany
22 Aug 1 — Southern France near Switzerland
23. 2 2. — No Ball, Paris, France
24. 4 — Oil Plant, Hamburg, Germany
25. 5 — Tank Plant, Madeburg, Germany (Magdeburg)

Lippert and Goldstein pictured after Lippert's return to Knettishall in December 1944.

Dong Ong's letter listing his missions to Earl Lippert's wife, Betty Ann, 28 October 1944.

42-107162 *Worry Bird* flown on the Ong crew's last official mission to Bourron-Marlotte on 18 August 1944.

END OF MISSION—Col. Dong Ong, Orlando, Fla., stands on the ladder of an F-100 Supersabre after completing a combat mission in the Republic of Vietnam. The 25-year service veteran is the deputy commander for materiel for the 3rd Tactical Fighter Wing at Bien Hoa AB and has been in Vietnam for six months. His supply squadron has been selected the best in all of Seventh Air Force.

Newspaper clipping detailing Dong Ong's combat sortie in Vietnam.

Dong Ong in his later career, probably taken in the early 1970s.

Old comrades, Ong, Peterson and Patten, May 2006.

The trophy

Trophy, front. Inscription with crest: "Outstanding Crew of the Month. 388th Bombardment Group".

September 1944 inscription. Johnnie Colburn is spelt wrongly as 'Jonnie'.

SEPTEMBER – 1944

JONNIE W. COLBURN – 1ST LT.
CHARLES R. WEEKES – 1ST LT.
MORRIS H. NEIMAN – 1ST LT.
ROBERT E. SIMMON – 1ST LT.
RICHARD T. HESLAM – 1ST LT.
WILLIAM R. TOBIAS – T/SGT.
GEORGE E. KRAGLE – T/SGT.
LEONARD W. GRANATH – S/SGT.
FRANK E. NUTT – S/SGT.

Percy Prentice holds the trophy. As a boy he was adopted as the 388th mascot at Knettishall; and even had a uniform made for him. He confesses to "missing a lot of school".

The trophy returns home. Pictured on remnants of the main runway, Knettishall.

The trophy pictured at Knettishall next to the war memorial of the 388th.

Two B-17s on the hardstands at Knettishall.

An example of a typical B-17 formation. The names in darker boxes denote planes that were lost.

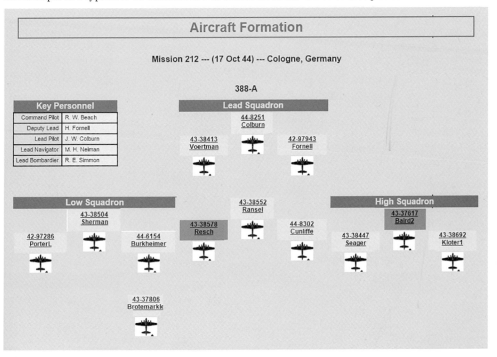

Aircraft Formation

Mission 212 --- (17 Oct 44) --- Cologne, Germany

388-A

Key Personnel

Command Pilot	R. W. Beach
Deputy Lead	H. Fornell
Lead Pilot	J. W. Colburn
Lead Navigator	M. H. Neiman
Lead Bombardier	R. E. Simmon

Lead Squadron

44-8251
Colburn

43-38413
Voertman

42-97943
Fornell

Low Squadron

43-38504
Sherman

42-97286
PorterL

44-6154
Burkheimer

43-38552
Ransel

43-38578
Resch

44-8302
Cunliffe

43-37806
Brotemarkle

High Squadron

43-37617
Baird2

43-38447
Seager

43-38692
Kloter1

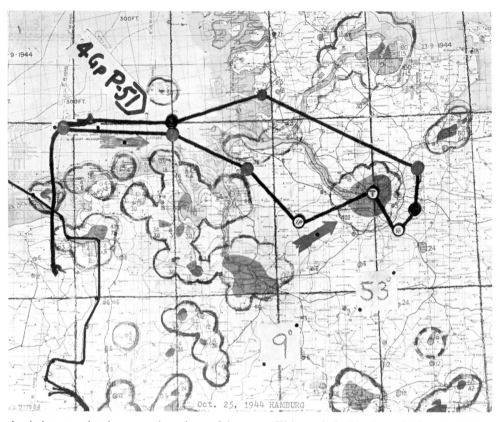

A mission map showing routes in and out of the target. This one is for Hamburg, 25 October 1944.

Chapter 11

A Beach Holiday

The first quality that is needed is audacity.
— Winston Churchill

Quite a few years ago, when our children were still small, we discovered France. This is not the discovery of the source of the Nile or some miraculous scientific enlightenment because, of course, France was never lost. A country that had previously been a stranger to us suddenly came alive and, although we have visited many times since, the more we go, the more we realize how little we really know it. We have an excuse for not travelling and knowing Europe better; we live in the far north of England and, by British standards, this is considered to be a long way. In terms of scale, the distance from our house to the south coast of England is similar to that between San Francisco and Los Angeles — so it may follow that our perceptions are indeed limited.

For the visitor to the United Kingdom, the English Channel is a mere wisp of water at twenty-two miles at its narrowest and most crossed point. However, the division culturally and politically may as well be several thousand miles. Remarkably, the English Channel also halted Hitler's insatiable European rampage of 1940. There are many reasons why the sea formed this barrier to the Nazis' master plan, not least that Germany did not have a large or developed enough navy to undertake a sea–borne invasion at this time. The English Channel became the 'no man's land' of a new kind of mobile warfare and air power, the arrows fired from each side's bow. The fighters of the Battle of Britain could cross the Channel in just over three minutes, bombers somewhat longer, but nevertheless there were instances of aircraft from both sides mistakenly landing at hostile airfields believing they were home. In April 1943, three Focke-Wulf Fw 190s tried to land at RAF West Malling in Kent with the result that one was captured intact and the other two were destroyed.

For the B-17 crews of 1944, the English coast carried with it the sense of foreboding on an outward trip and relief on the return leg. With the operation of assembling formations of bombers over the North Sea and then taking the eastern passages across to targets in Germany, there were extended periods of flying over water. To ditch or bail out over the North Sea was considered to be an experience from which you were lucky to survive due to the cold. Improvements in communications and sea rescue continued throughout the war as both sides recognized that returning aircrew were as valuable as whole aircraft. A fleet of fast rescue boats was established under the auspices of the Royal Air Force, a 'tip of the hat' to airmen that their rescue was not necessarily in the hands of the Royal Navy but that the RAF considered their rescue as important. Although provisions were in place for every returning raid, the odds against survival were a matter of chance. To find downed airmen in a small life raft, or worse still, individual men in a heavy swell and light rain – conditions not untypical of the seas around Great Britain – required good communication and a controlled descent.

My view on this day was of the White Cliffs of Dover gradually disappearing into the summer haze. My method of transport was much more sedate than an aeroplane; a ferry, and all thoughts of the dangers of war were far away from my travelling companions, who braved the breeze to capture the iconic cliffs on their cameras and phones. In the context of the trophy, my thoughts were very much on the passage of time and the contrast between this peaceful idyll and everything the coast signified in the Second World War. Our French holiday this year was really just for a few days and we decided to travel down to the Normandy coast and take a look at the D-Day beaches and the medieval capital of the area, Bayeux. Trish was a little less enthusiastic about my battlefield interests, so this trip was partially a beach holiday on some historic beaches.

Unlike some trips where both sides of the Channel were clearly visible nearly all the way across, Dover slipped into the sea haze and for a time we saw nothing but faint horizon before gradually the coast of France emerged. We had a little time on the drive to the guest house and at my bidding we made a short detour to the headland of Les Deux Caps. I'm particularly interested in Cap Gris Nez as this heavily fortified and bunkered promontory was the subject of Johnnie Colburn's first bombing mission on 4 June 1944. Not far away were the massive guns and huge concrete emplacements that launched their 380mm shells across the Channel. We parked in one of the well-planned car parks with the picket fencing so popular in coastal France. It was clear this was a tourist destination and, as we took to one of a number of footpaths heading towards the cliffs, it was clear that many others were enjoying this warm and sunny afternoon. We discovered this was a nature reserve, although the whole area was dotted with reinforced concrete bunkers and buildings of various shapes and sizes. The complex was all part of the Atlantic Wall, Hitler's armoured coastal belt designed to prevent an invasion. The paths skirt these concrete structures and one can still see bomb and shell depressions and the odd fractured remnant of a bunker less lucky than the rest.

Unlike many historical sites in Britain, curiously, there was no mention of the bunkers or the war on the information boards on the site. Instead, they waxed lyrical about the heritage of the sea, fishermen and the rural life of the past. The environment and the special vegetation that grows there were also featured. I couldn't help feeling that given the vast array of concrete, as a friend of mine would say, 'there was an elephant in the fridge.' In other words, there was a big issue that could not be ignored that everyone was trying not to mention. Perhaps the other thing that struck me on this late-August afternoon was, given the extent this area was bombed and shelled, there was nowhere near as much damage as I would have expected. Still, I found the walk very pleasant and the site worthy of a future visit when I had more time.

The next day, we set off from our guest house for the Normandy coast and our destination, the fishing village of Port-en-Bessin-Huppain. I have moved from the area of France where the 'phoney' war was waged in 1944 in the effort to distract Hitler into believing the Pas-de-Calais would be the invasion coast, to the section of France that became forefront in the invasion. It takes quite a few hours to reach on modern straight roads, so I can see why its location stretched the belief of the German High Command as to its suitability for a rapid invasion. Port-en-Bessin itself is fairly typical of small French ports, a small harbour lined with fishing vessels and yachts, and some bars, cafes and shops – nothing remarkable, but pretty. This port sat in the middle of the biggest sea-borne invasion in history yet, despite being in sight of Omaha beach, it was not suitable for beach landings and escaped a direct seaward assault on 6 June. German guns from the port fired on the beach and created a further nuisance to be eliminated. By the afternoon of 7 June, No.47 (Royal Marine) Commando had fought their way across the headland from Gold beach near Asnelles and had begun the operation to capture the port. Fierce fighting ensued but, despite mounting casualties, the many months of training and preparation resulted in the port being liberated the next day. There is no sign today of this firefight or indeed the momentous events that thrust Port-en-Bessin into the limelight; at least not in terms of things to see. The whole region has been, and will probably continue to be, the subject of an invasion several times the size of D-Day yearly – the tourist invasion.

The weather continued to be good during our stay and we would use part of our day to sightsee. Later we would find a beach with golden sand, not too difficult to accomplish, and sit and read or just snooze. Our closest sandy beach was the eastern section of Omaha beach and on the bluffs above stood the US 1st Infantry Memorial, and close by the large American Cemetery. Amongst the swimsuit-clad visitors it was hard to envision this stretch of beach as a battlefield. Instead of mined metal obstacles and spluttering machine guns, beach games of varying varieties were being enjoyed. A party of over-dressed visitors would suddenly emerge into view, walking slowly and deliberately, they were obviously trying to gain a bearing on D-Day amid the holiday frivolities. Sometimes a guide was with them pointing out the reference points and talking loudly about the events. It seemed two worlds were colliding, but the desired effect of the invasion was being played out; peace and freedom.

I had time to think through some of the events that crowded in on the airmen of the 388th Bomb Group during the immediate days after the landings. In history, singular events can become defining milestones in popular understanding. In the bar room history lesson of D-Day, the bombers missed the beach defences and as a result contributed to the bloodshed and near disaster on Omaha beach, possibly jeopardizing the whole invasion. Some elements are, of course, true but the close support bombing raids of those early days across all the invasion beaches achieved far more than some would have us believe. The first waves of bombers failed to silence the German guns and defensive positions overlooking Omaha beach. However, so did the guns and rockets of the Royal Navy and US Navy in the opening bombardment. There were five landing beaches that day and air power and the role of the bombers were, over the course of the whole invasion, very successful. German coastal radar stations were largely obliterated and communications and supplies seriously disrupted. I had names and faces for these actions in my two B-17 crews and it is clear reading memoirs of comrades of the time that the fog of war prevented most from forming a clear picture of how successful or accurate were their raids. Each carried its own demands and there was no time to question how necessary one raid was over another – the crews had to trust that someone had a grasp of the bigger picture.

A good deal of controversy remains about the later bombing of French towns such as Caen and whether or not these actions were misguided due to the loss of French lives. From the bomber crews' perspective, orders were orders and in terms of the physicality of a formation similar to the USAAF's B-17s, there was a need to fly accurately and bomb the target as a group rather than perform what we would now call 'a precision strike' involving single aircraft.

Whether it was visitors on a beach or gazing into the clear blue skies and trying to imagine formations of aircraft flying in to attack their target, my holiday was informative. It reminded me once again of the colossus of industries that went into the Second World War. The sheer quantity of men and material used is truly astounding. We took a walk along the beach at Arromanches as the tide receded and got close to part of the Mulberry harbour. These huge concrete structures towed into place to form an artificial harbour still dominate the beach and town. Like giant shoeboxes in the swell, they project the spectacular achievements of the D-Day planners and the might of industry behind them. Like the runways and airfields of the US bomb groups, they are disappearing back to nature. Their progress towards destruction may be slower, but the power of the seas over time will win. As we walked out across the sands, the nearest harbour section was one that foretold the fate of the others over time. Its sides had collapsed and it lay as a virtual shipwreck with twisted reinforced sections projecting from jagged edges. A vertical steel ladder still clung to the interior, suspended 30ft up a remaining wall. The huge collapsed section sat in its own moat of seawater, unable to hide its decay by sinking, it remains a spectacle. They are structures that generate an emotion by their size; a sort of fear and respect in common with many great buildings and structures that make us feel small.

There was a kind or irony in my travels and it was that I was seeing and experiencing on the ground the things that the bomber crews could not see and many never did see even later in life. Indeed, it came as a surprise for those still flying at war's end when opportunities arose to fly at lower levels and see the results of the bombing of Europe. It's easy to think that crews could see clearly what had happened over a target, but at 24,000ft with a sea of black smudged flak ahead and eyes searching the sky for fighters, it left little time to gaze downward. Even then, cloud and smoke would probably obscure any detail, even for quite a large target. For the fortunate, their war had ended effectively when the wheels of their B-17 touched down at Knettishall after their last planned mission. They were either assigned different duties or, more often, they returned to the States. Others had been less fortunate; they resided in prisoner of war camps and their eventual repatriation left no time for reflection or sightseeing.

A tourist town in summer has a life of its own. There's a sound, a murmur of people talking, the sound of footsteps; leisurely footsteps and not the hurried variety of a working city. The sun was picking gaps in the buildings and squares of Bayeux and, as the shoppers browsed or lounged in the outdoor cafes, all seemed relaxed and carefree. A man was standing in the doorway of the cathedral holding an old tobacco tin hoping for a coin or two. At first glance the visitor might have taken him for a member of staff at the cathedral, but his worn appearance gave him away. He stood for hours exchanging pleasantries and talking to regular passers-by. Begging is a way of life, but even here, it seemed a much more relaxed affair. I was standing in the square on the corner of Rue des Chanoines and under a boutique window close to the ground was a sign. It was a road sign with an arrow reading 'Littry' and 'Saint–Lô'. It seems insignificant but Saint-Lô was the destination of the mission on 24 July 1944, in which Johnnie Colburn's and Dong Ong's crews flew in the same formation. Johnnie was the lead pilot and Dong flew in the 'high' element that looked down on the formation on his left. They were flying as part of a huge raid to weaken German forces west of Saint-Lô to aid the break-out of Allied forces. As is often the case, when something as simple as a sign takes on significance it stands out and among the throng of my fellow tourists, I took a moment to think about it. One of the reasons I was standing outside a medieval cathedral rather than a rebuilt medieval cathedral, was that Bayeux did not suffer the destructive humiliation of its sister city along the Normandy coast, Caen. Bayeux was liberated from German occupation within forty-eight hours of the D-Day landings; Caen was heavily fought over and during the weeks immediately after D-Day was the scene of a number of battles. Finally, German resistance was overwhelmed and by 19 July the city was finally in Allied hands. The grip of the German army in Normandy was dealt a decisive blow as the Allies broke out west of Saint-Lô on 25 July.

My holiday was at an end but, like all good holidays, the memories lingered on. Perhaps some of the lighter moments in the sombre elements of remembering D-Day will also stand out in future. On the penultimate evening of our stay at Port-en-Bessin we had returned to our hotel and, sitting in the communal bar area, we suddenly heard the sound of bagpipes. The bagpipe is not an instrument that allows itself to be ignored and, as the noise became louder, we ventured out on to the street that followed the harbour basin. A few hundred yards away a group of middle-aged men were marching towards us with a piper in front. Outside the glass front of our hotel, the impromptu parade was halted and the men ordered to 'fall out'. This, it transpired, was a trip by former Royal Marines, not of the generation that fought during the Normandy landings, but a younger generation. The group were staying at our hotel and in their little parade they had also attracted a small group of French followers, who joined them for a drink afterwards.

Such are the pleasures of trips to places of remembrance. The sky, however, is a much bigger place and the traversing of this battlefield by thousands of airmen is harder to recognize on the ground now. There are very few plaques and memorials to airmen although they played a crucial role in so many instances. They have left their mark in places, the odd bomb crater remains, but chiefly their memory is carried by their children now living thousands of miles away and the stories they told them about their war.

Chapter 12

Nazi Heartlands

If Hitler invaded hell I would make at least a favourable reference to the devil in the House of Commons.

– Winston Churchill

With historical high insight, we can divide the combat flying missions of the Ong and Colburn crews into distinct phases. At the time, all the crews cared about was what the curtain revealed during the operations briefing. The groans and whistles of a long flight deep into Germany and its occupied echelons became an all too frequent sound effect of the curtain being pulled back.

As the two trophy crews started their combat career, D-Day was upon them and their first missions were considered milk runs. Johnnie Colburn's Soviet adventure at Poltava and his return through North Africa had created a break in the crew's missions and it was clear the focus was shifting off France and into strategic targets in Germany. For Dong Ong, the drift towards Germany was more constant; after all, since the 388th had arrived at Knettishall in July 1943 it had been on a conveyor belt of attacks on Germany. France and D-Day was therefore more of a welcome distraction to the regular crews, but as the Allies pushed inland from the beachheads the strategists once again lifted their heads towards Germany.

13 June 1944

Not a full week after D-Day, Hitler began flying bomb attacks against Britain. The V-1, Vengeance Weapon 1, was a small, unmanned flying bomb. It was really a cross between an aircraft, a missile and a bomb that was commonly referred to as a robot bomb, and it marked a watershed in aviation weaponry. For the first time, here was a weapon with a limited mind of its own that could act independently of its masters. The existence of the V-1 launching sites and capability was known to the Allies and for weeks before bombers had been attacking the launch ramps in northern France, but the bomber crews had no real idea what they were attacking. When the V-1s began to be launched, mostly against London, there was still a lot of work to be done to neutralize the threat. The V-1 was a simple device, using a pulse engine in flight that emitted a characteristic droning noise. It was neither a jet engine nor a rocket, the pulse engine was an ingeniously simple design that used a bent pipe and combustion chamber that, once the process was going, would suck in fuel and ignite it with minimal moving parts. The guidance system was more of a timing device that cut the fuel and thus the engine when enough flying time had elapsed. Keeping the V-1 straight and level was a gyroscope controlling flaps in the small wings. It flew straight to its target and it had no programming to access turns on the way there. As well as using belts of anti-aircraft guns, some of the faster fighters could catch a V-1 and after experimenting with shooting at them, which was effective but risked the chase plane in the resulting explosion, another method was perfected. By flying alongside, a fighter could tip the wing of the V-1 until it flipped on to its back. This tipped the gyro too, rendering it useless, and the V-1 would enter a steep dive and crash.

Some of the V-1s overflew Knettishall during this period. They were launched at night and their distinctive sound and the glow of the pulse engine at the rear made for an eerie experience as they droned on their unknown journey above. It was one of the sights and sounds that attracted onlookers and, emerging from huts and tents, it was easy to forget that there was an element of danger lurking. These particular V-1s were launched from Luftwaffe aircraft off the east coast of England, mostly from Heinkel He 111s with the V-1 slung underneath.

The Allies had three airborne fronts with which to contend: the support of the invasion in France, the destruction of the V weapons and the suppression of the German industrial machine that produced weapons and fuel for its armies. There was no denying that the then head of Nazi industrial production, minister of armaments Albert Speer, was a very capable man. Known as Hitler's architect, his plans for building post-war cities, particularly Berlin, were astounding. Speer, of all the Nazi leaders, escaped the war with his life and, to some degree, a reputation. Despite serving many years in prison for his role in using slave labour in the German factories, he denied knowledge or responsibility for the Holocaust. Maybe, unlike many of his Nazi colleagues, he appeared approachable, even likeable and at the Nuremburg trials expressed regret for his actions. He was, perhaps, the ultimate salesman in his ability to influence his fellow Nazis and yet maintain an air of tact and composure with his later captors. However, it was only after his death in 1981 that the true story of his complicity with the Final Solution became known. It was Speer's abilities that spurred on the diversification of war production into disparate geographical locations. He was making it harder and harder for the Allies, who by 1944 had near total domination of the air, to find Nazi factories. Some were moved to small towns, others were hidden underground. In the French Loire Valley, aircraft production was taken into the labyrinth of tunnels developed over centuries to store wine, cheese and grow mushrooms. Other factories needed a substantial workforce and large towns and cities became centres for manufacture. This in turn led to their destruction by Allied bombing and the loss of civilian life. The civilian was seen as a complicit worker in the Nazi industrial war machine and although modern society now considers civilian lives sacrosanct, there was little sympathy expressed at the time for German civilian targets. It is worth noting that many hundreds and sometimes thousands of slave labourers also lost their lives. One of the key factors in the Nazi expansion of industry was to transport large numbers of people to work in slave conditions. In scenes reminiscent of ancient empires, countries that were overrun were seen as ready sources of slaves. However, in the Nazi categorization, some races were seen as almost sub-human and therefore expendable.

What the emergence of the V-1 and, later, the even more fearsome V-2 did was to reinforce the Allied strategy of complete area destruction. There was no room for a measured response when the citizens of London were being dug out of rubble for a second period in four years. In fewer than three months, V-1s fired at London and Antwerp accounted for 22,892 casualties.

If Speer could hide his factories, there was one element much harder to conceal. The Nazis had fewer supplies of natural oil and, as the Allies closed in, this supply became further depleted. The answer was the increasing use of synthetic oil produced mainly from coal, a resource the Germans did have. The synthetic oil plants were big and impossible to hide but, perhaps given a ring of guns, fighter air cover and developing radar, they hoped they could keep the plants open. The Allies believed that killing the fuel supplies to a highly mobile army would cripple the German ability to resist. Raids on oil refineries in Romania on 1 August 1943 had been launched from Libya using B-24 bombers. The raid was costly in terms of aircraft and crews and the damage caused was later judged to be insufficient to warrant continued operations. From May 1944 and into 1945 the synthetic oil and other chemical plants became regular targets for the men of the 388th as part of a concerted battle against fuel production; the oil war. One of the targets, Merseburg, became known to the crews as 'The Little M' and was seen as just as dangerous as a trip to Berlin, 'The Big B'. The ring of guns was estimated to be more than 1,000 and the journey in and out was a long one, placing the B-17s in danger from other flak areas and fighters.

29 June 1944 – Wittenberg

With many of the Poltava crews still not returned from their 'summer vacation' via North Africa, Dong Ong and crew attacked a German target of some depth, an aircraft factory. The target was actually a secondary target, the first, the synthetic oil plant south of Leipzig named Bohlen, being obscured by bad weather. The Arado company had been producing aircraft since the mid-1920s and, although not as well-known as some of the other German aircraft producers, they were making some outstanding aircraft. The V weapons were not the sole area of concern to the Allies as Germany was beginning to manufacture jets in numbers. Arado was working on a jet bomber, the AR 234 Blitz. It is probably no coincidence the AR 234's first flight was in June and that Allied intelligence knew the aircraft was entering a production stage.

The Ong crew were flying B-17 *Joho's Jokers*, a plane named after pilot Harry Joho. The Joho crew had finished their thirty mission tally successfully in February and were well gone before the Ong crew showed up. Here was a successful B-17, a good omen if ever there was one. Bombing from 24,200ft, the target was bombed visually and the aircraft had all returned to Knettishall by 1253 hours.

7 July 1944 – Bohlen

Johnnie Colburn's crew were back in the hot seat after their 'excursion' to the Soviet Union. They were flying *GI Jane*, the B-17 they flew on their first mission which, although barely a month before, must have seemed like an eternity. Today's target was the synthetic oil plant at Bohlen. Johnnie was flying in the lead formation of the twenty-five aircraft supplied by the 388th that day. Dong Ong was flying in the low squadron and, as well as the height difference in the formation, he was positioned to the left of Johnnie and slightly behind. Today's mount for the Ong crew was *Miss Fortune* which, coincidently, was also the aircraft they flew on their first mission. The numbers of American aircraft in the raid was of a staggering proportion – but not unusual at this stage of the war. There were 1,129 bombers and 756 fighters. Of the bombers, 756 were B-17s and 373 were B-24s. This vast bomber stream was heading for multiple targets and, as well as synthetic oil plants, others bombed airfields, railways, factories and 'targets of opportunity'. Thirty-seven bombers and six fighters failed to return, which statistically represented a small loss given the total numbers flying. It also illustrates that, at this point in the war, even the most optimistic of German commanders must have known that being able to destroy the British and American bomber forces would be impossible. Taking into account the constant stream of new aircraft and fresh crews, it was an unimaginable strategic disaster that the Nazi leadership could not, and would not, address other than by issuing ever more harsh rhetoric.

Despite the simple mathematics, even in such a large formation of bombers, the effect of seeing thirty-seven shot down, out of formation or blow up must have played on the nerves and emotions of all who witnessed it. Up in the freezing still air being churned by thousands of propellers, engines creating contrails of thin cloud, each crew member with any view out was surveying the scene. As they approached their targets, the formations tightened up even further to try to prevent attack from fighters. The tighter formations made it easier to concentrate their bomb load too. As the action and flak intensified, some bombers fell behind, some turned back, some suddenly lost all ability to fly and began a slow tumbling spiral towards the earth. The lucky ones remained intact for those few seconds necessary for the crew to escape, others crumbled as wings folded up and tails broke off in a shower of glinting aluminium. In other instances there was a loud cracking sound audible above the bomber's engines, a flash, and a dark mushroom of black smoke where a few seconds before flew a complete B-17. Often the tail gunners witnessed the aftermath; small pieces of metal, objects and even people fell from the diminishing cloud and as they flew on, all that was left of the event was a smudge in the blue sky. Whenever something happened, everyone tried to count parachutes, but sometimes there were no parachutes.

Inside the bomber, the small universe that was the experience of the crew was frequently interrupted by the effect of flak. The aircraft lurched as it was caught in a near explosion and the hull was rattled as if someone was throwing gravel at it. Small holes of light could suddenly appear in the fuselage; equipment and clothing torn by pieces of metal in an instant. There were many casualties, but in the accounts of the veterans, as many, if not more, were near misses. Some, as in the case of the Ong crew, were hit repeatedly and the aircraft peppered with holes, yet Dong Ong said years later that he was proud to always bring his crew back and in one piece.

Colburn and Ong were part of the nineteen aircraft that made up the 388th's 'A' Group for that day. It proved to be a testing time for the command pilot, Bob Davis, and lead bombardier George Boozer. It was apparent the formation was late leaving the English coast by thirty minutes and, despite all efforts, it was not in its correct position even as the crews approached the target. Other groups began to jostle for position and the A Group was forced out of the bomb run by another group. They tried again, only for the same thing to happen before the lead bombardier decided to follow the formation ahead and finally they released their bombs from 27,000ft. Today was a good day for the 388th as all their B-17s arrived back at Knettishall by 12.56pm after nearly eight hours of flying.

11–16 July 1944 – Munich

Four days later, both the Ong and Colburn crews were flying to Munich. Dong and crew were flying *Betty Ann* for the first time, named after co-pilot Earl 'Corky' Lippert's wife. The crew's love affair with this aircraft stretched for seventeen more missions – it really was 'their' B-17. From 11 to 16 July, Dong and crew flew to Munich four times; an incredible marathon of airmanship and nerve jangling tension. The shear physical effort of flying nine-hour missions on a near daily basis, most of it in temperatures of -30 degrees and wearing oxygen masks is hard to imagine. Although Dong Ong's crew were credited with 'Crew of the Month' for August, this period in July was remarkable. Although few fighters were encountered, the flak varied from 'inaccurate' to 'intense accurate barrage'. It was on a Munich raid that Dong's plane was badly hit and lost two engines over the target. The crew even considered turning for Switzerland; but Dong made the call to go home.

Johnnie Colburn's crew also flew on two Munich missions on 11 and 13 July. However, a big change was coming to Johnnie's crew that effectively removed two members on a near permanent basis. Johnnie was selected as a lead pilot and this meant replacing Robert Ryan in the ball turret in favour of the Pathfinder Force equipment; an early radar bombing guide. Also leaving was John Schweikert, the left waist gunner. From here on in, the crew flew with only one waist gunner, Leonard Granath. New faces appeared to make the crew back up to ten men, a command pilot, who was a more senior officer, and also a member to operate the PFF equipment, known as a Mickey operator. The Mickey operators and command pilot were not rooted in one crew, they flew with the lead aircraft of the day. For the Colburn crew, this change was underlined by a training period with the 95th Bomb Group, based sixteen miles from Knettishall at RAF Horham. This meant Johnnie and what remained of the original crew, flew only two combat missions in the next month.

The attacks on Munich marked a new level of ferocity and, although not all elements of the raids were on the city itself, the hammer blow to the city and the region around it was immense. Firemen from around the region's towns were summoned to help and try to limit fires. Three of the raids – 11, 12 and 13 July – were 1,000 bomber raids while the 16th saw 213 B-17s attack an engine factory. All were flown by the Ong crew. For the bomb groups, the 12th was the most costly in terms of losses with twenty-four bombers downed of the 1,271 despatched, four more returning but damaged beyond repair. The damage figure was more alarming, with 297 bombers listed that day.

Munich was a transport hub and had many factories and military sites around it. Owing to the intensity of Axis activity, it was seen as a viable target, not just for specific targets, but the city itself. It was deemed that the city provided the workers for industry and disrupting life in the city was a key war goal. July 1944 also saw a shift in policy, particularly by American forces, from targeting strategic war elements such as factories and airfields to area bombing. The success of the Allies on the ground would lead to a German retreat towards its own borders and this had the effect of galvanizing the Allied leadership into believing that one last push against the civilian population might topple the Nazis from power and save the lives of Allied soldiers on the battlefields. Taken in the light of the enormous loss of life in the First World War, it is not surprising that the generation who saw the carnage first-hand had no wish to visit the terrors on the next generation of their soldiers. The end justified the means and, put into crude terms, the 'they started it' mentality had no serious challengers within both British and American governments. Ultimately, politicians decide policy, not soldiers and few elected representatives considered the lives of the German civilian population to be anywhere near the value of their men – and more particularly, few wished to face the pain of grieving parents in their constituencies.

By 11 July, the Allies were clearly well established in Normandy and although the city of Caen had proved troublesome in providing the breakthrough the Allies so needed, many Wehrmacht commanders knew that given the weight of forces facing them, the dam could break at any time. More worrying for many senior German officers was the near unstoppable track of the Russians on the Eastern Front, who were now in full advance against them. If the Allies wanted the Nazis deposed, they had to hope that either the military or civilian population – or both – would rise up in revolt. Little did the Allies realize that the plot to assassinate Hitler was well developed. On this day, Wehrmacht Staff Officer Count Claus von Stauffenberg was summoned to brief Hitler at his Austrian mountain retreat, Berchtesgaden. Although he did not carry it that day, Stauffenberg was already in possession of a briefcase bomb that he intended to use on the 15th. Plans changed suddenly as Hitler was whisked away to the headquarters at Rastenberg where, after following, Stauffenberg finally planted the bomb on 20 July. Although the bomb exploded, Hitler was shielded from the blast by the large wooden table that the officers were gathered around. His remarkable survival led to a characteristically brutal reprisal against those involved in the July plot. The suspicion of further treasonable actions by the Wehrmacht led to an intensification of Nazi influence and further powers being ceded to the SS.

The attacks on Munich also had significance in striking at the heart of the Nazis. Munich was the birthplace of Nazism and was considered its spiritual capital with lavish parades and ceremonies held where many SS recruits were sworn in. The Nazis created a shrine at the beer hall at the heart of the early movement and art galleries and civic buildings celebrated Nazi achievements. If the city could be reduced through bombing and the citizens driven to rebel against the Nazi authorities there, it could be the model for the collapse of Nazi Germany, or so the Allies dared to believe. During the five days of attacks, the sound and percussion of the bombing would be heard at Dachau, fewer than than ten miles from Munich. Just as

Munich was the model Nazi city, Dachau was the representation of what the Nazis were prepared to justify on their journey to fully establish their Third Reich. Dachau was a forced labour camp that killed thousands of inmates by hard work, execution, starvation, disease and medical experiments. It was the destination of many political prisoners from both Germany and the occupied countries. Even clergy who were seen to disagree with the Nazis were sent there. Here, where hope was in very short supply, the progress of the Allies could be seen and heard daily – but salvation arrived too late for many.

18 July 1944 – Kiel

The pace for the Ong crew was unyielding and, after only a day's rest from their marathons to Munich, the target marked on maps for that day was Kiel. Germany was short of coastline compared with its island adversary. Kiel was an important port on the south-western shore of the Baltic and was part of the U-boat building programme. The Germans were losing the Battle of the Atlantic by this stage of the war and losing U-boats at a faster rate than they could build them. The 388th provided eighteen bombers as part of another enormous raid of 1,349 bombers and 476 fighters, and the Ong crew were flying in the lead formation of the 388th 'B' group. B-17 *Betty Ann* was with the crew and must have provided a comforting stability in a very busy period. One hundred and seven B-17s were tasked to strike Kiel, the massive formation splitting into parts to strike other targets. Losses were low with only three bombers failing to return.

19 July 1944 – Schweinfurt

The name Schweinfurt, a town on the Main river in Bavaria, is rarely heard outside of the historical context of the losses suffered by the American 8th Air Force. It is the place that nearly derailed the whole concept of daylight bombing and threw into serious doubt the design of the B-17 to fly and defend itself as per its original design. Schweinfurt was the site of an industrial complex that produced ball bearings; an apparently innocuous product, but essential for all manner of engines and machinery. On 17 August 1943, nearly a year earlier, a large raid of B-17s to Schweinfurt and the Messerschmitt Bf 109 plant at Regensburg had resulted in the loss of sixty B-17s and fifty-five crews. The main problems had been a combination of fog in England delaying the bomber waves and a force of 400 German fighters. In 1943, the Allies did not have a fighter escort capable of flying the whole mission and the Germans had only to hold off and wait for the fighter cover to turn for home. The result was a severe mauling of the B-17s, but they did strike their targets successfully and inflict disruption to production. Although escort fighters such as the Spitfire were equipped with additional drop tanks, these were a hindrance during a dogfight. Pilots chose to jettison the tanks to engage German fighters and the Luftwaffe pilots soon learned the advantages of feigning an attack to limit the range of the Spitfires.

For the 388th, an attack on a ball bearing factory at Stuttgart on 6 September 1943 proved to be the most costly mission for them of the whole war. Of twenty-four aircraft dispatched, eleven failed to return; a disastrous blow to a relatively new fighting unit. A second attack on Schweinfurt on 14 October also proved very costly for the 8th Air Force with the loss of seventy-seven B-17s. A halt was called as a direct result of this raid and it would be a further three months before a resumption of operations of this type. The introduction of the long range fighters the P-51 Mustang and P-38 Lightning changed the landscape of the conflict; not only could these fighters fly all the way and back on escort duty, they had enough fuel to fight, too. Schweinfurt continued to be of marked strategic importance and altogether was the subject of twenty-two raids.

The raid of 19 July 1944 was Dong Ong's eighteenth mission and he was over the halfway point towards his thirty mission target. There is no doubt the going was tough, but it must have been some encouragement that the 388th had lost few aircraft in the past weeks. The Munich raids had passed without a loss. However, death waited around every corner and all manner of complexities faced the crews on every mission. Today would be no exception. As the aircraft were climbing out and attempting to get into their correct positions, 42-30851, *Little Boy Blue* descended in the formation and, after trying to regain height, was effectively cut in two by the propellers of an aircraft arriving above, a 96th Bomb Group plane flown by Lieutenant Ralph Colflesh out of Snetterton. There was a suggestion that a supercharger problem with *Little Boy Blue*, led to the misbalancing of the engines, leading to an uncontrolled loss of height. Pilot Walter Malaniak had already survived the Poltava episode, but he could do nothing to recover the tail-less plane and the crash near Bury St Edmunds resulted in the loss of all but two of the crew. The waist gunner and tail gunner escaped and parachuted to safety from the severed tail. After dumping his bombs in the North Sea, Ralph Colflesh and his crew made it back safely on this occasion but, by cruel irony, ten days later their plane snapped in two after being hit by flak after trailing behind the formation for half an hour on a raid to Merseburg.

The loss of the Malaniak crew must have focused the Ong crew on the risks; they had begun their combat tour together in 560th Squadron. Their first combat missions were only twenty-four hours apart and the Malaniak crew took *Betty Ann* on three successive missions. *Little Boy Blue* was a veteran, perhaps seen as a 'lucky' plane and lost on her ninetieth mission. She had first flown in combat in September 1943 and was an 'F' model B-17, considered an old aircraft. She was also the aircraft Dong Ong had taken to Berlin on 21 June, his first to 'The Big B', while his compatriots had headed for Poltava on a separate mission. While a crew completed, if they were in luck, thirty missions, these older aircraft seemed to thumb their noses at danger and survive periods thought unlikely. Their very presence encouraged crews to believe that maybe they too could make it through.

Little Boy Blue had been flying just a little behind Ong in *Betty Ann* and the drama of this mission was still being played out. Ong was in the high squadron and to his right Charles Maring took considerable flak damage to his aircraft, *Blind Date*. Such was the condition of his aircraft, Maring decided to perform a wheels-up crash-landing at RAF Honington on his return. The crew were safe and even the unlucky *Blind Date* was repaired, but when pressed into service again on 7 October, she crashed on take-off with a full bomb load. The pilot on this occasion, Harold Resch, and his crew got out before fire took hold and the aircraft eventually blew up. The incident caused an area not far from Knettishall to be cordoned off and some damage occurred to properties closest to the explosion. It was only Resch's second mission and the misery continued as he was shot down on his next, ten days later over Cologne. One crew member was killed, but the others, including Resch, were taken prisoner of war.

20 July 1944 – Wetzlar

Dong Ong and his crew with the fearless *Betty Ann* were airborne again and heading to the Leica factory in Wetzlar, north of Frankfurt. Leica was world renowned for the manufacture of cameras before the war. The demands of military production saw the making of optical devices such as binoculars and gunsights. In a small town such as Wetzlar, the arrival of the bombers must have had a particular terror as, although the formations passed almost daily, they were invariably heading to the bigger towns and cities. However, the railway had been hard hit in the town, even if the medieval centre survived. Unlike many other German companies of the time whose reputation was damaged by the Nazis, Leica had Ernst Leitz II at the helm, the son of the founder. Leitz had been in charge of the company since 1920 and he did not greet the rise of Hitler in the 1930s with enthusiasm. He employed many Jewish people and through the late 1930s and before the border was sealed in 1939, he helped many Jews escape by making them sales employees with oversees placements. Some of these 'employees' had no previous links with Leica, so it was a deliberate and well thought out plan to help this persecuted minority escape the Nazis. Although Leitz's activities were not known fully until after the war, the operation is now known as the Leica Freedom Train. Leitz's daughter, Elsie Kuhn-Leitz, was caught by the Gestapo and roughly treated for helping Jewish women escape into Switzerland. Later in the war, after her release from custody, Elsie also got into trouble again for trying to improve the living conditions of 800 Ukrainian women slave labourers who were forced to work at the expanded Leica plant.

Ironically, Wetzlar was also the site of a new holding camp for recently shot down USAAF crews. As part of the Dulag Luft transit and interrogation camp system, every captured airman went through one of the Dulag Luft camps before being assigned to a prisoner of war camp. Some remained in the Dulag Luft for years and the main interrogation centre was at the Oberursel Camp, twenty miles to the south. Thousands of feet up in the air, the Ong crew and their compatriots in the formations would have little or no idea that they risked the lives of the very friends who, perhaps only days earlier, had fought alongside them.

24 and 25 July 1944 – Saint-Lô area

The switch back to strategic attacks in France must have seemed a sudden move; it was certainly dramatic. The whole of the 8th Air Force was called upon to carpet bomb an area around Saint-Lô, a town south of the Cherbourg peninsular and the place of Generals Bradley and Collin's intended break out. The action was known as Operation Cobra and was designed to punch a gap through the German forces to enable an irresistible wave of men to swing south.

The 388th provided thirty-six aircraft in three formations, A, B, and C. Whether Johnnie Colburn's crew were trained fully in their role as a lead crew is unsure, but nevertheless, they were leaders of the 388-C formation. Of the Colburn crew, Morrie Neiman was lead navigator and Bob Simmon lead bombardier. In some senses, they had already proved themselves as a good crew. To lead was an honour, but also having good men in front was a necessity. They were flying *Borrowed Time*, a new B-17 that had the PFF incorporated during its manufacture. This aircraft also flew the next day on a similar mission, in the same position and with a different lead pilot, Herbert Moore. Having completed his first tour of duty, this raid was the first of his second tour and first as a PFF lead pilot. This might suggest that the PFF crews were still under training when the Saint-Lô call came.

Dong Ong was being led by Johnnie and tucked up a little higher and to Johnnie's right in the C formation. The weather was not good on the 24th and over the target area it worsened. Nevertheless, bombs were away at 1311 hours and all the aircraft landed safely back at Knettishall by 1603 hours. Despite damage to the German forces in an intense raid involving 1,600 Allied aircraft, the poor visibility took its toll with twenty-five American servicemen killed and 130 wounded in 'friendly fire' or, in this case misguided bombs. The raids were called to a halt once it became clear that the conditions were becoming too difficult and the ground offensive was delayed for twenty-four hours. It would be wrong to assume the Colburn crew were stood down the next day because of this incident; it would have been impossible to tell which units of the bomber force had caused this problem. As mentioned, Moore led the next day in Colburn's place and it seems both lead pilots were fresh in the role.

25 July 1944

Operation Cobra was relaunched with a ferocity hard to envisage in the post-war era. Some 1,800 heavy bombers and 600 fighter-bombers attacked a narrow strip of land along the Saint-Lô to Periers road. For the 388th, it was almost a carbon copy of the action the day before. Dong Ong was positioned in the same slot in the 388-C Formation, this time led by Moore instead of Colburn. The Allies were serving notice that they were coming through the German lines and the recipients of this most potent message were the Panzer-Lehr Division. The bombing run inflicted heavy losses and almost as soon as it was over, 1,000 Allied guns pounded their positions. Ahead of them, 140,000 men began to engage the Axis forces in a huge battle to push out of the area of the D-Day beaches and into northern and central France.

It was a key moment in the Second World War, for, just as landing on the beaches had been a tremendous triumph, the liberation of Europe depended on the march towards the German border and the rolling up of the German army. The Allies had to break through. The Nazi high command knew the war could be lost if the Allies broke out, whereas holding them in a confined area at least kept some hope alive that one day they might be able to push them back into the sea. Air power had changed warfare forever and, where the First World War had led to artillery duels on a huge scale and men leaving trenches and charging towards their opponents, today's fight was led by aeroplanes thousands of feet in the sky.

29 July 1944 – Merseburg

After the brief French intervention that had delayed deep Germany operations, the Ong crew were going to Merseburg. The bomb groups that attacked it had many stories of the flak and fighters. Today would be no exception with flak described as 'intense and accurate'. Ong flew in the B Group and escaped the brief but intense sudden attack of some forty-plus Me 109s and Fw 190s on the A Group ahead. Although the escorting fighters were quickly on the problem, Russell Boyce and crew were shot down and seven of them, including Boyce, perished. An account of the incident was published in the 388th Association's newsletter in 2008:

Lt. Russell Boyce's a/c no. 42-39866 was hit by three ME-109Gs from the rear, setting the two inboard engines on fire. Lt. Boyce was forced to break formation and dive in an attempt to put out the engine fires. His B-17 was seen to disappear into the clouds at an estimated 14,000 feet; they were not seen by the formation again. Only co-pilot 1st Lt. Darrell Hornesby (on his 28th mission) and navigator Emmett Lawless (on his fifth mission) were able to bail out. They were taken prisoner shortly after landing in a barley field. The bodies of the rest of the crew were found still in the aircraft by

Germans from a nearby air base after it had crashed and burned. Killed with Lt. Boyce (on his 30th mission) were S/Sgt. Alfred Japhet, top turret gunner (29th mission); S/Sgt. Kevin Ernster, ball turret gunner (31st mission); T/Sgt. Calvin Leitz, waist gunner (30th mission); and S/Sgt. Norman. Hubbert, tail gunner (30th mission).

Ironically, they were flying 42-39866 *Heaven Can Wait* and in the fortunes of war it seemed heaven could not wait any longer. The Boyce crew were at or very close to their final mission before their tour ended.

On return, Ong's fellow 560th pilot James Fitzpatrick had landed his plane, taxied in and had left the B-17 when another aircraft from RAF Fersfield lost control and crashed into it. Crew Chief Wells was killed in the accident – another stark reminder that even being back on the ground could be a dangerous place.

31 July 1944 – Munich

In the facts and figures it's sometimes easy to forget the simple details that affect young men. The day of a raid meant a very early start and, even in the height of a British summer, before dawn. Sleeping in was not an option and for Dong Ong and crew the intensity of the missions, with so many packed into a short space of time, meant the added pressure of trying to get rest.

After the normal hours of preparation and briefings, take-off today was at 8.45 am onwards. The weather proved to be an issue in this Munich raid with the formations relying on their PFF equipment to bomb through the cloud. In the clear dazzling sunshine and azure blue skies the business of war at times seemed far away. Yet the unbroken cloud beneath the formations proved to be an added challenge – bombing using the early radar guidance system was far from an easy task. The other bomber formations were making themselves known today and multiple contrails meant the 388th group had to climb a further 1,000ft to get some clear air. The flak was heavy and accurate, and demonstrated that the Germans were improving the radar control of their guns. Dong Ong and crew were flying in the B Group and in the low formation on the left-hand side. They were at one of the more exposed parts of the formation and of the other two aircraft immediately with them, Floyd Doherty flying *Stardust/My True Love* was in the centre and, slightly ahead and to Ong's right, was Ora Castrup flying *Devil's Luck*.

In any mission, the immediate run to the target is the most intense time of danger. Flak and fighters were their principal enemies, but in the target area the flak was the real aggressor. The flak on this target run had crept in amongst the 388th formation. A little further across in the formation, Sergeant Byron Cook, a waist gunner, had remembered to bring his camera with him, which was against regulations. Cook recounts in the book *388th Anthology Vol II* how he was moving about from side to side in his aircraft trying to get a shot or two somewhat hampered by turns on to the target run:

I noticed that a ship flying off our left wing (Lt Castrup) had caught a hit in the oxygen system. It was trailing blue flame. I couldn't get the camera in such a position that I could see the plane in my viewfinder, so I simply held it up to the window, pointed it, and snapped the shutter release.

Cook had lost sight of Castrup's *Devil's Luck* for a crucial few seconds. The B-17 blew up. His next shot remains one of the most poignant in the 388th photo archive and shows an intense black cloud of where a B-17 had once been. The Ong crew flying on the right and quite close must have witnessed the whole incident and heard the blast of the exploding aircraft. One of Ong's waist gunners, Carl Lindorff, flew only three more missions after this one before being 'retired' with an apparent stress disorder. The combination of so many missions in short order and incidents such as the loss of the Castrup crew must have placed a huge mental strain on the crewmen.

Both the Colburn and Ong crews had been flying combat missions for just under two months. As they took the war to Nazi Germany, there was no shadow of doubt that this was the toughest challenge they would face. They also knew that to have the time to take stock of what was happening, they would first have to survive. Despite the skills they had spent months perfecting, the simple truth was that chance and circumstances beyond their control played a big role.

Chapter 13

Fear, Loathing and Duty

The only thing we have to fear is fear itself.
– Franklin D. Roosevelt

From the earliest days of seeking out the airmen of the trophy and their descendants, I was sure that there was more of a story to tell than tales of comic book flying heroes. There was something impressive about the names and yet I had little doubt that now, seventy years on, there were elements of the story that would be painful. All the names survived the war, but how well did they survive life? What part of their combat experiences coloured their behaviour afterwards, their choices, their careers and their relationships? I have spent the last fifteen years studying the First World War and I am convinced the trauma of the trenches turned an optimistic, forward looking nation that once maintained the largest empire in history into an emotional shadow of its former self. Some talk of a 'lost generation' but those who did not come back did not contribute anything further to society. It was those who returned who dictated the pattern and prosperity of Britain, and the mood had changed. Clearly, the class system had been shaken, but also, and perhaps more importantly, the effect of trauma and sorrow left an indelible mark. Britain lost its spark and while America continued in the path of the American Dream, a generation of British men lost confidence in themselves.

As a young child in the 1960s, I grew up with Sunday afternoon war films where the plucky Brit always triumphed over the nasty Hun. The story always featured a central hero with a stiff upper lip and a sense of fair play. American war films always had a flamboyant but ill-tempered and insubordinate hero who spat his lines out like he fired his gun. In the films, men who showed fear were always those who died first and if a hero died he died in the arms of his buddy. Germans were portrayed as brutal, but ultimately not very bright and would suffer defeat after defeat. The films portrayed the victors and with each film one could expect a stirring theme tune. Perhaps so soon after the war the film makers were wanting to give everyone the story of what happened, but the grim intense reality of battle was something the public did not and could not understand. My school playground imitated these films with 'Tommies and Jerries', 'Japs and Commandos' and 100 dogfights fought with arms outstretched as we ran and weaved in our pretend Spitfires. Our arms would shake to emphasize our firing guns and the louder we shouted the more accurate our fire.

In short, in boys' play there was no place for 'cowards' and there were no casualties requiring medical assistance – you 'died' or not, that was it. If you died, you could come back into the game a few minutes later. While there is much criticism now of computer gaming, guns and killing for fun, times then were really no different. Instead of a screen, we carried plastic guns and threw stones as grenades. All around us was a generation that as young men had gone off to war and were now fathers. I never heard of anyone talking about how bad war could be or what they had experienced. I wonder now what these veterans made of their sons running around the streets and gardens of Britain making machine gun noises and emulating, albeit in innocence, some of their darkest experiences. One of the turning points in the media in Britain was the release of the television documentary *The World at War* in 1973. Although I was only ten, my parents let me watch it and, for me, it was one of the first windows in to the reality of war. This was the first expansive attempt at a no holds barred documentary series and proved to be ground-breaking. It was the start of the quest for greater realism and, with it, questions not only about how men survived the physical elements of combat, but how their minds and well-being were affected, too.

As newly-weds, Trish and I rented a ground floor flat in a small village just outside the town of Cockermouth on the edge of the English Lake District. Our landlord, Jack Harkness, lived above and one day Trish looked after a friend's baby for an afternoon while its mother went shopping. Jack and his wife Betty soon found out, in fact I doubt whether much could pass them by, and they offered the use of the small garden outside in which to entertain our guest. As we stood, the ladies fussed the baby and Jack and I got talking. He was retired and for the latter part of his working life had driven a farm feed truck around the local farms. As a result, he knew everyone and had more than an amusing tale to tell, but Jack was not a gossip; he had a quiet and serious nature. I was interested to learn he had been in the army during the war and he told me how he had ridden up through Italy on a motorbike.

Jack then uttered a few words that have stuck with me, not for what they explained, but with the purpose he said them. I knew they were heartfelt thoughts:

War is a terrible thing. War changes you forever. You see things as a young man that no one should ever see; it changes you.

I didn't ask what he had seen; his tone told me immediately that whatever sights and experiences he had would be locked within him. They bore no relation to his life afterwards as a quiet man in a rural environment. They were sights, sounds and experiences alien to anything he would experience afterwards, but, nonetheless, he carried the sadness with him. In our process of social awareness of the Second World War, we had reached the point where a man could confess that war was terrible. We had not yet reached the acceptance that a man could be mortally afraid and maintain honour.

Harry Patch was the last British survivor of the First World War trenches. In a 2003 documentary Harry said: 'If any man tells you he went over the top and he wasn't scared, he's a damn liar.' This quote was a variation of what had been said by many veterans from many wars but, perhaps because of the high regard for a man who lived until he was 111 years old, Harry's version is particularly emotive.

With the passage of time, we now understand far more about fear and stress than in previous generations; we now have the phrase 'post-traumatic stress disorder' as a peg on which to hang this hat. However, to label it is not to fully understand it and, despite our certainties of its existence, treatment and help is far more difficult to administer. Fear is a subject that has engaged man for centuries and, in the realm of battle, it is considered to be the attribute of losers. Bravery, on the other hand, is considered a fine attribute, the stuff of numerous books and films and a basis of a good story. Few ask the question whether a man who is filled with fear can win a battle – it seems a stupid question. However, there is a difference between a man who is filled with fear and a man who becomes consumed by fear. Many servicemen testify the quality of their training and the camaraderie and loyalty of those they served with carried them through. In terms of the bomber crews of the Second World War, nearly all confess to being afraid at some point. The fortunate thick-skinned personalities say that fear was present, but did not trouble them unduly. Many confess that fear stalked them constantly, at times from far away, at other times it took control and threatened to render them useless. Most were able to fulfil the task they were trained for throughout the fearful times and even hid it successfully from their comrades. The life of a bomber crewman was endangered by mechanical failure, pilot error, enemy fighters, flak and even the weather. There was much to overcome and, in addition to physical harm, he had to contend with the damage of the mind.

Many veterans have testified to physical injuries healing, but scars of the mind remaining. The definition of fear is also hard to reach. Was a certain decision made from operational prudence, sensible self-preservation or illogical fear? Sometimes, in any one event, all three aspects manifest themselves. The accompaniment of fear is often guilt and this can be even more difficult to control. The tendency to blame oneself for circumstances that, being objective, were not in your control, is commonplace. The guilt of surviving is not unusual and many veterans live with questions as to why they survived when so many others around them did not. For those with faith, the realization that God had preserved them for a reason was a humbling experience; for those without, chance seemed to be a fickle mistress.

A former RAF Lancaster tail gunner, Harry Dobinson, who lives in my home area, witnessed a large flash and explosion one night behind him in the bomber stream. Only later did he realize that he had witnessed the sudden destruction of a Lancaster hit in the bomb bay. For those who fought at night, the terrors were all around, but often invisible. The imagination of what could happen was a significant mental strain. The empty beds of the missing and lockers being cleaned out did little to reassure crew that they had a future.

For the men of the 388th Bombardment Group, the terrors could be witnessed in clear daylight. There was little need to exercise the imagination. They could see bombers being hit, dropping out of the formation and, all too often, see them fall down or blow up. By mid-1944, the raids had gained incredible strength; 1,000 bomber raids were not unusual and these formations were defended by nearly as many fighters. The downside to these vast armadas was that the chances of witnessing bombers shot down became much higher. The statistical probability of being shot down might have been reduced as the war progressed but, in terms of mentally grasping the true situation, the eyes served only to exaggerate anxiety. Few express much feeling or understanding for their targets on the ground, principally because they were flying so high.

Without doubt, 1943 had been an enormously testing time for the 8th Air Force in Britain. It had come within a whisker of abandoning the concept of the daylight raid. For the 388th Bombardment Group, the confidence and enthusiasm of entry into the European theatre of operations had diminished quickly. Too many crews went missing to get any feeling of security. In our world of instant news coverage it is more difficult to take a step backward into the experience of an airman of the time. If a plane fell out of the formation badly damaged it may have been possible to count some parachutes, but the uncertainty of the crew's survival meant they effectively went missing. Nothing more was heard unless a postcard was sent from a prisoner of war camp and even then this news could take months to arrive. Unlike more modern smaller wars, such as the first Iraq conflict, there were no TV reports or captured airmen giving forced interviews at the hands of their captors. From a ground crew's perspective, one day their plane would not land and, with no news or sightings, all would be assumed lost. For aircrew, the training and replacement conveyor belt was in full operation. They knew their failure to return would be marked as briefly as possible.

Speaking in a video interview in 2011, 388th radio operator Larry Goldstein recounted his training and eventual arrival at Knettishall. As part of his three-month crew training he was part of a thirty-crew group, 300 men, many of whom came to Knettishall. Of the thirty crews, Larry's later research showed only five made it through the war. When Larry and his crew arrived at Knettishall in autumn 1943 they arrived at 8.30 in the evening and were shown their beds. In a thirty-man billet, twenty-four beds were empty and when they asked why they were told they were all men who failed to return.

For some, the odds seemed impossible and perhaps it helped to discuss their chances of survival. These were young men and perhaps in among the bravado and promise of heroism, they were able to stave back the feelings of raw fear. My natural inclination was to write of the heroism and bravery of the two trophy crews; perhaps forty years ago this book would read very differently. Now, as this generation fades from us and we lose the first-hand accounts of this war, it is essential to reflect as true a picture as possible of their story. My early concern in the research was to find out if everyone returned from combat out of the Colburn and Ong crews – all did. The second concern was whether any had been seriously injured and, again, it seems all returned without serious incident, although it seems inevitable that some suffered minor injury at times. The most difficult area of the research was to assess the mental damage to the crews and this is far more difficult given the time that has now elapsed.

In terms of relationships, it appears a number suffered marital breakdowns and some possibly drank a little too much or were unwise in their choice of life partners. However, given the social changes and pressures of the twentieth century and, men being men, it is impossible to quantify whether the statistical incidence of these problems was higher among those who saw active service in the two trophy crews to others who had not. The accounts of their children are helpful but not conclusive because they could not compare the man before he went to war with the man who returned.

Gene C. Peterson, a 561st Squadron pilot and close friend of Dong Ong, perhaps his closest friend, certainly had significant problems with a crew member losing his nerve. It seems Dong Ong might also have had some early crew problems of this kind, but not anyone mentioned on the trophy. Peterson later recounted his experience in a poem written in his simple and light-hearted style. Having had two engines knocked out on his twentieth mission, the same happened on his twenty-third over Hamburg on 4 August 1944 flying 44-6171 *Cutie on Duty*. Peterson described his navigator as a 'bar room hero' and in the crisis of 4 August his navigator lost the plot until he became 'a nightmare' and an 'uncontrollable mess'. After he had 'stopped screaming', Peterson had asked for a heading and it became clear the navigator had no clue what to do. Peterson recounts that his co-pilot suggested he went down and shoot the navigator right there and Peterson took control of the situation and told everyone to keep calm. Out of the formation and limping home, a third engine began to stream oil and over the Dutch coast they were down to 2,000ft. They were fired on by a ship over the Channel and their only comfort was the company of a 'Little Friend', a P-51 fighter that had latched on. They could see rescue boats in the English Channel, but by some luck and good flying they made it to land. On landing, a burst tyre pulled them off the runway, but they were safe, at least physically. Peterson immediately requested the navigator be removed and, by some quirk of fate, he conveniently fell off a bar stool that night and broke an arm. The navigator was returned to the States shortly after – he never flew again with the 388th.

In a later memoir, Dong Ong says that for this mission Peterson should have been awarded the trophy. Although Dong Ong had a reputation for humility in his achievements, it is clear the incident made a deep impression. If the nerve of a crew was at all suspect, it would sometimes manifest itself in an aborted mission. These were normally for some technical reason rather than a particular crewman losing his nerve, although there were cases of crewmen being inventive with technical issues to facilitate an abort. Both the Ong and Colburn crews were outstanding in not aborting missions and in Dong Ong's case, this stretched right into his second tour. After fifty missions, he set something of a record for the least number of aborts – listed as only one due to an aborted take-off after an engine problem on mission number five.

One recollection of Johnnie Colburn's crew is that of Navigator Morris Neiman (also known as Morrie) coming on the intercom to report his oxygen supply was faulty. Oxygen was an essential commodity and it would not be possible to continue with the mission without it. Unlike some Hollywood depictions where pilots are seen at high altitude with their oxygen mask hanging down, it was impossible to function without oxygen and hypoxia and resultant unconsciousness would follow rapidly. Johnnie suspected Neiman might be losing his nerve and was trying to force an abort, so he sent another crew member down and found a rather blue and oxygen-deprived Neiman. Emergency oxygen bottles were available and Morris recovered. The incident became part of the crew's repertoire of amusing stories and Colburn and Neiman carried on to become lifelong friends.

In the many hours spent searching for trophy crew members and their relatives, Penny Warner, daughter of Ong crew waist gunner Carl Lindorff, was a great help in forwarding information and letters written by Carl through the war. Penny had herself served in the US Air Force and had spent much time researching her father's military career. Carl was close to his sister Marie and it is chiefly this correspondence that gives us an insight into the training, the combat and the struggles to cope with the aftermath. Interestingly, it was Marie who talked of Carl to her children and described to them the condition we now know as post-traumatic stress disorder. It is worth looking at Carl's experiences in a little more detail, as in many ways he was a typical recruit who went through months of intensive training with the uncertain promises of combat.·

Carl, known as Chuck, Lindorff arrived at the Las Vegas Army Air Corps Gunnery School (LVAGS) on 27 April 1943 to become an aerial engineer/gunner. It was the dual role of these gunners that proved them to be a valuable asset. Not only did they train how to operate the guns, but they would act as the eyes and ears for the pilot in identifying and, if necessary, correcting faults and battle damage while in flight. The five-week course at LVAGS was to direct them to the B-17 and normally the air engineer would occupy the top turret. Others in the crew were cross trained in gunners' positions, the radio operator would train on the ball turret and the other gunners would have a secondary training, too. Part of the *raison d'être* of the B-17, the Flying Fortress, was the principle that the aircraft would be bristling with guns that would provide an interlocking arc of fire with which it could defend itself. Combine the 'Forts' into a formation, each with their own 'basket' of defence, and it was thought that a fighter would find it very difficult to attack.

In May 1943, during the course, Chuck wrote to Marie in reply to another letter in which Marie must have asked a few questions:

Well, that contraption as you call it, is a ball turret. It is a little round ball set in the bottom, top, side or tail of a plane. It has a little door to get in to it and lock. About 2/3 of it sticks outside the plane. It has two 50 calibre machine guns in it with the barrels sticking outside. It's only about 3 or 3 ½ feet in diameter. It has controls in it too you can move it up or down and turn it around 360 degrees as far as you want to. It has glass windows, supposed to be bulletproof, all around it. You sit or rather lay in it just like you would in a ball. Someday when you see a bomber fly by, look and see if you can see one sticking out on it and you'll get more of an idea of what I mean.

In the same letter, Chuck referred to his brother's marriage and his expectation of a posting to Europe:

If they're going to get married I wish they would before I go across. If they don't I maybe won't get to see the happy family. Hell, if I leave I only got from 1 to 3 chances in a 100 to come back as a A.G. They claim the life of one is an average of 8 seconds in actual combat and only 9 out of 100 come back. It used to be 4 seconds and 10 out of 100 came back. They changed it since I got in. I guess that's why they only take volunteers for it and they

can refuse to go up in the air when they want to (as if they'd refuse) some
of them get scared out and quit. Oh well I haven't as much to lose as a lot
of others and I want to go before next year and by then they'll have a
lot of planes for protection. It won't be so bad if I get in a B-17. *I'll be*
O.K. They're fast, fly high and better protected, too. I stand a good chance
because I passed the high altitude test we had in the chambers. I'll get higher
ones in advanced training.

There are a few noteworthy elements in this extract. Firstly, the statistic
quoted of a ninety per cent casualty rate is very high. This is May 1943 and
the extent of losses were unknown to the rank and file of ordinary servicemen.
The true statistics were strictly classified as they would be useful for the
enemy. Although there was plenty of first-hand knowledge available, the true
extent of the risks varied from unit to unit and aircraft type, location and
mission types also played a significant part. It would seem that the emphasis
was in obtaining crewmen who would volunteer on the basis that they faced
what appeared to be a very high probability of death or substantial injury.
The positive outcome of what might be classed now as 'scaremongering' is
that when a higher rate of survivability was achieved, it increased the moral
of the crews. The negative element was that crewmen were entering the
shooting war with an elevated level of anxiety based on the statistics given in
training. Many testify to having an indestructible belief in themselves right
up to the point of their first combat mission, after which, and normally in
the light of a baptism of fire, their mental strength collapsed. At least one
crewman of the 388th confesses that the pent up anxiety of his first bomb
run led to him involuntarily soiling himself as he heard the 'bombs away'
message. Others found the steel helmet provided to protect against fighters
and flak was useful in which to vomit.

For Chuck Lindorff, it seemed the danger was offset by youthful
enthusiasm and he believed that he had not got as much to lose than
others. However, in the light of what happened to him, perhaps in his case
the upscaling of the casualty risk played a significant starting point in a
psychological battle. The actual statistics for B-17 crew losses in combat were
far less than Chuck quotes. An analysis of figures of the 95th Bomb Group
based at Horham throws up some interesting facts. It would appear that
the risks faced in relation to the position and role in the B-17 were roughly
equal. The gunners did have a slightly higher percentage point record of

deaths or injury but, broadly, they were not significantly more overall than their fellow crew members. The oft-quoted story of the tail gunner being in the most dangerous position does not appear to be correct in statistical terms, although in the 95th the ball turret operator had a rough time. The element of risk posed by fighter attack reduced as the war went on and by late 1944 many formations reported seeing no fighters at all. With flak, the risk to the crew was universal and, in the event of bail outs, the gunners in certain positions had some advantages in making a speedy exit.

The Germans knew they faced stiff opposition in the Fortress but, just as the Americans had worked hard to cover all angles of attack, so they studied to find out at which angle they were most likely to succeed. The favoured approach became known to the Americans as the '12 o'clock high'; a head-on attack, but ten degrees above the horizontal to reduce the risk of collision. Renowned German fighter pilot Lieutenant Franz Stigler described a 1944 attack against B-17 bombers:

With high speed built up in a dive, my aircraft made a very fleeting target and the more vertical my descent, the more difficult it was for the top turret gunner to get an angle on me. I targeted the pilot's cabin, the engines and wing's oil and fuel tanks. On this type of approach, the firing time was extremely limited. I could get in only one short burst. But I was going so fast that I was also harder to hit and the real danger was that I might collide with my quarry. I was through the formation before he even saw me and climbing back for another pass.

Chuck Lindorff looks to advancing technology to keep him safer and in his letter he particularly expresses his confidence in the B-17. His mention of 'chambers' is interesting as it illustrates how the use of decompression chambers in training was preparing flying crew for the rigours of altitude. The chambers were used for training in recognizing the effects of hypoxia and helped in the selection of those deemed to be physically capable of high altitude flying.

The newly qualified Aerial Gunner Carl Lindorff sent another letter to Marie:

Pvt Carl Lindorff
Class 43-22 Bk9 2-16-20
Las Vegas Army Gunnery School
Las Vegas, Nevada

June 1, 1943
Dear Marie,

Thanks for the cookies. They made a nice graduation present. You see we graduate today and get our wings (aerial gunner wings) and pay. I sent $40 home to mom. I only got $62 this time. I get my flying pay next time. We were flying all week and was it fun!

We leave tomorrow so I got to pack again. Haven't much time to write. Just wanted to thank you for the cookies and tell you not to write till I get a new address which may not be for a week or so and maybe longer.

How's Harry and Albert coming along? Say hello to grandpa and ma and pa for me.

Luck to you all,
A G (Aerial Gunner) Carl
My silver wings make me want to fly home

Chuck's most significant posting is to Rapid City, South Dakota. The U.S. War Department seized 341,726 acres from Pine Ridge Indian Reservation to establish Rapid City Army Air Base (RCAAB), a B-17 bombing and aerial gunnery range.

Chuck was about to meet Dong Ong and the crew who would form an integral part of his life for the coming months:

Sgt Carl Lindorff 37549176
Combat Crew Training School
Military Training Section
Crew A-40 R.C.A.A.B.
Rapid City, South Dakota

January 20, 1944 (Rapid City)
Dear Marie,

Well, I'm in a new camp now. Just got here this morning.

I'm in crew 7617. Got a Chinese pilot. He's a swell guy. Got a swell crew all around anyway as many as I've seen so far. The radio guy is kinda quiet,

*though. The bombardier is a happy guy with a red moustache. The co-pilot's
a swell egg, too. The one A.M. (second engineer) is from Texas. Him and
I been together since we left Salt Lake. We get along O.K.. Good thing as
I'm first engineer and I might need his help. It's funny they made me first,
he used to work on the line. I'm the youngest I've met of our crew so far. The
oldest is 27. I get my pick of the guns. Think I'll take the top turret.*

*I'm only 520 miles from home now. Want to try to get a 3 day pass. They
claim you can't here, though. We get a class A pass and can go in whenever
we're off duty.*

*Ong (pilot) said he'd try and arrange a trip so we could go to St. Paul.
He and I get along O.K. We're the only two who have worked on B-17s
before.*

*Maybe one of these days I'll be flying over your place. If I do, I'll try to
find something to drop out.*

How's Loren coming along? Bet he's smiling as usual. He's sure cute.
Guess I'll close for now.
Love, Chuck

Chuck's army life was changing as the training intensified. He wrote as a
promoted sergeant and it is clear that in the past six months his training
stream had been on B-17s. In this letter he expected to get the top turret,
which implies he would act as the regular engineer on the crew. Things were
going well for him and he was clearly riding high:

Jan. 24, 1944
Dear Marie,

*This is a soldier's paradise if there is such a thing. No one blows a whistle
to wake you, no reveille, retreat or formation. They tell us a day ahead of
time when, where our next meeting is. Got Class A passes and can leave
camp any time we're off duty.*

*I'm First Engineer on a ship and got my pick of guns so I took top turret.
That's the best one and got the most business. Good thing I got the full
insurance, ma will be collecting that in the future, well 9 chances out of 10
she will.*

*That was my last furlough when I was home. I won't get another for 6
months and by then, I'll be over as we only got 90 days left here starting the
first (of March 1944).*

Look Marie, I didn't make out any will – you think I should? My bonds and insurance are made out to ma in case anything happens we get 6 months' pay to give anyone and I made that out to ma. Pop's second beneficiary on it all. If anything would happen I wish you'd see to it ma gets all my things to do what she wants to with, will you? If I make out a will, I want to make you administrator or whatever it is, OK? I don't think there's anything to worry about but you see a lot of us won't leave this field. Some planes get smashed up in training and you never know who is next. One guy here is the only survivor out of two of them (planes). There is also a chance I may ship across any day. It's a slim one but it's there. We're just replacements for overseas squadrons and can ship out anytime they need us. May be here for 6 months but that's very doubtful. Don't get excited, I'm just telling you in case.

Ma wrote and told me she hurt her knee. She sure has tough luck.
I got to take a shower before all the warm water's gone.
Love, Chuck

Chuck had an on-off relationship with his future wife, Jane, and it is true to say that Chuck's parents did not really approve of her. However, with the pressures of war and imminent posting overseas, Jane agreed to marriage in February 1944 and before his training period was out in the United States, she was pregnant with their first child. Insurance was a voluntary decision and, once again, six months after he wrote from gunnery school, he was repeating the nine out of ten statistical casualty rate. The training accidents only reinforced the thoughts of danger ahead. However, it's clear Chuck was enjoying the ride and getting free from some of the rigours of basic training. By this date, Rapid City had lost thirty-three B-17s in fifteen months in training incidents. Perhaps as Chuck was writing he was recalling the accident of a day earlier involving a pilot, Donald Lowe, in B-17F 42-5446 ,which appears not to have been overly serious, but was a stern reminder of the risks.

Chuck's next letter was to his brother and it seems there was a certain amount of anticipation as to their next move:

Sgt Carl Lindorff 37549176
Combat Crew Training School
Military Training Section
Crew A-40 R.C.A.A.B.
Rapid City, South Dakota

Feb 17 1944
Dear Harry,

   Well, everything but the thing is done. I think we'll wait till about the 3rd of March.

   I got enough time in for flying pay for this month and last month so I'll pay you back when I get paid.

   Flew yesterday and was supposed to this morning but it was stormy out. Fly tomorrow night now.

   Passed my Eng. (engineer) test here. I had an instructor Eng. go along yesterday and check me out in the air. I think or rather am supposed to get another stripe out of here. Boy will that be swell.

   Am I behind on my writing! Got 26 letters I haven't answered yet.

   I got to go again.

   So Long, Chuck

In the chain of correspondence, there was now a significant break in surviving letters and sadly all the letters written covering Chuck's transit to England and his operational flying from 7 June to 4 August 1944 seem to be missing. His next letter came on 11 September and he had been grounded. He had flown twenty-two missions towards the thirty necessary to finish the tour of duty. The rest of his crew with Dong Ong finished only two weeks later and were rotated back to the United States with leave and a lifetime's worth of honour. Chuck remained at Knettishall as a ground engineer until the end of the war. He returned a different man and his nephew recounted that he was always nervous, very thin and smoked his pipe constantly.

   The challenge seventy years on is to piece together what happened to Carl Nels Oscar Lindorff and perhaps we shall never fully know. However, his letter of 11 September leaves the reader in no doubt as to his condition by his own assessment:

388 BG 560 BG
APO 559 c/o PM
Ny NY

Sept 11, 1944
Dear Marie
*   I wonder what kind of guy the folks think I am. Here you say it was Mom's birthday and I didn't know it. I couldn't of sent her a card but I could of at least sent her a letter. I missed Pop's, too. It's good you and Harry went over. At least someone remembers them anyway.*

*   Yes, I got two oak leaves for my Air Medal. I won't be getting no more medals and no more flying pay. I guess I'm a washout and always will be. If it weren't for Jane and Jr, I'd give up and call it quits. I guess I'm licked all over just because I'm nervous. I can't help it that I'm shaky and everybody figures there's something wrong with me. Now the Doc grounded me permanent and said I got combat fatigue. We call it flak happy but it's the same as shell shocked. That's why I went to the rest home (flak house). I haven't flown since. You can't tell them it's natural. They ask me how I got this far if I always had it. Well, maybe some of it came from flak happy but everyone gets a touch of that after what I've been through. Well, anyway, he grounded me and request I be sent back to the States.*

*   They say its combat fatigue cause they can't find anything wrong. My pulse and everything's OK. Well, I guess I could of expected it. The doc says I did good to hold out as long as I did. Well, skip it, maybe it's a good thing if I get home. I'd sure like to see Jane and be there when Jr. is born.*

*   You know, Marie, Jane does mean everything to me. I made up my mind that she'll never be sorry she married me.*

*   Love, Chuck*
*   Say hello to Harry and the boys for me. Don't send any packages to me as I may not get them. Write though.*
*   S/Sgt Carl Lindorff*

It appears the shaking was noticeable and persistent, and remained with him throughout his life. There was nothing unusual about the 'flak house' and most crews were given the opportunity to relax for a few days. The houses were not specialized care homes in the modern sense of the word, but often the larger houses of land-owning families who made them available during the war for rest and recuperation. The 388th Group men visited at least two houses of this sort.

From the operational record, we can see that Chuck was flying on 4 August to Hamburg, but not the next day's mission with the Ong crew to Magdeburg. This in itself is remarkable as it points to an event that precipitated a decision to stand Chuck down. Records are not detailed in this respect, but perhaps some clue comes from his uncharacteristic absence from the Ong crew for a few days after 20 July. During the Saint-Lô operations on 24 July there was a maximum effort with all available crews flying, but Chuck did not fly. Instead, his place was taken by J. Polka, a man who flew his last mission with Ong having racked up an impressive forty missions with the Montgomery crew. The next day, the 25th, Chuck was back with the crew and this suggests a possible rest day or a time when he was recalled from a flak house visit.

From the time of his training letters to the point of his stand down from flying, there were a number of key events in Carl's life. Perhaps the most emotionally challenging was the movement from a bold aviator feeling he has less to lose than others to the married man expecting a first child. Something changed within Chuck's role on the crew, it may have been a subtle change, but it appears he wanted to be the principal engineer with upper turret duties. On all the combat missions, he flew as a left or right waist gunner. Whether he minded this change, we will never know. However, the position of waist gunner brought with it the ability to look across the formation and it gave a depth of vision that some other members of the crew did not have.

What is clear from the records is that the Ong crew flew more often than many of their compatriots and finished their thirty-mission tour at breakneck speed. It appears on paper that Chuck was the only airman in Ong's crew to crack under this intense pressure. However, George West flew fifteen missions with the Ong crew before disappearing from the flying roster of the 388th. We don't know what happened to West and whether injury or sickness grounded him. Ong requested specifically that his crew were not asked to return to flying duties after their thirty-mission tour. Indeed, he made it a pre-condition of his return to the unit for his second tour. Radio operator Ken Gardner also came back from the war as a noticeably nervous man – war had changed him.

What evidence is there, therefore, from the flying logs that might suggest life-changing pressures? The Ong crew, like the Colburn crew, flew their first combat missions on or near D-Day and from then on the diary seems like a race towards important targets, and perhaps for the crew a race to see how quickly they will be shot down. By all accounts, the Ong crew seemed to suffer more structural damage than average. It seemed if anyone got hit, it was their aircraft and the stress of flying with such damage, possibly falling out of formation or struggling to make it home, must have been wearing. In the period Chuck was on flying duties there were thirty-nine losses of B-17s and, even after stripping out the unusually high number of eleven at Poltava, it still reads as twenty-eight losses in ten weeks.

Although numbers are important, it is worth taking note that the losses had faces attached to them; familiar names, men they had trained with, and aircraft they had become familiar with and had flown in. It is possible seventy years on to piece together certain incidents that Chuck would have witnessed, although we can only speculate as to which affected him the most.

Chuck passed away in 1989 so recent testimony is hard to come by. However, his nephew Loren, recalls being told of a time when Chuck witnessed a crewman with a severe abdominal injury, he was 'trying desperately to hold his intestines in'. It was believed this was an Ong crew member but, with the exception of George West, no names seemed to fit this description. Ong is on record as saying that he was proud he brought all his crew safely home *alive*. A breakthrough in investigating the identity of the man was a conversation with the last survivor of Ong's crew, Morris Fleishman, in January 2015. As recounted later in this book, Morris identified the man as Staff Sergeant Joe Payne, one of a number of men who filled in individual roles. Joe Payne only flew two missions with the Ong crew; his injury coming during the second flight.

From the time of preparation at Knettishall to the end of his flying, Chuck had the opportunity to witness many tragic events. Some were ground crashes, such as the Schneider incident where the plane made an emergency landing, but came off the runway killing two 560th ground crew, others were in the air. The Bryant crew started combat flying on 28 May, but by 8 June 1944 they were all killed after being hit over Tours. A fire started and despite making it very close to home, their aircraft blew up near Thetford, only a few miles from Knettishall. Taking account of the general pressures with crews going down or missing, an examination of the records and the Ong crew's position in particular raid formations leads to some interesting possibilities about incidents that Chuck may have witnessed.

The raid on Magdeburg on 20 June resulted in three aircraft being lost or written off, two of which made it back to their home base. Every aircraft had been hit by flak on this raid. Ong had been the spare plane in the formation and was instructed to turn back when it was apparent enough B-17s were mechanically fit. One aircraft did not return, *Pride O the Yanks* flown by Joseph Patrick. Like Ong, they had begun their flying careers on or close to D-Day, and as a 560th crew they shared living space and squadron facilities. Having been hit over the target they dropped out of formation and struggled on before being forced to ditch in the North Sea off the Dutch coast. The B-17 sank in less than one minute, taking three crew members with it. The rest were picked up and taken prisoner.

On 19 July, as the 388th bomber formation was assembling, *Little Boy Blue* flown by Walter Malaniak was sliced in half by another B-17 from an arriving lower formation after he lost altitude. Malaniak and all but two of his crew perished. *Little Boy Blue* had been flying to the left and lower than Ong, quite close, and whether the full drama was realized then is unknown. Malaniak and his crew were also contemporaries of the Ong crew; they arrived together and they served on the 560th Squadron together.

Chuck missed the next mission on 24 July and this could tie in to the above events. It was an unusual event for a man to miss a mission if he were part of a regular crew; they liked, wherever possible, to start and end together.

On 29 July, the mission to Merseberg, a tough target, resulted in the loss of a B-17 shot down by fighters. It was an event witnessed by most of the formation as *Heaven Can Wait* tumbled out of the sky. There were only two survivors. The other aircraft returned safely only for a B-17 from the 388th satellite airfield at Fersfield to make a poor landing and collide with 44-6096 on the hard stand. The Fitzpatrick crew had fortunately left the aircraft, but a 560th crew chief was killed. The Fitzpatrick crew were yet another crew who joined the 388th with the Ong crew. This time they had been very fortunate, but it must have illustrated to everyone how fragile was their situation.

Perhaps the most dramatic event happened two days later, on 31 July. The mission was one of four that the Ong crew undertook to Munich in as many days. They were flying in the low squadron on the far left and, across from them on the right, was Ora Castrup and crew flying 42-320030, *Devil's Luck*. Chuck Lindorf was in his regular position of the time, right waist gunner. This position gave him a good view of *Devil's Luck* close by. In the account of Byron Cook earlier in this book, *Devil's Luck* was hit over the target by flak and exploded shortly afterwards.

Chuck's last mission was to Hamburg on 4 August 1944 and records say that seventeen aircraft were hit by flak. It must have been obvious by now that his shaking and disposition would probably ground him. What does remain is that Carl N. Lindorff's name was engraved on the trophy for August, even though he flew only three of the nine missions the Ong crew undertook in that month. From the photograph of the Ong crew under a B-17 holding the trophy, it's clear that Chuck is in his ground overalls while the rest sport their flying clothes. It doesn't take the imagination to travel too far to imagine the scene where the photo is being taken and perhaps the reticence that Carl felt in being pictured this way after his grounding. It is also a testament that his crew felt he was very much part of them and that there was no question of him not appearing on the trophy or on the celebration photo.

Having built up a compelling set of circumstances that might explain Chuck Lindorff's apparent post-traumatic stress disorder, another possibility comes into the frame, and in an unexpected form. The man standing behind Chuck on most missions in the left waist gunner's position was Morris Gumpel, who apparently suffered no visible ill effect of his combat experiences. However, in a conversation I had with Morris' brother, Dr Roy Gumpel, in early 2015, Roy recounted that Morris suffered with Parkinson's disease in the last ten years of his life. Dr Gumpel believed that the combination of hypoxia and possible exposure to carbon monoxide was a contributing factor to his brother's condition. When I mentioned that Carl Lindorff suffered an uncontrollable shake, Dr Gumpel wondered whether this was indeed an early onset of a form of Parkinson's brought on through hypoxia. Certainly Carl's last letter has a telling phrase:

I can't help it that I'm shaky and everybody figures there's something wrong with me.

Could it indeed be that Chuck's shaking was primarily a physical problem that led to a diagnosis of a nervous problem? Certainly Chuck's remark that: 'They say it's combat fatigue cause they can't find anything wrong. My pulse and everything's OK,' raises the issue further up the ladder of possibilities.

Could it even be argued that any nervous disposition was fuelled by the experience of being grounded and being told that a nervous problem existed? We shall never know, but perhaps there is room for future research into the incidence of Parkinson's disease among high altitude flyers of the Second World War.

Chapter 14

Down on the Farm

If history were taught in the form of stories, it would never be forgotten.
— Rudyard Kipling

Driving through the lanes of Suffolk was proving to be a much more enjoyable experience than we had anticipated. Trish and I had decided to take a few days away, and the end of October is traditionally a cloudy, grey and wet time. In previous years we had endured freezing cold temperatures, rain and storms and, together with the change of times out of British Summer Time, early darkness. This year was, we were assured by the media, the warmest on record and we were not to be disappointed. The trees were still in late leaf and, even though the cloud was quite low when we started out from a holiday let near Sudbury, soon the sun was glinting through the clouds and creating kaleidoscopic effects through the golden colours of autumn.

We had set a day aside to visit two old airfields; one of course, had to be Knettishall, the airfield at the heart of the trophy story, and the other was at Tuddenham. With the advantage of Google Earth, I had been able to locate Tuddenham easily and, with the function of looking at historic photos from December 1944, see where the airfield had been. Trish was armed with a good book in the event of serious boredom setting in, but it all proved to be interesting enough. RAF Tuddenham was our first port of call and as we drew near the area I kept a lookout for the characteristic concrete access roads that are now part of the agricultural landscape. My reason for seeking out Tuddenham was simple. Bob Simmon, Johnnie Colburn's bombardier, had written his account of their actions on D-Day. On their return from a second mission of the day the weather was closing in and, as darkness crept in, finding Knettishall was difficult. Out of the low cloud, another B-17 appeared in front and flying directly towards them. Johnnie took instinctive evasive action and avoided the collision. In this process, all sense of direction was lost and, after pressing on a little, they used their emergency radio call and were given a bearing for RAF Tuddenham. By this time, it was past midnight and getting very dark, even with June being the lightest month of the year in England. There was little time or fuel for manoeuvre and firing flares, some of which were mistakenly red, signifying injured crewmen, Johnnie touched down at Tuddenham. Fuel was low and the approach was too high, resulting in a late landing. The result was the B-17 screeched and skidded down the runway before disappearing into the gravel at the end. It took a little time for the RAF to recover the B-17, although no damage was done to the aircraft. Bob Simmon recalled that as they taxied to a parking area, two engines quit due to lack of fuel. The RAF was not amused by the distress flare colours, but Johnnie and crew stayed the night at Tuddenham before transiting the fourteen miles to Knettishall next day.

RAF Tuddenham was at that time home to 90 Squadron, which was operating heavy bombers from the base. It had just been re-equipped with Avro Lancaster Mk Is and IIIs in May after flying the Short Stirling. Casualties for the squadron had been significant and it was a seasoned operational unit. What its crews thought of this stray B-17 cavorting down their runway into their safety zone is probably unprintable, especially when they too were in the full swing of operations. Undoubtedly, the hospitality given to Johnnie's crew would have been welcoming, and probably the odd bit of humour and back slapping ensued. The friendly rivalry between Brits and Americans was often apparent and with these Brits now operating what many considered the superior Lancaster bomber, there was room for colonial leg pulling.

I had identified where the end of the runway would have been at Tuddenham. The runways have now gone and agriculture has taken over, making it nearly impossible to judge where they were. I had also looked at the wind direction on that day and, being such an auspicious day, there are plenty of detailed maps and records. If Johnnie had landed as he should into the wind, he would have used the main runway running roughly east to west. There was the possibility that he landed after a downwind approach, which may have explained his run-off into the gravel. However, I was giving Johnnie the benefit of the doubt. He proved to be a very capable pilot and it would seem improbable that he would make a basic error of approach. It was also very likely he was already approaching from the east, so even a direct landing would have been into the wind. I was hoping that I was not using too much historic 'artistic licence' and Johnnie, as of a few days before my visit, could not remember the details.

One thing Trish and I realized about Suffolk and the agriculture of this area was that the pig industry was an important factor. We drew up outside a wide entrance that had once been the intersection of the boundary roads, or peri tracks as they were known. In the fields around us, hundreds of pigs roamed around and doing what pigs do best, rooting in the soil, squealing and playing, with a bit of aggression thrown in for good measure. Across the road stood a large pig standing motionless in a big pool of water, as if he were examining himself in his reflection. On the former airfield itself it seemed all was given over to arable crops. The first thing that greeted our visit was a small sign, Private Keep Out. Before us, though, was an open gate and an invitation to walk along the former peri track towards the area I had identified. Under normal circumstances I would obey such signs but, having undertaken a 300-mile journey, I decided to risk the wrath of the farmer. We pulled on walking boots and headed out along the straight leg of the track. Normally, as is the case at Knettishall and many other old airfields, the boundary tracks are concrete and bomber bases had wide tracks. These led to wide dispersals, semi-circular bays where the bombers would park. Around the dispersals, engineers would work and often live in tents through all the coldest, dankest weather England could throw at them. The tracks at Tuddenham are not concrete or tarmac and appear to have been crushed stone; hardcore as it is known. The passage of tractors for more than sixty years has now turned these into muddy tracks, but the course remains the same.

We were a bit nervous as it seemed several farm workers were busying themselves with various tasks in the boundary fields, so we waited to be challenged. Trish was wearing a rather obvious red coat, which she took off and we strode like wanted criminals with a guilty purpose. Finally, we rounded a corner and walked across a home straight to where the end of the desired runway would have been. The remainder of a wide concrete runway greeted us at a confluence of fields. Just on the edge of the concrete strip stood two grain silos and beyond them, where the gravel run-off area would have been, was now a grassy field with agricultural equipment strewn about. The idea was simple enough, take a few photos and then walk back the half mile around the edge again. A few hundred yards away across the old airfield were a couple of tractors and men working. Within a couple of minutes our hearts sank as we saw a tractor turn towards us and come down the track opposite at some pace. There is something particular about the way a vehicle is driven that tells you that they are coming to see you.

As the large green John Deere tractor approached, Trish had her back turned and it was up to me to do the talking. It was immediately apparent as the tractor drew up and the side door opened that this was a friendly encounter. I explained why I was there and the young man, or at least significantly younger than me, took a keen interest. He explained that he and his father had only taken up tenancy of the land a year ago and he didn't know much of the war – or even the course of the runways. The story of the overshooting B-17 stirred his interest further and it was good to contribute something to the local history of the area. In all probability, no one ever knew of Johnnie's D-Day exploit except for ground crew at the base. They were long since gone and probably didn't recount the event to anyone – it was not that unusual. The tractor driver told us he had found some unexploded training bombs and had them taken away. They were small smoke bombs used for target training practice and I was quite familiar with them as they were used on some of my local airfields in Cumbria. In this case, the tenure of the bombs probably pre-dated 90 Squadron, which arrived in late 1943. No.3 Lancaster Finishing School was in residence earlier before moving to RAF Feltwell. Looking across these flat farmer's fields, there was nothing to indicate the wartime drama and sacrifice of the young who flew and died from this field. To the untrained observer, it is now nearly impossible to distinguish this from any other group of fields in the area. In recent years more attempts have been made to preserve and record historic sites but, in a small area like the United Kingdom, there are far too many sites to comprehend the scale of recent history. Even the information-filled internet does not have much to say about 90 Squadron and, hopefully, as years pass and relatives wish to know more of their family history, some of these gaps will begin to be filled.

The bombers have long since gone, of course. The hero of the hour for the British was the Avro Lancaster, which, like the Spitfire, captured the public eye more than some of the other capable types such as the Handley Page Halifax. The bombers that thundered down the runways of Tuddenham were consigned very quickly to the scrapyards. Some of them were sent there within weeks of the end of hostilities in Europe, but certainly by late 1945 holding areas were at bursting point. In my own home area, airfields such as RAF Kirkbride and Silloth were crammed wing tip to wing tip with every kind of combat aircraft. There were more than 1,000 on each airfield, which led to planes being dispersed into farmers' fields close by. The scrapping was accomplished at an industrial scale and a few pictures from the archives reveal Lancasters and Halifaxes in large numbers waiting for their ignominious end. In the years after the war there was the stark realization that some types of aircraft had been scrapped to extinction. There is only one complete example left of a Halifax in Britain and that was made up of composite parts. Even the Lancaster has few surviving examples. Their metal ended up in post-war reconstruction, aluminium clad temporary housing and, as the baby boom gathered pace, the demand for pots and pans grew. In America, too, the huge numbers of aircraft being reduced to scrap in the 1950s led to a boom in products such as aluminium siding for houses.

We took more photos, perhaps pretty unremarkable landscapes showing broad flat land and a scrubby grass field, but there was a story to tell elsewhere. We walked back with heads held high and enjoying the autumn sun, past former ground fuel tanks now used for storing water, and to our car. A quick drive through the nearby small village of Tuddenham St Mary half a mile away revealed once again how these airfields of 2,000 to 3,000 men must have turned life upside down. The accommodation sites for Tuddenham also bore a resemblance to Knettishall, scattered over quite a wide area. Most were either wooden huts or Nissen type buildings, the curved, metal roofed sheds that still survive around farms of the area.

Tuddenham is only three miles from the large American air base at Mildenhall, and we drove on towards Thetford and out into the countryside again to our second disappearing airfield of the day, Knettishall.

The sun had disappeared slowly behind a hazy murk and the scenes before us were a lot more late autumnal. The weather is always changeable in Britain and today was proving once again that nothing can be taken for granted. What has struck me as remarkable on these bomber bases was the lack of covered space in which to work. The airfields around my home area in northern Cumbria have huge hangars, some capable of taking the largest aircraft. Here at Knettishall there is a distinct lack of hangars and even with the post-war clearance of the smaller buildings, of which nearly every one has gone, normally I would expect to see a number of hangars remaining. There is one remaining hangar on the west side of Knettishall, but another, a hangar where Glenn Miller and his band played, has gone. The truth of the matter is that nearly every servicing and maintenance function on the B-17s was done in the open. Many arrived back with significant damage and yet hangar space could barely squeeze in four B-17s. Today, even with the grey cloud about, was reasonably good weather, but the prospect of bringing the bombers up to readiness in a biting wind or lashing rain chills me to even think about it. We parked the car next to the small black granite monument that commemorates the 388th Bombardment Group. At its original dedication, I knew that Bob Simmon, Johnnie's close friend and bombardier, had stood here a few years earlier. Numerous others who would have answered so many of my questions would have visited here and yet, in many senses, I was too late. The monument is located on a corner of a small coppice, an area that was used as a headquarters site during the war. Some of the buildings were built in the small copse and we started our visit with a short walk through these trees, but found it hard to imagine anything had ever been there. However, towards the edge of the trees we started to find pieces of rusty metal, parts of a building frame and small pieces of concrete. The only recognizable item was an old watering can that had been used for pouring tar and, given its age, it seemed certain it was some tiny part of the airfield maintenance. Also in the gathering leaves were pieces of steel hawser, often used in towing and for tough jobs. It was probably somewhere here in a Nissen building that the trophy resided, perhaps on a shelf, perhaps in the officer commanding's office. So far, there were no clues to its exact whereabouts during its tenure here.

Stepping out of the trees on to the field opposite I startled a large hare – the hare startled me, too. In an instant it was off across the field in the jangling run so characteristic of the animal, its white and black ears flashing as it went. Next to the HQ site was the accommodation area of 562nd Squadron, Johnnie Colburn's home for his duration. The field now looks virgin with green grass and flat seemingly undisturbed vistas. It is hard to believe that such a developed area can be returned to agriculture with such precision, but with the will of a farmer anything is possible. Knettishall characterizes the order of the day with the 8th Air Force. It was here for a purpose and it never intended to stay for a moment longer than it needed. Even though airfield 136 was built under the vast British airfield building programme, it had none of the vestiges of permanence that some of the finer airfields enjoyed. There were no impressive brick–built buildings, no married quarters, of course, and no significant office spaces or lecture rooms that the pre-war airfields enjoyed. Knettishall did have concrete runways and peri tracks, and some of this infrastructure remains, but two of the three runways have been dug up and have disappeared entirely. Knettishall was more akin to a camp than a permanent base, quite a sophisticated and well equipped camp, but with so many of the engineers under canvas and the crews under tin sheet, this was never a place built to last.

I took some photos of the 562nd field to send on to Johnnie and relatives of other crew. We took a drive along the road that now cuts across the airfield. Undoubtedly this was an original and ancient road across the heathland that was closed to the public during the operation of Knettishall. It was probably some relief when it was reopened after the war. We transected some of the boundary roads and took a few more photos before moving on to where the road cuts the course of the old runway. It is here, and for only a few yards each side of the road, that one can see the cracked and disintegrating remains of the main runway. I had a task to do that I failed to do on my first visit some months before. Taking the trophy out of the car, I placed it on the old concrete and took some photos. It has a gentle poetic significance that each of the names engraved were propelled down this stretch of concrete on numerous occasions and, thankfully, all came back; all returned home after the war.

We made our way back to the small crossroads that marks the corner of the memorial and turned towards the village of Hopton. We passed (and photographed) the small St Mary's church in Coney Weston, which stands on its own and quite a distance from the village. Part of the roof is thatched and there is no tower; it stands as a building of practicality with the signs of many alterations over the centuries. *The Domesday Book* lists a church in the village in 1086, and this structure dates from 1350. Being such a distance from the village it serves is curious, but not too unusual. In some cases, a more ancient village stood around or near its church, a village that disappeared in favour of a new village. At times, older villages were deserted due to the Plague, or Black Death as it was known. The remnant of the old village was often the thing that could not be moved, the church and burial ground. For the young Americans, this church, a short walk from the airfield and almost on its boundary, must have been one of the oldest things they had ever seen.

We made our way to Hill Top Farm, Dave Sarson's home, and also the place of the small museum of the 388th. My last brief visit had been with company, but today we had the place to ourselves. Dave was very helpful and suggested I make my way through the guest book to see if any of my 'names' had visited. After a little while, I found a 'Ken Gardner' who had visited on 4 April 1998; he had very helpfully written his full address. Kenneth L. Gardner was Dong Ong's radio operator and a name I had not been able to trace to a home address. A subsequent phone call to the States revealed it was a different Gardner family but they were related to a Charles McGehee, who was a pilot who began his combat career just after Dong Ong returned to lead his second crew.

Dave Sarson also had a photo album and some address lists provided by the 388th Association, all of which were very interesting. Undoubtedly there were people to trace and, like a tree with many branches, there were possible connections in many places. Each of these men had been connected during the war. Some had retained or retraced their connections since, but there was also a large group of family members who never met or knew of these other young men. Their father, uncle or brother had come back from the war and married, started or resumed their careers and had children. Their children were now at retirement age, and the names on the pages mean less and less to the next generations. This is not to say that they care less, arguably, the later generations are taking a keen interest in their family history, but they rarely had the chance to meet any of the names their forebears knew so well.

Time is the great enemy of investigation and, with our time spent at Hill Top Farm at an end, we wended our way serenely back through the country lanes to Sudbury. There were, as usual, so many things to think about, so many details and clues that I could not afford to miss. The next day we avoided doing anything aviation related, or nearly. We always enjoy exploring new areas and a trip to Bury St Edmunds with a pub lunch was an easy way to spend a day. As we drove back to our accommodation, I looked out for the old airfield at Sudbury. As 'luck' and perhaps some guidance would have it, we passed right outside the site and somehow the car turned, of its own volition of course, down another road even closer. It was a familiar story; a B-17 base of the 486th Bombardment Group with four squadrons located there, 832nd, 833rd, 834th and 835th. They participated in many of the actions and missions that tied all these USAAF bomb groups. After all, to put 1,000 planes into the air required many airfields and a wide dispersal geographically.

The predisposition to ignore prohibition signs took hold of me and, as we passed an airfield entrance, we drove in. Trish was rolling her eyes almost immediately, had I no shame? There was a public access road that had several small factory units and a council recycling centre. However, there was a gate open that led to the boundary tracks and, with little hesitation, I drove through and around the perimeter of the old airfield. There were other businesses located on the site so I felt if I appeared confident of my right of passage, I would be ignored. We bumped and weaved around large potholes and Trish was very much in 'why are we doing this?' mode. It was clear that here, too, the concrete was being taken up and I felt my little pilgrimage was just another nod of appreciation to the young men of seventy years before. My visit also allowed me to get a feel for the plan of the airfield and confirm it was largely the same as many others in structure. My short journey around the boundary track led to a wired compound and there inside was a concrete crushing machine. Piles of reduced concrete sat around this motionless dragon as this was the new history of the twenty-first century. Sad as it is for the fans of the 486th Bomb Group, time and necessity are marching on, land is valuable and sometimes there is too much history crammed into too small a country to consider preserving it.

Thirty years of marriage have taught me not to 'push it' and we fairly quickly retraced our journey and got back on to public roads. Still, it was another tick in my imaginary book of airfields visited. In this part of Suffolk it was possible to open a window and spit, and still find an airfield. I know I'm not alone in my appreciation of old airfields but, like sites of lifted railway tracks, it takes a switched-on imagination to hear the sounds, smell the fumes and see the spectacle in the mind.

We knew our short trip into East Anglia would be the last before the onset of winter and, as the dark evenings closed in even further, I was spending many hours trawling numbers, names and databases that would lift the lid on the trophy story. The room I write in is euphemistically called 'the office', but houses all the things that don't fit into the rest of the house. It is also cold in comparison to the rest of the house and, despite a large radiator, its chilly conditions can numb the extremities.

As Christmas approached I was getting to grips with the positions in the formations of each of my crew on each mission. To aid my work Trish had bought a blanket for me to wrap around during my spells of writing. It was slightly laborious, but out of the data a story of who saw what and who did what started to emerge. It was possible to place Ong or Colburn's B-17 into the bigger story and focus in on some of the events that happened close by, or even at times alongside them. Bombers were hit, crews were lost, flak was intense, fighters attacked, but my two crews always returned. There is an expression that history is written by the victors. However, in the trophy story, it would have been very possible that a crew could be recognized in this way, names engraved, and yet all could have perished the next week. They survived and some of the names went on to fly in Korea and Vietnam, but all returned. The aircraft they flew often did not return from raids. Some endured to the end and were scrapped in the post-war period, but many familiar B-17 names of the 388th did not survive. Like a game of Russian roulette, the chamber was empty when the trophy crews flew, but other crews were sometimes lost in the same aircraft a few days later.

Chapter 15

Follow my Leader

I looked up in the sky and trusted in God.

– Anne Frank

The combination of crews finishing their tours and losses meant that finding and selecting flyers capable of leading formations successfully was a constant process. It is probably true to say that, at the end of their conversion courses on B-17s, the instructors already knew who the brighter stars were. However, being a good pilot and leader could as easily see you dangling beneath a parachute over Nazi Germany as enjoying the plaudits of your comrades.

Johnnie Colburn was moved on to the formation leader's track after about twelve missions, but the story is also about the quality of the crew as Bombardier Bob Simmons and Navigator Morris Neiman also featured in the lead roles. In the form of flying and bombing, the formation, often around twelve aircraft in number, followed the leader's course and actions. Bombs were dropped on the leader's cue as the goal was not pinpoint accuracy on a specific target, but a close concentration of bombs on the target; a 'Shack'. There were too many variables in this form of technology to guarantee the accuracy we now expect. Although targets could be identified by Pathfinder Force equipment (*PFF*) through cloud and poor visibility, an accurate attack could span some acres of ground. The 1990 movie *Memphis Belle* features the captain telling his crew they are going around again on the bombing run so that they don't hit a school next to the target factory. This kind of singular accuracy was not possible on formation bombing and rare in all but specialized squadrons. Perhaps the RAF's 617 Squadron is best known for these activities, gaining a special reputation for the raids, on German dams.

Johnnie flew three lead missions in France to support the Allied breakout from the Normandy area in a lead pilot capacity. His second operation to Mery-sur-Oise, the V-2 rocket storage facility in France, must have presented some challenges as three of his immediate six aircraft in the lead squadron failed to complete the mission. Two aborted due to engine troubles and oxygen failure respectively, but the third, *4th Term*, flying on Johnnie's immediate left, was hit in the nose and its plexiglass was blown away. The pilot, Donald Balboni, and all but one of his crew bailed out and became prisoners of war. Balboni was shot at from the ground as he came down and was badly injured. He was taken to hospital in Paris but died a few days later. The crewman remaining with the plane was the co-pilot, Willard Spangler. Why he stayed with the ship is uncertain. Perhaps his parachute was damaged or he had another similar reason for staying. He managed to crash-land the plane south-east of Pontoise, where it was destroyed. Spangler too was taken prisoner.

For Johnnie's crew, leading could prove to be a lonely business, however, the added presence of a command pilot must have been an important factor in boosting experience on the flight deck.

The third lead mission to France was flown in *Fickle Fannie* on 13 August and it seems the crew adapted this name as their own and painted their flying jackets as such. They flew the plane only twice, but it seems likely that some in-joke prevailed as they retained this identity as a crew and even made reference to the name into their old age. Johnnie was leading the 388th A group with B and C following on attacks fairly close to Paris on multiple targets. Dong Ong and crew flew in the C group and they were only five days off finishing their tour; this was their penultimate mission flying *Millie K*. It was another maximum effort day to aid the Normandy breakout. All along the Seine from Le Havre to Paris the German forces were attacked from the air. Nineteen German divisions were beginning to fall back, and the effort was both to aid the Allied advance and destroy as much of the retreating force as possible. Garrison troops in Paris began to disarm the French police and it was becoming clear that the weight of Allied forces would be upon them before long.

Compared to the missions in France, a more demanding test would have been leading the raid on Zeitz in Germany three days later on 16 August 1944. The 388th was tasked to lead the 45th Combat Wing and 101 B-17s were following in Johnnie's wake. Zeitz was a synthetic oil refinery, a key target in the oil war against Germany and one of many similar attacks for the 388th. Defensive flak was always intense over these targets and today was no exception with twenty-two of the 388th planes being damaged. The aircraft lost this day was not an action of flak or fighters, but a mid-air collision between two of Johnnie's lead squadron aircraft. The Colburn crew must have wondered what was going on around them as they faced a second major incident in so many missions. Elroy Gierach was flying 42-97328 *Heaven's Above* to the left of the Colburn crew and, near the target, Gierach allowed his plane to drop and stray into the path of the three aircraft immediately behind in the lead group. Richard Timberlake, co-pilot of the plane immediately behind and right of Gierach's errant path, recounted the incident in his book *They Never Saw Me Then* (2001). His pilot, Larry Locker, was not watching to his left, he was concentrating on keeping formation with Jack Sarten on his right who was flying *Girl of My Dreams*. Jack Sarten, in turn, was keeping a close watch on Johnnie Colburn a few feet ahead of him. They were tucked in close on their bombing approach. Timberlake saw Gierach coming lower and lower dropping towards them and, realizing Locker had not seen him, took control and took evasive action by dropping their B-17 down out of harm's way. Sarten was less fortunate and, although he took some evasive action, he was too late; he was struck from above by Gierach. His fin broke away and the B-17 entered a flat spin from which it never recovered. None of the crew survived, although some reports suggest some bailed out successfully, but were killed by German civilians on the ground.

Frank Nutt, Johnnie's tail gunner, must have witnessed the incident from only a few feet away but it appears he did not say anything about it to his relatives later in life. Gierach and his damaged plane completed the mission and returned to Knettishall. It is not recorded if disciplinary proceedings ensued against Gierach, but he and his crew were shot down on 28 September on a raid to Merseburg. They are listed as a returned crew after crashing near Liege, but did not fly again with the 388th. Liege was still under German occupation at this time and it seems likely the crew were harboured by the Resistance, causing a delay in return.

By their nature, all targets at this point in the war were tough. The expression 'milk run' was still used, but gone were the days of quick missions with sparse defences. The next mission for the Colburn crew was to Brux in Czechoslovakia on 24 August and, again, it was against an oil refinery. Johnnie was leading, and once again the going was tough and not without cost. Although his immediate formation saw fewer incidents than on the last two missions, he had still lost 'Pappy' Olson, who aborted due to engine troubles. As they tightened up on the bombing run, the formation was a small space and once German shells were fired accurately at the formation things could be very hairy. In his memoir, Richard Timberlake remembers the flak at Brux as being particularly aggressive:

We formed in the usual manner, and crossed the North Sea toward Germany. The weather was completely clear with visibility unlimited. We approached the target from the west. The flak was the closest and heaviest we had seen to date. On most missions the roar of the engines drowned out exterior noises. However, the flak was so close at Brux that we could hear the crashing of the shell bursts as they exploded with an ugly red flash and boiling black smoke.

Charles Edwards and his crew flying *Belle of the Brawl* were hit and shot down over the target. They had been flying on the left of the low squadron behind Colburn and their crash site near Hrdlovka is not far from the target area. Edwards, together with four other crew, were killed and the remaining four taken prisoner. This was a tough call as the Edwards crew were only on their second mission; their operational career had lasted six days. Being harsh, they were probably hardly recognized at Knettishall. They were a new crew and going down so quickly robbed them of the recognition enjoyed by more established crews. Their tenure at the base was only a few weeks as they flew practice flights and acclimatized to the tasks ahead. Given the intensity of flak, it was perhaps miraculous others did not go down, although four had major damage and nineteen minor damage.

Zeitz and Brux were mentioned specifically on Colburn, Simmon and Neiman's commendation for the Distinguished Flying Cross in October 1944.

The routine at Knettishall was well established for informing crews they would fly operations the next day. As well as direct instruction, other simpler methods such as small flags placed in the mess rooms reminded crews not too indulge too heavily and that the night would be short. The exact target would not be revealed until the small hours in the crew briefings, but the routine of early waking remained similar for most missions. August was waning for those taking note and counting down their missions. When the curtain was pulled back from the target board at briefing on the morning of 27 August, there was no doubt a rumbling groan. Berlin. Next to 'Little M', the 'Big B' was everyone's least favoured target. Taking off at 10.00 am, Johnnie Colburn was deputy lead pilot and on his first trip to Berlin, a target he knew would catch up with him before he could end his tour. It was not that he and his crew had not flown deep into Germany. Indeed, the Ruhland trip, just south of Berlin, had gone deeper than ever – Poltava. As they crossed the enemy coast it became apparent that dense cloud was going to hamper the mission to a critical extent. The recall order was received but, happily for the crews, they had advanced far enough for the mission to be counted against their total. Flak en route still damaged four B-17s of the group.

Although the Colburn crew flew further flights deep into Germany, the Big B eluded them; they were not tasked to fly against it again. It was their work in leading that earned them the September Crew of the Month accolade. Had it not been for the outstanding Ong crew, their ranking in August would have seen them well placed to qualify for the title.

Chapter 16

Conversations and Recollections

Memories are the key not to the past, but to the future.
— Corrie Ten Boom

The first time I had spoken to Morris Fleishman, Dong Ong's engineer, was in August 2014 and, in accordance with the flow of other calls made at the time, I had no expectation that it would be him who answered the phone. So many calls were dead ends, answer messages or redundant numbers. It surprised me to find a number and speak to Morris so easily. I was also ill prepared and did not have an organized set of questions or ideas to talk about. He had told me that it had been a long time ago and he did not remember much of the war.

Mid-January in England is normally the coldest point of the year and 2015 was proving much of a norm. Between rain and sleet showers, I decided to venture out into the hot tub outside. The hot tub has been one of my best ever purchases and, being involved in the building trade, it has proved to be a life-saver for restoring circulation after a day in the cold. Although a normal convention in the USA and Canada, the hot tub is still something of a novelty in the UK and, although popular, it is considered in certain misinformed circles to be the playground of the swinger and party animal. Its peculiar mention here in a book about aviation is to give this humble contraption the credit it deserves in helping me think through many of the twists and turns of the trophy story.

On this particular evening, the clouds began to part and gradually the stars broke through. I had spent many hours thinking through portions of the book and the research; the hot tub being a useful companion. Morris was the only living member of Dong Ong's crew left and I began wondering if he might know a few more details. I realized that I should call him again, but this time with a list of questions, and see how good was Morris's memory.

Later that evening, I dialled Morris's number in Texas and, once again, he was quick to answer the phone. He apologized that his hearing was not too good, but he did pretty well in keeping up with me. I asked a few questions about the crew and he told me he was best friends with Carl Lindorff (waist gunner), and also spent a lot of time with (John) Arvid Estrom (ball turret). Morris was the engineer, but Carl was a trained engineer too so they had much in common.

He told me about how quickly their combat tour had gone; it may not have been a USAAF record, but it was pretty close to one. It seemed to Morris that they did not make many friends, their bonds were in the crew, but it's also clear that crews came and went. Morris could not necessarily remember individual missions, although he could remember particular incidents. He remembered the plane getting hit badly at times. I asked whether anyone was injured and he said only one, and that man was a 'ghost'. The expression was used to describe someone taking a regular crew member's place and these men were often making up their numbers towards their final total. Some men coming to Knettishall had been posted in as replacements, but they were not part of a designated crew. Others arrived and were allocated to a crew that was perhaps halfway through their thirty missions and, once completed, it left the lower tallied man without a crew and needing to make up his numbers. Morris's account substantiated a memory from Carl Lindorff's relatives that a crewman on Ong's crew had a serious abdominal injury. However, looking through the records, I could not see who it might have been. I had concluded it might have been someone who Carl had helped on the ground from another crew. The statement that Dong had always brought his crew back still held some sway. However, Morris's information was key – the man had been a ghost, a one-off traveller with them, and not part of the regular crew. This made the man's plight even more unfortunate, not only to be seriously injured, but perhaps close to, or even on, his final trip to make up his mission numbers. It seems from searching the records, this man was Staff Sergeant Joe Payne, who flew two missions to Munich with the Ong crew and was listed as a nose gunner. His combat service was marred by loss and misfortune. He had lost his regular crew after a raid on Ludwigshafen on 30 December 1943 when their plane crashed into the sea not far from the Isle of Wight after being hit by flak and attacked by fighters. A number of the crew died, including the pilot and co-pilot. After the ditching, Joe's next six months were spent filling places in other crews and, with aborted missions stacking up, he must have wondered when he would finish his thirty missions. His final mission of twenty-six, on 12 July to Munich, records he was wounded by flak near Brussels on the return leg. Joe survived his injury, but clearly it was a very serious one. He died in 1974.

I asked whether there was one particular mission Morris remembered. Munich was a target where he recalled getting hit badly and losing two engines. There had been some debate among the crew over whether they should make a break for Switzerland. Dong made the call though. 'We're going home,' he said. Looking through the records, the Ong crew flew to Munich five times. The first four were in quick succession with *Betty Ann* and there seems no break in her flying dates that would suggest a down time caused by the damage remembered by Morris. The fifth trip would therefore be the most likely and in a break with the norm they flew *Mary's Sister* on that mission on 31 July 1944. *Mary's Sister* was the plane I looked for traces of in a field above the Channel Tunnel terminal in Kent, where she had crash-landed in January 1945. There was also a down time in her flight records after 31 July until 8 August, the kind of break that would suggest some repairs.

Other casualties were the Crider crew, who were only on their third mission. They too were hit close to the target and made the decision to break for Switzerland. Unlike Ong, their damage was too severe and the crew bailed out not far from the Swiss border in Germany, near Legau, south of Memmingen, where they were taken prisoner of war.

I asked Morris what they did in their spare time at Knettishall and he told me they had visited London 'five or six times', which equates to quite a frequent event in the weeks at Knettishall. Morris recalled that they 'had a good time and drank beer', although they had a few near squeaks with V-1 flying bombs. Our conversation turned to events after their flying tour was over. Morris told me they all volunteered to return for a second tour, but this was never taken up. One of the reasons might have been that Dong had specifically asked that his crew were not recalled as a condition of his return. Whether the request of a humble first lieutenant carried much sway is difficult to assess, but only Ong and Lippert, the co-pilot, returned. Morris volunteered for the South Pacific, but it seemed the USAAF had enough airmen for this theatre of war so he was sent on a number of training courses before hostilities finally ended. The week after he was discharged from the Air Force he had married his sweetheart, Joyce Crystal. His father, who served in the First World War, had advised against marriage in wartime but Morris wasted no time in making good his promise once released from the service.

They bought a farm and settled down to enjoy a family life. When Joyce died in October 2014, they had been married sixty-nine years.

With the encouragement of such a valuable conversation with Morris Fleishman, I decided to pursue another Morris on the Ong crew, Morris Gumpel, a waist gunner who became Dong Ong's bombardier in later missions. With a little hunting I found his family in Connecticut and, in particular, his younger brother, Dr Roy Gumpel. Morris Gumpel, it seems, said very little about his time in the Air Force, whereas his other brother, Hugh, spoke all the time about his time in the Navy. Through my conversation with Roy, a picture emerged of Morris as a man who, with all kindness, would not necessarily make the rank of staff sergeant under normal circumstances. It seemed he coped well with the stresses of the battle he had been through and, unlike his fellow crewman Carl Lindorff, showed no ill effects of the war immediately afterwards. However, it appeared he had problems settling into regular work, although Roy suggested this trait was apparent even before the war.

I emailed some information to the Gumpel family, but it seems the Ong crew photo did not feature Morris. Some days later, I heard that Roy and his son Stephen had gone through every photo on the 388th website, but had not spotted Morris. He was a man who was not seeking the limelight although it now seems likely that, as the only crew member missing from the Ong photo, it is most likely he was taking the picture. Indeed, the man identified as Morris Gumpel on the 388th website, albeit with question marks beside the name, was not Morris. I thought at first it appeared to be the man whom I thought was the most elusive, the tail gunner Daniel Visconti. Morris was 5ft 7½in, but this man in the Ong crew seems to be the most diminutive. There was information that he was known as 'shorty', for obvious reasons according to the photograph. The clue came some months later when, looking through enlistment records, I realized that Arvid Estrom, is listed at 98lb, a featherweight 7st. Ironically, the record does not give his height. Arvid was the ball turret gunner, so it seemed being a small man would have been a distinct advantage in that cramped environment.

One interesting facet of my conversation with Dr Roy Gumple was his belief about Morris's condition before he died. He lived with Parkinson's disease for the last ten years of his life, and Roy felt there was a possible link between a lack of oxygen and exposure to carbon monoxide. It appears that both elements have been linked to Parkinson's, although whether servicemen in the high level flying environment suffered more incidents of the disease is unknown. It appears no formal studies have been carried out. However, Roy felt it was a strong contender as a cause of Morris's condition. Whether the effects of hypoxia contributed to Carl Lindorff's shaking and subsequent diagnosis of being 'flak happy', we shall never know. However, both men were the waist gunners and were subjected to near identical factors.

Morris Gumpel remained a bachelor for most of his life, but he did marry later on and he remains a character remembered with great affection.

The tradition of naming an eldest son after the father had worked well in my research. It wasn't always a given but it was a starting point. Richard Heslam Jnr was one such son easily found but, for a little time, hard to reach by phone. I had his number and left a couple of messages, but I'm no lover of messages and I was always afraid I was talking to the wrong answer machine. On more than one occasion the likeness of a home town name had fooled me and when I talked to my intended subject, he kindly informed me I was wrong and I had the wrong family. It felt like a knock-back when this happened, almost as an actor auditioning for a part is told he is not required. The same went for emails, although email contact is very much less personal and therefore slightly less disappointing.

All phone calls can sound abrupt at first and like a salesman, which my wife assures me I am at heart, I tried to get enough information into my first sentence to awaken curiosity. Richard Heslam Jnr was very helpful in my quest for information. His father had served as a Mickey operator on the Colburn crew although, as mentioned earlier, these early radar operators were not assigned to a single crew, but flew a number of PFF-equipped lead aircraft. Richard Heslam was named on the trophy with the Colburn crew, so it is clear his exploits and skills were seen as a vital part of their success. As with many father and son relationships, Richard Snr did not seem to talk in great detail of his time in the manner that historians would like; in one great monologue of remembered history. That's not how life is and particular memories are brought up in the context of a conversation, often beginning 'that reminds me'. Certain tales will therefore emerge quite a few times and be retold and reflected on in a different way that may divorce the story from aspects of date and time. Richard Jnr told me of his father's experiences and one story in particular that brought home a universal thought process among those in the flying front line. Why me?

This recollection of Richard Snr is of flying as Mickey operator on the lead plane when it developed a technical fault as they closed on the target. The pilot therefore dropped further back and exchanged places with the deputy in the formation, who took on the lead. Some time later, perhaps only minutes later, the new lead ship was hit by flak, fell out of the formation and was lost. How easily it could have been for the original lead plane to be in that position. The names and dates are not as important as the more fundamental question of the life changing circumstances that could have ensued.

Tackling the finer detail of the story is not as important as understanding the emotion. My job was to do both, but primarily in the retelling to ensure the facts were straight. So which mission, which plane and who was flying was an important set of questions. It appeared 'out of the gate' that it did not seem to have been a mission in which Johnnie Colburn was flying. There were a couple of planes shot down from his lead group, but in the case of at least one, Paaske, the crew did not have anywhere near enough experience to be deputy leaders. Heslam flew twenty-nine missions of which nine were with Colburn, the most with one single crew. The temptation for an author to favour possible links to a character that would benefit the theme of his book can be his undoing. As I could not tell exactly which crew and which mission to which the story fitted, it was going to be necessary to guess the best possible match. Fortunately, due to the hard work of previous researchers such as Ed Huntzinger, who trawled the records of the 8th Air Force and produced a highly detailed history of the 388th, most of the statistical work has been done. Bringing this established work up to date has been the work of Dick Henggeler who, in terms of a searchable web database, has produced an online resource second to none.

For Richard, or Ted Heslam as he was well known, to recount the story so clearly points immediately to an event in which he felt connected intimately. It did not take long to look through Heslam's mission record and understand that a good number of missions resulted in no planes lost. By autumn 1944, the stranglehold in terms of air superiority in favour of the Allies was being firmly administered.

One mission fitted all the criteria of the story and I believe is recorded clearly. On 9 November 1944, Heslam was tasked to fly as a PFF operator to Saarbrucken to attack railway marshalling yards. He was assigned the lead aircraft in the 388th B group that day with pilot Orville Kroening. Immediately behind was Lewis Panther acting as deputy lead in *Vagabond Lady*, a regular ship for the crew. Approaching the target, Heslam realized his PFF equipment was not working correctly and the deputy lead aircraft exchanged places with Kroening; he took Panther's place in the formation. Over Saarbrucken the flak is recorded as 'moderate accurate tracking flak', which in practical terms suggests radar controlled gun aiming equipment. After the bombs were away, Panther's plane was hit directly in the nose, blowing it away. The incident and resulting crash claimed the lives of the bombardier, navigator and radio operator. The rest of the crew took to their parachutes and became prisoners of war. The tail gunner, Tony Rosetano, had a remarkable escape story which was recounted in the 388th newsletter of summer 2004:

Rosetano had heard the bombardier report flak at 12 o'clock when the plane suddenly lurched and surged downward. Rosetano saw the gunners at the waist start for the hatch, and that the right inboard engine was on fire. He knew he had to bail out. After struggling into his parachute, he tried to open his escape hatch, but it wouldn't budge, wind pressure was keeping it shut. As the plane fell, the tail section broke off with Rosetano trapped inside. Rosetano frantically tried to force open the hatch, but nothing worked. Then the horizontal stabilizer surfaces that extended outward, one each side of the rudder fin, began to act as wings and the separated tail section assumed a flight attitude and levelled off enough to break the spiralling fall. The hatch then opened and Rosetano bailed out. On hitting the ground in German territory, Rosetano was captured when an old man in Volksturm (home guard) uniform pointed a Luger automatic pistol at him.

Heslam was clearly shaken, for not only would his plane have been hit, but in the location of the casualties, he would probably have been killed. Although he did not know this at the time, he did realize that it was his call on the faulty PFF equipment that led to his pilot Kroening, exchanging places with Panther. The disintegration of Lewis Panther's plane may well have been reported to Heslam. In war, certain events are inescapable and, just as in sport, a simple decision taken in a few seconds can influence the whole outcome of a sporting event and the careers of the participants.

The wonder of the internet was illustrated to me time and time again in the search for trophy information. Rob Simmon, the son of Johnnie Colburn's bombardier, and Darlene, Johnnie's daughter, began to send me photographs. Many came from the late Bob Simmon's files and featured the Colburn crew in formal poses next to the aircraft or more light-hearted moments in crew life. In one, co-pilot Russ Weeks seemed to be wrestling Bob about and another showed Johnnie stripped to the waist outside a medical hut; probably for injections of some kind. A sign read 'keep off the grass', but, ironically, the photo seemed to show only mud. In others men were shown reading or relaxing in their bunks. Bicycles featured in some photos propped up against nearby walls. I asked Rob whether he still had his father's old camera, but he hadn't. However, Darlene sent me a picture of Johnnie's wartime camera, a box brownie adorned with a badge and motifs. Other pictures were more serious, including Bob dressed in an inexpensive suit; a photo taken to enable downed crewmen to obtain forged identity papers from the French Resistance movement.

One photo showed Johnnie and co-pilot Russ Weeks showing off the rear of their A2 flying jackets. The backs were adorned with 'Fickle Fannie' the crew name and it appears that lines of painted bomb shapes denote completed missions. One bomb remained unpainted, so it is likely that this photo was taken either just before or just after their last mission.

As time passed in this research project, I began to think there would be names and families I was not destined to find. One, with a distinctive name, was Ulysses B. Ganas, Dong Ong's bombardier. I tried for months and thought I might have found a telephone number for a John Ganas in California. I knew Ulysses was born in 1915, but he died in 1977 in Santa Clara so the passage of time was against me. Eventually, after some months, I came back to the telephone number and an older man answered my call. He was very hard of hearing and took me for an insurance salesman for a while. He later confessed his hearing aid had broken, but all was forgiven because he was Ulysses's younger brother. They were nine years apart, so John was about 91 and he told me he was living in a retirement community. Ulysses had come back from the war to the home of his parents and his two younger brothers, John and Chris. John had served in the army in Italy, but the war had interrupted his studies. He persuaded his brothers to go to college and improve their education; after all, what was there for them? All three went to Miami and studied and, although John was the youngest, he was ahead of his brothers. Ulysses graduated and began a career in teaching, but was recalled in the services for a time where he met his future wife, who worked for the Red Cross. Settling in Sacramento, Ulysses taught mathematics, but the couple did not have children. They did have a favourite nephew in John Ulysses Ganas and I would have liked to have spoken with him. However, John Snr told me that his son had passed away only two days before, so the timing of my call was at a sad time. It was a great privilege to find and talk to John, tucked away in his quiet corner of California.

Days later, I was on the trail of another 'evadee', Dong Ong's radio operator, Kenneth 'Kenny' Gardner. Despite a number of attempts to find his family, I could find only a death record that showed he passed away in 1985. I was thirty years behind Kenny and I had to hope I could muster a breakthrough. Having decided not to subscribe to the numerous person search websites that charge a fee, I was at a disadvantage. Perhaps I was being too much of a purist? I had wanted to see how an average person could trace historical characters without significant monetary outlay. However, all was not lost as I found I could search the US 1930 and 1940 census for free. This led me to Kenny's family and, in particular, his younger brother Robert who was born in 1927. Finding Robert's phone number was relatively easy and, with the normal trepidation, I called, first leaving a message and then calling again the next day.

There was a certain amount of surprise that anyone would be calling after his brother after so long. I guess that's a normal response, but Robert was helpful, although he said he knew very little. This was because Kenny had said nothing about his service in the war; nothing at all. Just one incident came up in the conversation and it puzzled me a good deal. According to Robert, Kenny had parachuted out of his plane and, as he pulled his ripcord, it snapped leaving him holding the D-handle and cord. The chute opened but not correctly and terrified Kenny above any other experience. He landed safely enough as it seems he is not listed as injured. The puzzle was that in contacts and remembrances of Dong Ong's crew, no one had said the crew had to bail out. It sounded as if Kenny had bailed out of a damaged plane over England, perhaps a plane that would have endangered the crew on landing. As in all stories, I wondered how true this could be as it did not seem to fit.

Robert gave me the telephone number of Kenny's son, Kenneth Jnr, and I wasted no time dialling the number. I found Kenneth driving to Denver as part of his work as a puppeteer and he too, perhaps naturally, was very surprised that anyone was calling asking after his dad. Kenneth told me he also knew nothing of his father's service – he did not talk about it, apart from one incident. Kenneth told me the story of the bail-out and that his mother had been given the D-handle and cord after the war.

With this meagre but fascinating account, I looked again at the 388th database and found Kenny had flown one mission with another crew. Could it be that his luck was out the one time he flew with someone else? Sure enough, Kenny flew a mission with pilot Arthur Pohl and crew to Houppeville, France, on 17 July 1944 to bomb V-1 weapon sites. Pohl and crew had the misfortune to have twelve aborted missions, which by any standard was a lot. This meant that by the end of their tour they had ventured out on some forty-six occasions. Some returns, particularly in the early stages of the tour, were due to them getting lost, so all did not bode well for the crew. It seems that their regular radio operator therefore finished his tour and left the crew before the rest. So, on the last few missions they had stand-ins, Kenny being one. The trip to Houppeville was far from a quiet one for Pohl's crew; they were hit by flak over Rouen, a busy northern French city and port not far from their target. It is clear the pilot feared for the safety of the plane on landing. An extract from *The 388th At War* by Ed Huntzinger summarizes the incident:

> *Lt. Pohl in A/C 42-37849, landed safely at this base after his entire crew, except the co-pilot, had bailed-out over the field. All crew members are safe. The ailerons of the aircraft had been shot away by flak and Lt. Pohl gave his crew the choice of bailing out or staying with the plane for an emergency landing. All of our a/c returned to base by 2305 hours.*

Expanding this summary a little gives us some further insight into Kenny's terrifying parachute jump. Firstly, we know from the time of the raid and return of the aircraft to Knettishall that, even for a damaged plane being given priority in the landing pattern, it would have been dark. British summer evenings are light, as are the mornings, but light would be fast fading by 2100 hours and they were still over Rouen at 2040 hours, four miles from Houppeville. Further to this, we know that the weather that day was cloudy so the challenges of dark and cloud cover add to the drama. I talked to a friend who had served with the Parachute Regiment and asked him, given that the task was dropping the men over the airfield and not scattering them over the whole area, what height would be optimum for the task. The opinion seemed to be around 1,000ft as long as they were quick in leaving. The crews had one parachute each and no reserves, so Kenny would have no option but death if the parachute failed to open. His terror was probably short-lived as the ground would come up to meet him fairly rapidly – but no less frighteningly.

The records show Kenny was flying to Kiel the next day with Dong and crew, and it was a very early start. Bombs were away at Kiel at 0842, so Kenny would have caught very little sleep before his next mission. This also brings up the issue of what effect such experiences engender; Kenny had no time to rest and process what had just happened before the next potentially life-threatening experience came along. Robert, Kenny's brother, told me that Kenny returned from the war a nervous man. I asked him if he was nervous before the war and he said he was not. He was a married man and obviously had worries and considerations with which to contend. Although Kenny did not talk about his experiences, he refused to fly in an aircraft again after the war and, for an aviator, this is very telling.

Chapter 17

The Trophy Missions – August 1944

A Bridge in France.

– Dong Ong

It seems clear the operational record of Dong Ong's crew combined good flying, a refusal to turn back and a quantity of missions in a confined time. Looking through the records now there are elements regarding the number of missions undertaken that seem as if he were chosen above others to do more. Whether this is statistically true remains open for debate, but both the Ong and Colburn crews outperformed the averages of the day. The fact that they both started their combat career around D-Day probably accelerated the pace significantly. The brake on the Colburn career was two-fold, firstly the Poltava debacle and secondly the selection of the crew to fly as Pathfinders.

Dong and crew were clearly foot soldiers in this process. They did not lead, but they performed well and distinguished themselves. Being realistic about the place of the trophy, the award seems to have been a simple morale-boosting exercise. It carried no official weight, but it remained an inter-squadron award at Knettishall. It was a matter of pride for a relatively small number of men in terms of the history of the 388th and perhaps served the purpose of allowing the commanding officer to add something of merit outside the official medal and awards system. Some might argue it was a rather insignificant award and, in terms of its disappearance for seventy years, it illustrates its amateur nature.

In the role of the trophy, August is therefore Dong and crew's month. It started with a mission that was unusual for a heavy bomber group of the time and on 1 August they were tasked to drop supply canisters to the burgeoning French Resistance in southern France. Accompanying the drop were eight men of the Office of Strategic Services, OSS, led by the larger-than-life Major Peter J. Ortiz. No account of the day can justify mentioning Ortiz without an examination of his life and military career to this point. Born in

New York City in 1913, Peter Ortiz was the son of an American mother and French-Spanish father. He and his sister were sent to France as part of their schooling but, by the age of 19, Ortiz had decided against further study and joined the French Foreign Legion in search of adventure. He experienced action against the Moroccan Rif Berbers and was awarded the first of two Croix de Guerre of his career. Leaving in 1937, he returned to the United States as a technical advisor for Hollywood war films. The outbreak of war saw him re-enlist in the Legion, where he fought and was injured in the battle of France in 1940 before being taken prisoner. Being a POW did not suit him, and he escaped after eighteen months and made his way back to the States, where he eventually enlisted in the US Marines in June 1942. This unusual character very soon attracted the attention of his superior officers and he was commissioned shortly afterwards. A man so fluent in French and knowledgeable about North Africa was an immediate asset for what we would now term special forces, or secret agents. Six months later, he returned to Morocco as an 'observer' for the naval attaché and Marine Corps. His role was a cover for his participation in covert operations with OSS and the British SOE on the Tunisian border, an exercise named Operation Brandon. Several notable operations followed where Ortiz was involved directly in fighting with German forces. He was injured and repatriated to the US where once again his masters were particularly keen to see him in action once again, but this time helping the French Resistance forces and their organization.

Further special training in 1943 saw him complete 154 parachute jumps, professing to preferring jumping out of a plane to riding in one, which made him air sick. In January 1944, he was parachuted into the French Haute-Savoie department in the Alps as part of a three-man group called Union 1. The two others were a British colonel, Henry H. Thackthwaite, and Frenchman Andre 'Monnier' Foucault, considered one of the best SOE radio operators available. Their job was to assess the strength of the French Maquis and investigate how the Allies could further aid them. They found plenty of willing fighters, but too few supplies and weapons. Ortiz made a point of changing from his jumpsuit into his Marine uniform together with a pair of sunglasses shortly after he landed and cut a dashing figure, as perhaps his Hollywood influence dictated. With his uniform adorned with his badges and combat medals, his presence attracted attention from all quarters. Thackthwaite later wrote:

Ortiz, who knew not fear, did not hesitate to wear his U.S. Marine captain's uniform in town and country alike; this cheered the French but alerted the Germans, and the mission was constantly on the move.

Ortiz went on to hijack German vehicles and commit sabotage in a way that particularly infuriated his enemies. In one account, he even confronted German officers at a bar and made them drink a toast to the American president and a second round to the Marine Corps at gunpoint before slipping away into the night. His efforts were designed to demoralize the German forces, but also encourage the French into more outward opposition. He and his team were airlifted out of France shortly after 20 May and another operation, far more ambitious than the first, Union II, was planned.

Unlike Union I, the second mission was to be far more aggressive in approach. As well as airlifting in more men, large quantities of material would be dropped at the same time. The scene had changed dramatically, too; the Allies had launched the Normandy landings and were threatening to push east. Operation Dragoon, the invasion of southern France, was planned for 15 August, just over two weeks hence. The German forces in the south already knew that it would be hard to contain any kind of aggressive move by the Allies in the region.

The OSS men of Union II gathered at Knettishall on the night of 31 July 1944. As part of a larger group the 388th was tasked to drop canisters of equipment, and also Ortiz and six other men, Sergeants John Bodnar, Fred Brunner, Charles Perry, Jack Risler and Robert La Salle of the Marine Corps; Frenchman Joseph Arcelin, whose papers identified him as a US Marine; and Francis Coolidge of the USAAF. The first the crews saw of this maverick group was at the early briefing and Sergeant Fred Brunner was assigned to drop with Dong Ong. The others were each assigned a B-17 and this in itself points to a very small drop zone where each parachutist needed accurate 'aiming'. The aircraft took off at around 1000 hours and reached their drop zone far in the south of France by 1500 hours. The formations seem to have been unharried during the trip and the fighter escort was described as very good. The trip was not without incident though, and the fighter escort reported seeing and shooting down a B-17 with German markings that attempted to join the formations.

The drop was also to be carried out at a much lower altitude than even the OSS men were familiar with. A normal drop was low at 1,000ft but, due to the dangers of enemy forces nearby, it was decided to drop at 400ft. The drop zone was a mountain pasture that required the B-17s to weave through valleys on the approach – it really was something that later fictional characters such as James Bond would have been expected to do. Each man was carrying 50,000 French francs ($1,000), but Ortiz carried 1million francs for the Resistance, a tidy sum if captured. The lead pilot was guided by a ground radio operated by the Maquis, and confirmed the landing ground was clear. Jack Risler, one of the OSS men, recalls they were so low that not only could he see the cows in the pastures below, he could hear their bells, too. Risler was flying with Gierach's crew and was ushered out of the rear door by waist gunner John O' Flarity with a hearty slap on the back. He recalls the drop being very short and landing with a thump. Ortiz dropped from the lead pilot's plane, *Fickle Fannie*, flown by Calvin Samson with Lieutenant Colonel Chester Cox as command pilot. It must have been a little crowded as the B-17 was carrying a group navigator and a Mickey operator; twelve in all including Ortiz.

Dong Ong dropped Fred Brunner successfully, but the mission was not completed without cost. Robert La Salle had wrenched his back badly and was not able to participate further in the mission but, worse still, Charles Perry's chute had failed to open after the static line broke. He was buried the next day with full honours with a grave adorned with drop canisters. Local French women painstakingly made an American flag overnight, which they placed in the grave with Perry.

As well as the human cargo, the formations of B-17s also dropped 864 canisters of weapons and material to the Resistance. One 388th pilot recalled positioning for the drop and suddenly seeing another formation of B-17s heading straight for them dropping their canisters, too. Miraculously, in the ensuing melee of B-17s and canisters, the aircraft escaped unscathed. The reason for the near disaster was that a group of B-17s had missed the drop zone and had decided to turn around and come back in the opposite direction from the rest of the stream.

With such a prominent air drop, it is unsurprising the Germans knew of the Maquis reinforcement. Through a series of aggressive German patrols, the Union II mission began to unravel. Their task had been to take and hold prominent sites to prevent German destruction in the face of the invasion forces. After two weeks of training the Resistance in weapons and strategy it was clear the Germans were closing in on the Marine contingent. Entering the small town of Montgirod, they were shelled by the Germans, but made their escape. Entering the town, the Germans took revenge on the civilian population and burnt the town; it was nothing short of a massacre. Although the OSS group had escaped, it was not long before they were compromised again and surrounded. Once again, under the cover of darkness, they escaped through the enemy line. By this time Operation Anvil, the invasion of southern France, had begun and the Germans were on the move. Arriving in the village of Centron, the OSS group's luck finally ran out as they encountered a German motorized convoy. A fierce firefight ensued with house to house fighting. Brunner and Coolidge made their escape across a river, the others fought to hold off a battalion. Realizing the situation was impossible, Ortiz and his remaining men offered their surrender to the German commander, Major Kolb. Knowing that Centron would probably suffer the same fate as Montgirod, Ortiz requested the safety of the town in exchange for his surrender. Major Kolb, convinced he was facing an American company of men agreed, but was infuriated when he found only four men stepped out under a white flag.

Perhaps surprisingly, Ortiz and his men were spared, but they were wearing uniform and clearly identifiable as combatants. Ortiz had gained a reputation in both Union missions and, even if the German commander had wished to vent his frustration on them, he was in no doubt of the prize he had in his hands. At this point in the war perhaps the German commanders were also looking over their shoulders as the prospects of a German victory were sharply diminishing. Ortiz and his men were taken to a POW camp near Bremen, but even then Ortiz made numerous escape attempts and in April 1945 he was at large once again and searching for Allied lines. They were still too far away and he and his men returned to the camp to find only limited efforts at guarding it; the prisoners were effectively running the camp. They were liberated on 28 April 1945 by the 1st Scottish Armoured Division and Ortiz, together with Bodnar, Taylor and Risler, immediately requested a return to his unit. This request was denied and Ortiz's war was finally over. After the war, Ortiz returned to Hollywood as a technical director and later an actor who featured in a number of prominent feature films. He was close friends with director John Ford, another OSS man, and starred alongside John Wayne in *Rio Grande* (1950).

What became of Fred Brunner, Dong Ong's 'man' who escaped over the River Isere at Centron under fire? Splitting from other members, he made his way north, made contact with friendly forces and within weeks was flown back to England, where he continued his OSS work. He was awarded the Silver Star for his action in Union II. While his colleagues languished in a POW camp, Brunner was tasked for another mission, this time deep inside Germany. It appears the goal was to establish contact with an embryonic German resistance movement that revolved around a communist miner turned intellectual, Karl Macht. Flying from RAF Harrington in a smaller but agile A-26 on 19 March 1945, the drop zone was deep inside Germany at Hamm. The aircraft took off into the night in poor weather conditions. It is not known what happened after this point, but the A-26 disappeared seemingly without trace. The wreck and remains of the crew were found after the war on high ground on Grosse Moor north of Osnabruck in Germany. It is believed the aircraft was not in the best mechanical condition and the crew had not flown together before. Frederick John Brunner is buried in the American War Cemetery in the Ardennes, Belgium.

Of course, the Ong crew knew nothing of the Ortiz story at the time. It was another mission, albeit an unusual one, and once the parachutist had left the door, it was time to set course for home, another mission completed.

There was no time to reflect as the next day, 2 August, the crew were dispatched to the V-2 storage area at Mery-sur-Oise. This was the mission where Colburn was leading in the formation just behind Ong and where the Balboni crew were shot down. In the letter Ong wrote to co-pilot Earl Lippert's wife in October 1944, he lists this mission as a 'no ball'. Whether they were unable to drop their bombs on the target or had to divert is unknown. The group as a whole are recorded as bombing accurately.

With barely forty-two hours' rest, if such a short period can be called rest in these circumstances, the morning briefing of 4 August showed Hamburg as the target. Hamburg was the subject of many raids during the war, it featured as early as September 1939, but was first 'bombed' with propaganda leaflets. As well as a busy port with submarine facilities, the area was a key industrial area; in short, the Allies could not and would not ignore it. The most notable raid was on the night of 27–28 July 1943 when 787 RAF Halifax and Lancaster bombers hit the city centre, creating the first recorded firestorm of its kind. Unlike a similarly weighted raid of two nights before when 1,500 died, this raid created an enormous death toll, some 30,000 in a single night. Subsequent raids shortly after also added to this and, by the end of Operation Gomorrah, 42,600 people had died. Strategically, it had the effect of displacing a further 1.2million people from Hamburg and the surrounding area, crippling many industries. Perhaps it is of note that such losses did not affect the Nazi war machine in the way the Allies hoped. Pre-war analysts predicted that such losses would compel the surrender of a country suffering in such a way. It is telling that Germany under the Nazis was not behaving in a way that fitted any political model envisaged up to that time. It was a regime willing to commit its citizens to slaughter, with a high disregard to any personal suffering endured in the pursuit of its monstrous goals.

So it was that industries were rebuilt, often with the use of slave labour, and, a year after the 1943 raids, the Ong crew were once again attacking the area. The target was a familiar one, an oil refinery. The records show that no aircraft was lost and all returned from the fields of flak. The ground crews were kept busy though as out of twenty aircraft dispatched of the 388th, seventeen were damaged to some degree and it seems highly likely that the Ong crew were hit, too.

The next day, 5 August, the Ong crew were in the air again. Indeed in the first eight days of August, they flew seven missions; all in their favourite B-17, *Betty Ann*. The target on the 5th was Magdeburg and the Krupp armaments factory, which manufactured tanks. It was another long haul, with intense and accurate flak over the target. One of Ong's regular crew was missing, waist gunner Carl Lindorf, who had been retired permanently from flying duties due to battle fatigue. In his place was a stand-in gunner, Francis Fenstermacher, who at this point in his war was seeking a regular place on a crew.

Krupp was a distinguished and a very long-standing business still within the reins of the original Krupp family. First founded by Friedrich Krupp in Essen in 1810, as a steel producer and heavy manufacturing business, it flourished in developing armour plating for battleships in the arms race before the First World War. Its place in gun and shell making was renowned, and this high profile industry ensured members of the Krupp family were never far from political intrigue and controversy. The head of the business from 1909 was Gustav Krupp, who effectively gained the surname by marrying Bertha Krupp. She had inherited the empire at the age of 16. As committed royalists, it came as somewhat of a surprise that

Gustav and Bertha were wooed by Nazism. Their initial opposition to the National Socialist Party warmed to outright support, with Gustav helping to expel Jewish members of the German Chamber of Commerce. Whether their appreciation of Hitler was fully heartfelt is not known and Bertha in particular tried to avoid meeting him on visits to Krupp works. If Gustav and Bertha's Nazi sympathies were adopted for business gain, their son, Alfred, was far more committed. He joined the SS in 1931 and was firmly ensconced in the Nazi regime by the time his father was forced to retire after a stroke. Alfred was rewarded by Hitler by ensuring all the company shares were transferred to him, dispossessing his siblings.

The use of slave and Jewish 'extermination by labour' was commonplace at Krupp. Some 100,000 of 278,000 people working for the company were slaves working in terrible conditions. Unlike the Zeiss factories, the owners at Krupp were more than satisfied with the working arrangements of their 'employees'. The Magdeburg plant was by this time one of many factories in the industrial group. In the lists of targets it is hard to think of one so deserving of the attentions of Allied bombers as Krupp in terms of its production of arms and its Nazi leanings. The only downside of such raids was the loss of life in the slave worker community.

The punishing pace continued for the Ong crew and, after Hamburg and Magdeburg, the ultimate target of displeasure presented itself on 6 August. The 'Big B', Berlin, and another tank factory, was the intended target. This time it was the Daimler-Benz works, which was producing one of the most potent tanks of the Second World War, the Panther. In considering the threat of the Panther tank, it is worth quoting the *Tanks Encyclopedia* website, which comments:

Military historians still debate which the best tank was of the Second World War, but for all the polls and specs comparisons, the Panther is always one of the pretenders. Given its speed and off-road capabilities, tremendous firepower, protection, sophisticated ultra-performing targeting sights, use of equipment far ahead of its time (like infrared vision) and, last but not least, its production of about 6,000 machines, the Panther could be compared to a main battle tank years before the British Centurion appeared. Being one of the best-balanced designs of WWII, it performed accordingly, with a fear capital almost rivalling that of the Tiger.

The Ong crew had been to Berlin once before as one of only three crews sent from the 388th on 21 June. The rest of their number had been dispatched to the Ruhr and on to Poltava in the Ukraine. Dong lists this as their twenty-sixth mission, the official records say it was his twenty-eighth, but the discrepancy comes due to Dong not recording 'legal aborts' as missions. These were occasions where the crew flew as back-up to make up numbers in the event of other planes turning back due to technical issues. At times they were not needed and returned to base as a 'legal abort'.

This mission to Berlin must have been a psychological battle as the twenty-sixth mission was the first of five added on to the original target set of twenty-five for those flying a few months earlier in the war. Berlin, too, was an enormous fortress of flak guns by this point in the war. The guns were positioned not only on the boundaries of the city in green spaces, but within the city itself. Three enormous flak towers, fortified reinforced concrete structures, were built with the guns on top. They served as command and control centres, and had shelters built into them.

This intensive flak claimed a B-17 flying just ahead of the Ong crew during this raid. As often happened, the real damage was inflicted during the bombing run. Pilot Donald Kluth was standing in for regular pilot Robert Rowe, who had been shot in the foot during the Hamburg raid a couple of days earlier. The Rowe crew under Kluth were on their twenty-seventh mission when they were hit in the flight deck shortly after bombs away. Oxygen bottles exploded and Kluth ordered the bail out shortly afterwards. All the crew became prisoners of war. Ong and Lippert must have seen the drama unfold from their pilot's seats; another B-17 dropping out of the formation and failing to return. As news was slow to arrive back in the case of crews taken prisoner, everyone had to assume the worst in such cases. As far as they knew, the plane that dropped out could have killed everyone. This was why the practice of counting parachutes was so important, not only for the record on their return, but each parachute counted towards an individual sense of survivability. All too often parachutes were not seen but, even then, the crews were often struggling to keep the plane airborne for some time before bailing out. The efforts included jettisoning all gear, including guns, that might impede the efforts to keep her flying and often the plane was well out of sight of the formation before the end came.

For Donald Kluth, the drama and tragedy of war did not end with his release from capture. The *Manitowoc Herald Times* of Saturday, June 9, 1945 reported that after months of detention in Germany he returned home to the elation of his family only for their joy to be cut cruelly short. News of his brother Frederick's death in the Pacific was received the same day. His brother was also a pilot, flying B-25s.

Six 388th aircraft aborted their mission to Berlin. It is not possible to draw definitive conclusions from this, nor would it be fair on particular crews experiencing technical difficulties. However, six is an above-average number of aborts and, in the light of the mission the next day to Fismes in France where no aircraft aborted, there is room to speculate that the 'Berlin effect' had bitten hard. Perhaps after three straight difficult German targets, the Ong crew might have been hopeful of a few days' rest. Allied command had other plans and as the attempt at break out in Normandy was in full swing, there was a concerted effort to prevent the German forces from retreating in order. Fismes was a key railway area east of Paris and the destruction of bridges was as much to prevent escape as to prevent reinforcement of German forces. For the crews it must have been considered a milk run compared with their deep penetration raids of the last few days. There was little chance the Luftwaffe would trouble them for little remained of any effectiveness in France at this time. Even flak over this provincial town would have been negligible.

The swing in action once again into Normandy and the urgent call for heavy air power as the Allies tried to push east guaranteed a much quieter end to the Ong crew's tour than they perhaps anticipated. They were called into action on 8 August to support the Canadian-British offensive to break through the German line holding the French town of Caen. Operation Totalize was a significant attack in the area of the Verrières Ridge. The Canadian commander, Guy Simmonds, devised a number of unusual methods and formed his attack into six motorized columns that struck on the night of 7–8 August. Some of the vehicles were fitted with radio direction finders and, in the dark and dust thrown up in the attack, Simonds had artillery fire markers in the direction of the advance and 40mm Bofors guns fired tracer rounds over the advance to maintain their direction. The RAF was bombing the German line across the whole Caen perimeter. As daylight broke, the advance continued, successfully taking the Verrières Ridge. The participation of the USAAF was planned to kick in to support the advance, although its timing and targeting turned out to be unfortunate in some respects.

One German strategy that was employed widely was to launch a counter-attack as soon as possible after ground had been lost. This characteristic had been a mainstay of its operations throughout the First World War and it was often used with great success in the Second. SS General Kurt Meyer, commander of the 12th SS Panzer Division, had decided the time was right to move his tanks into a counter-attack. This movement began at 1200 hours and, although the counter-attack failed, it did delay the Allied operation. Dong Ong and the rest of the 388th, as part of the 45th Combat Wing, pressed in for their bombing attack, but the haze and dust of battle obscured their view. They had been ordered not to bomb if they could not visually identify the target. A number two aircraft of the 388th had a malfunction and bombs were dropped by accident at 1342 hours, with a further six aircraft following its lead. The raid as a whole pressed on and hit the German positions. However, because Meyer had moved his Panzers north, they were not hit in the USAAF attack. Although the German counter-attack had failed, these tanks then held up the advance of the Polish 1st Armoured Division. As in many actions of the time, the operation as a whole was a success, but did not achieve all its objectives and this, in turn, led to a second wave of actions being necessary.

As an interesting postscript, Major General Rod Keller was badly wounded at the headquarters of 3rd Canadian Infantry Division after it was hit by 'misdirected bombs' during the American air attack. Whether these were some of the 388th bombs that were dropped out of place is not known, but it is an interesting coincidence. Ironically, Keller had not distinguished himself in Operation Totalize and was effectively stood down from command for the rest of the war.

The mission on 8 August was also the last the Ong crew flew in their beloved *Betty Ann*. She had served them in eighteen of the last nineteen missions and she flew the next day with the Harris crew to Nuremburg. With only two missions left it appears on paper a little unusual that the Ong crew did not get her back. The answer seems to be that *Betty Ann* may have been badly damaged even though the raid did not reach Nuremburg. As Ed Huntzinger reports in his record *The 388th at War*:

As the formation crossed from Holland into Germany, it encountered a front with clouds from 17,000 to 30,000 feet. The Wing Leader made two 360 degree turns in an attempt to get under the clouds, but being unable to do so, turned back in the vicinity of Maastricht at 1025 hours. Very accurate flak was encountered from Liege and Aachen. The Group received a lot of battle damage with three aircraft receiving major damage.

There is a break in *Betty Ann*'s operational record from 8 August until the 24th and this inordinately long time on the ground spells major repairs. One can only imagine the Ong crew milling around *Betty Ann* looking at the damage. They themselves had experienced heavy battle damage and it must have saddened them that, with only two trips to go, their old warhorse would not be with them. The photograph taken of the crew with Dong holding the trophy is underneath a B-17. In that Carl Lindorf and 'Goldie' Goldstein are featured in the photo although they were not 'on' the crew by that time, it points to an organized photo shoot. It would seem more than probable that they would choose to take the photo under *Betty Ann* and perhaps the fact that a cowling is off and a ladder is in the background suggests she was still under repair.

There was a maximum effort on 13 August as nineteen German divisions were in full retreat. The 388th attacked roads and railways near to Paris with good results on four out of the six assigned targets. Even then, although the flak was described as 'meagre', it was accurate and damaged two aircraft significantly, and six to a lesser extent. The Ong crew were flying *Millie K*, which was on her eighty-fifth mission and was possibly considered a lucky bird by this time. Did the Ong crew 'catch it' once again on this mission? *Millie K* was on the ground for five days afterwards, so it is possible. Sadly, her luck eventually ran out on her ninety-seventh mission on 28 September over 'Little M', Merseburg, with the Frawly crew. They had to abandon her when she was hit by flak over the target.

So it was that the Ong crew's thirtieth mission had finally come, on 18 August 1944. It was no deep dangerous thrust into the heavy industry of the Ruhr but again, in tune with the times, a raid into France to prevent German withdrawal. This time it was an attack well south of Paris and not their primary intended target for, as they crossed the French coast, the message came through that a previous wave had bombed the primary successfully. The target was then changed to an area near the village of Bourron-Marlotte and, although it seems there could have been little there of significance, there is a bridge on Route Nationale 7 over the railway. The opportunity, therefore, presented itself to block a highway and a railway in one measure.

The crew had been waiting for this day to arrive because with it came the promise of home leave. They also received their 'Lucky Bastard' certificate, a simple printed sheet with their name on it, but something many would treasure for the rest of their lives. They had done it. They had survived. Before the crew's return to the States, there had obviously been some formal approach to Ong and Lippert regarding their return. This was likely to have been a standard procedure involving all leaving pilots, but there was an emphasis that a second tour was a voluntary element to their service. The majority took their Lucky Bastard certificates and decided to take their chances back in the States as to whether they were re-trained and reallocated. Many expected a posting to the Pacific if the war continued. Ong and Lippert decided to come back to the 388th for a second tour after their Stateside leave, although interestingly, as has already been mentioned, Ong made it a pre-condition of his return that his crew would not be recalled.

There were no pretences of added heroism in the completion of their tour, Ong simply lists the last mission in his letter to Betty Ann Lippert as a 'Bridge in France'.

Chapter 18

The Trophy Months – September 1944

The leaves fall, the wind blows, and the farm country slowly changes from the summer cottons into its winter wools.

– Henry Beston

The weather over Stuttgart was clear and bright on 5 September and yet again the Colburn crew were at the head of the A group. It was becoming a regular slot and it suited them to fly at the pace and direction that they chose. Of course, there were parameters of navigation and course to follow, but the concentration on having to fly in formation was lessened; they were the 'mother goose' with all others trailing after. The navigation led by Morris Neiman and bombing led by Bob Simmon was accurate; the crew were distinguishing themselves.

No fighters were seen and, with German resources in this area being stretched to breaking point, the skies were becoming clearer and the ground a more deadly place to be. However, flak was still taking a harvest nobody could ignore. Although the group dodged flak going in and out of the target, the concentration at Stuttgart was to claim the life of Lieutenant David Rosenthal, bombardier of Victor 'Pappy' Olson's crew, and injure four other crewmen in the group. Sadly, the Olson crew suffered further disaster when they were shot down just over three weeks later. Olson lost his life while the others became prisoners of war.

Just behind and to the left of the Colburn lead aircraft was a new crew led by pilot Raymond Paaske flying *Moonlight Serenade*, a B-17 named in honour of Glenn Miller and to commemorate his concert at Knettishall only ten days earlier. Miller was pictured underneath the all-silver B-17 at Knettishall. Like the Edwards crew at Brux, they too were only on their second mission when they were hit over the target and turned away out of the formation after losing engines number three and four. In such circumstances, fighter cover was quick to pick up lost souls and Paaske was accompanied by 'Little Friends'. It appears he flew further south, perhaps with his eyes fixed on

Switzerland, but gravity won the battle over the Vosges mountains after the number one engine caught fire and the crew bailed out. Paaske was left floating in his *Mae West* in the middle of a lake before he was captured. The rest of the crew survived, some captured and some evading capture. Sadly, co-pilot Garis Jacoby died in captivity in November. The Paaske crew's combat record stretched only three days but highlights the risks all faced, however experienced or inexperienced. The flak that hit Paaske could easily have disabled Colburn's aircraft in similar fashion. The luck of the draw, the spin of the wheel, the mystic hand of fate, are all euphemisms that could be bandied about and perhaps it is no wonder that the award for the crews surviving their thirty-mission total was membership of the Lucky Bastard Club.

The bombing of Stuttgart took place at 11.15 am and the target was the Daimler-Benz plant at Untertürkheim. It was an important and large site that today is the headquarters of the Mercedes-Benz motor company. Historically, it had been the founding Mercedes factory and, by this point in the war, substantial efforts had been made to disperse production and tooling to limit damage. Aero engines were a key product and Daimlers featured in many Axis aeroplanes, mostly the DB605 engine and its variants that powered the Messerschmitt Bf 109, Bf 110 and Me 210C fighters.

The factory had been the subject of repeated raids, but statistics showed the resilience of the plant in withstanding bombing. In attacks in November 1943, only 3.2 per cent of its machine tools were destroyed with 4.8 per cent damaged. March 1944 saw raids destroy six per cent of tools destroyed and 5.8 per cent damaged. This raid on 5 September 1944 resulted in twelve per cent of tooling destroyed but, with forty-three per cent damaged, the results were far more impressive for the Allies. It was reported, too, that sixty per cent of the factory floor area was destroyed. The bomber force was only 203 in number and in terms of some attack sizes, quite small. It's clear though that through Colburn's accurate flying, Morris Neiman's navigating and, just as importantly, Bob Simmon's accuracy as lead bombardier, the 388th crews scored a significant hit against the Daimler factory's potency.

The net was closing around the Nazi empire and the unstoppable forces in the west and to the east were beginning a vice-like movement to crush Germany. The 3 September saw the liberation of Brussels amid riotous rejoicing and speculation about the speed of advance led to a further breakdown of Nazi control throughout the region. By September in the Netherlands, 65,000 Nazi collaborators fled into Germany in what became known as *Dolle Dinstag*, 'Mad Tuesday'. Antwerp had fallen on the 4th and wild rumours circulated that liberation was close. Dutch national flags were being prepared and a rail strike called as the population became far less intimidated by the occupying forces. Dutch hopes were dashed though later in September as the Allies failed to accomplish their target of taking bridges in Operation Market Garden, with Arnhem remaining in German hands. The result was that the rest of the Netherlands had to endure another occupied winter with a severe lack of food to the point of starvation. In the east, the Warsaw uprising was approaching a crucial stage as it became apparent to both sides that the Soviets were not going to help the Polish resistance fighters. The German army, however, was in no doubt that the Soviets would continue their onslaught regardless of the outcome of Warsaw, but were equally determined to show no measure of mercy on the Poles.

The weather in Britain and across Europe had cooled from the August highs and the role of the Pathfinder aircraft became more pronounced in these September days. Cloudy and unsettled weather would endanger any hope of bombing visually and, despite the misconception that bombs were dropped indiscriminately, there were times that bombs returned with the aircraft if the target had not been found. There were primary, secondary and last resort targets listed, and the value of the navigators became more pronounced during times of poorer visibility.

The Colburn crew were back in the air in their lead role on 9 September heading for Dusseldorf. It was yet another early morning start with a 7.00 am take-off with the formations bombing by 10.29 am. They were flying the unnamed PFF aircraft 42-97760, a fairly new B-17G model with the PFF equipment built in. She was an all-silver aircraft with the 388th Bomb Group 'H' on the tail and the code letter 'K' underneath the serial number. The Colburn crew had several pictures taken with her on a sunny day, probably in August on their return from a raid. The target today was an armaments factory close to the centre of Dusseldorf. The daylight bomber force was split into three sections as 1,140 heavy bombers attacking multiple targets. Johnnie had twelve aircraft following his lead out of a force of 251 B-17s heading for Dusseldorf. All aircrew comment on how cold these high level missions were and, even with heated elements in the flying suits, it was far from comfortable.

One airman from another bomb group recalled that this mission was one of the coldest they experienced at forty-eight degrees below zero at 26,000ft. The Colburn crew carried a new Mickey operator, Robert Heslam, and it was Heslam's name that is recorded on the trophy as part of the Colburn crew for September.

The 388th suffered no losses on this mission and in some ways it was a typically satisfying mission to complete. Other bomb groups were far less fortunate and, for one in particular, the 390th flying out of Framlingham in Suffolk, the raid on Dusseldorf was a dark day in their history. A direct hit on a plane in their low squadron resulted in an explosion that knocked nine of the twelve planes out of the formation – many destroyed completely. There was something about the bombing altitude of 26,000ft that the crews did not like and 390th Bomb Group pilot Robert Longardner recounts his memories on the subject on the 390th Group website:

Clay Perry, a 43J classmate of mine, assigned to the 568th Squadron of the 390th, and I studied the German 88 and calculated a probability of accuracy that their rifle had at various altitudes. At 25,000 feet the 88 was most deadly with accuracy of better than 50% chance of hitting the target with four rifle batteries firing sequentially. At 28,000 feet, the accuracy of the 88 fell arithmetically and was rendered to firing a barrage pattern. Based upon the muzzle velocity of the 88, a four-barrel battery firing sequentially to 25,000 feet would explode in track approximately 100 feet apart. Therefore, by kicking the rudder at the first flak shell explosion away from the burst, the following burst would trail off target. With this knowledge, and by swinging the squadron back and forth under the lead squadron, we had been successful in avoiding any serious battle damage in the low squadron position since we started leading August 16 on a mission to Leipzig.

Planning the Dusseldorf raid did not allow favourable flying as far as altitude in relation to dodging the 88mm guns below and it was clear the crews were not happy about this during their briefing. Whether similar views were shared at Knettishall is unknown, but it seems likely the briefing at Framlingham would not have been an isolated experience:

At the briefing on the morning of September 9, 1944, we were given a bombing altitude of 26,000 feet. The combat crews erupted in vexation, grumbling about the severity of such altitude in 'happy flak valley', Surely the targeted factory could have been hit from 28,000 feet as well as from this defenseless altitude of 26,000 feet which meant that the low squadron would be flying at 25,000 feet until the initial point of the bomb run.

Orders were orders and, sadly for the 390th, their calculations as to the accuracy of 88mm guns were correct. Flying B-17 *GI Wonder*, the Longardner crew survived due to extra armour plating being fitted to their plane:

We were to bomb with the pathfinder, provided the target was 9/10 to 10/10 covered, if not, we were to bomb our secondary to keep from being shot up too badly. We reached the bombing altitude of 26,000 feet just before the I.P. and started a run in toward the target which was 6/10 covered. The flak didn't look too bad. Over the target before "bombs away," a direct burst caught Hobbie's ship in the bomb bay which was loaded with 12 x 500 pound bombs. It blew him and eight other ships out of formation. Hobbie was flying the element directly below G.I. Wonder.

When the explosion occurred from the direct hit, we had not yet pulled the low squadron out from below the lead in order that we could bomb on the pathfinder drop. At the instant of the explosion, G.I. Wonder *was tossed tail high, riding the ball of overpressure while the bottom of our aircraft was battered by debris and shrapnel. The intense heat and noise of the explosion drowned the senses of the crew, and it seemed an eternity before I was able to command control of* G.I. Wonder. *After righting the aircraft from the dive attitude, I observed an engine nacelle at ten o'clock to our aircraft. The sky was full of other exploded aircraft debris that was avoided by some of the wildest manoeuvres ever flown in a B-17. Had* G.I. Wonder *not been shrouded with all of the armor steel, the cockpit would never have withstood the effects.*

Four days after the mission to Dusseldorf the Colburn crew were tasked to fly deep into Germany again. Their placement in the formation was more of a supporting role with a back-up PFF aircraft and they flew to the right of the leader, Charles Cooke. They also carried the deputy commander,

Joseph Andrecheck, who, after flying thirty-four operational missions, was undertaking his last flying role with the 388th with the Colburn crew that day. Andrecheck had served as a co-pilot on a crew that changed its pilot on a number of occasions before he was called forward to take command. In regard to the trophy, Andrecheck's mission on D-Day had Dong Ong as co-pilot on his first 'experience' mission.

The intended target on 13 September was in the Stuttgart area but on the bombing run of the attack, which was being conducted visually, poor visibility over the target area led to it being aborted. The secondary target looked no better and eventually the bombers made their way to Darmstadt where they bombed the railway marshalling yard and locomotive works successfully. Darmstadt was in the process of grieving as, fewer than two days earlier, on the night of 11–12th, a raid by 226 British Lancaster bombers had created a firestorm that destroyed the historic centre of the city. More than 12,000 of Darmstadt's inhabitants had died and 66,000 were left homeless.

Yet again, there were no 388th losses and, despite the hazards of flak, no fighters were seen. The statistics on Luftwaffe fighter losses bear witness to the grim harvest to which they were subject. From January to May 1944, the Luftwaffe lost 2,262 fighter pilots, some ninety-nine per cent of their average available force over the period. January had seen 292 lost, but by May the figure had climbed incrementally to 578, some twenty-five per cent of the force in a single month. German factories were continuing to produce aircraft at an astounding rate despite the constant threat of air attack. The Germans produced more fighters in 1944 than in any other year; indeed with production at 24,981, they built more fighters in 1944 than they had for the previous five years combined. Pilot losses are actually more important in considering the Germans' ability to resist Allied bombing. The Battle of Britain in 1940 had shown how wafer thin the odds became if trained pilots were not available, even if aeroplanes were. Bombing German oil refineries, the Oil War, had also reduced the amount of fuel available for pilot training and, with the pressure on, the Luftwaffe had failed to set up a relief system for experienced pilots. In short, they flew until they died. As 1944 progressed, Allied fighter pilots were finding Luftwaffe pilots were far less experienced and, as a result, far more likely to be shot down. For the 388th, and all other bomb groups, the skies were not filled with enemy aircraft as they would have been in 1943.

The 19th of September saw the Colburn crew in their familiar position at the front of their formation providing a lead for the 45th B Combat Wing. Their intended targets were rail centres in the Ruhr Valley, but again visibility led to a diversionary target, a marshalling yard in the town of Dillenburg. Reports suggest a very accurate bombing pattern in the railway area. No flak or fighters were reported and it seems the attack was somewhat of a surprise for the inhabitants of Dillenburg, who did not frequently attract the attention of Allied bombers. However, it was a railway centre that dealt with iron ore smelting products from the region and undoubtedly registered on the Allies' target lists. It suffered heavier raids during early 1945. Bob Simmon was the lead bombardier on the Colburn crew, and he remembered that day and target in later years. His son, also Robert, was serving in the Air Force in Germany, and in 1976 Bob visited him and took the opportunity to visit Dillenburg. Robert recounts how, while in Germany, they got into conversation in basic German with another older man about the same age as his father. The war featured in the conversation; perhaps naturally enough as Bob was the tourist. They found the German man had been an anti-aircraft battery gunner and Robert wondered whether they might have stumbled into a tricky situation. It turned out the man was quite affable and it seems he harboured no ill feelings for those attempting to drop hundreds of pounds of explosive on his head.

This raid, with its tight pattern of bombing, yet again distinguished the Colburn crew and certainly went some way in the decision to award them the Crew of the Month title. Their newcomer, Mickey operator Richard 'Ted' Heslam, was a big part of the team as he tried to 'see' through the deep waves of undercast below. To be a good operator required knowledge of the equipment, but principally an ability to interpret what he was seeing on the tube of his H2X set. The sets were only fitted into B-17s from April 1944 and, as with all new technology of the time, sometimes it was a hit or miss affair to get them working correctly. The 'screen' was a small round tube that produced fuzzy green images, not a picture as we would recognize now.

The group navigator flying with the Colburn crew on this raid was Ed 'Goldy' Goldstein, who trained and flew with Dong Ong's crew and features in their crew photo.

As the month of September began to draw to a close, the Colburn crew flew two more missions. The first, on the 25th, was to the I.G. Farben plant in Ludwigshafen, which was an important chemical producing company. Farben consisted of six firms, including some still well known today, such as BASF and Agfa. Pre-war it had pioneered many chemical processes including the development of dyes. However, the company will forever be remembered for its Nazification and the product that, although it did not invent, it held the licence for: the pesticide Zyklon B. The disgrace of I.G. Farben was complete with its plant at Auschwitz and the use of Zyklon B in the murder of millions by gassing. The plant and town of Ludwigshafen were subject to many bombing raids and the attack of the 25th was conducted through cloud using PFF from 24,000ft. The Colburn crew were leading the 388-A group, now a familiar position.

The next raid, on 27 September and the last in the trophy month, was on railway marshalling yards at Mainz and Johnnie Colburn was in the PFF role leading a formation from the 34th Bomb Group. The 388th had its own aircraft out on the raid, but the two PFF aircraft were helping other bomb groups. The Colburn crew were flying a brand new B-17, 44-8146, on its first combat mission and a plane which made it through to war's end in May 1945 after forty-one trips. It was also a plane used by Dong Ong when he returned for his second tour as a lead pilot. The weather meant that PFF was essential and another veteran, Bud Neath, from the 96th Bomb Group at neighbouring Snetterton, recalls how they attached themselves to another group to take advantage of PFF leading:

Our bomb group got cut off from our assigned bomber column position by another group and our C Squadron got split away from the A and B Squadrons. The C Squadron leader had PFF and those twelve planes went in and bombed through the clouds with good results. We were flying in the number two position in A Squadron. Neither A or B had functional P.F.F. so we attached on to another Group, making a 60 plane formation and we also had success getting our 12 – 500 pound bombs on the assigned Railroad Marshalling Yard.

Unlike the Ong crew, who finished their missions in their trophy month, the Colburn crew were to carry out four more missions before their tour ended. It seemed they were not allocated missions frequently at all in the following weeks and did not complete their tour until 16 November 1944.

They were assigned Mainz once again on 9 October, but they were not allocated a PFF lead role. They flew once again with their old friend Robert Ryan in the ball turret, a man displaced previously by the need to carry PFF equipment. It was Ryan's last combat mission, although he had flown only sixteen.

Perhaps Johnnie and crew were partially rested during this period; they had certainly topped the previous twenty-five mission target. The crew's services were restored on their next mission to Cologne on 17 October – and it was a rough ride. They bombed Cologne at 9.09 am from 27,000ft, but the flak was described as 'moderate' to 'intense'. Statistically, the 388th took a hammering. Of twenty-six aircraft on the raid, twenty-three were damaged by flak, ten with major damage, thirteen with minor and, more seriously, two shot down. Those downed were the Resch and Baird crews. Both planes were flying in Johnnie's formation; Resch closest to the Colburn crew and tucked in behind their aircraft.

The Resch crew had a miserable combat career that lasted only eleven days. They flew their first mission on 6 October to Berlin; their only successful mission flying 43-38578, which was brand new and also on its first mission. Their second mission the next day ended in disaster before it had started as they crashed on take-off. The plane, *Blind Date,* was a regular on her seventy-seventh mission and was written off. The local police report stated:

At 0840 hours on Saturday, 7th October 1944 an American Fortress Bomber made a forced landing on a field at Holly Tree Farm, Walpole.

This a/c was on an operational flight, laden with ten 500lb High Explosive bombs and developed engine trouble soon after leaving its home station at Knettishall, W. Suffolk.
    The crew of this a/c all escaped uninjured and were at once taken to the USAAF Station Holton St. Peter.

The a/c caught fire immediately on landing and owing to the close proximity of houses on the Bramfield Road, it was necessary to evacuate the occupants of eight houses.

The Bramfield Road was closed and the road leading from Walpole Lane towards Halesworth was also closed.

At 1030 hours the main bomb load exploded and minor damage was done to 14 houses in Walpole.

At about 1430 hours the 6218 Flight, RAF Bomb Disposal Unit, Coltishall, arrived and Sgt. Plunkett made a reconnaissance of the area of the forced landing and rendered safe one 500# U. X. B.. This bomb was then removed to USAAF Station Holton St. Peter and the area was declared clear.

At 1445 hours, the roads were opened to the public and at 1500 hours the evacuated persons were returned to their homes.

The crew were recalled ten days later on the Cologne mission, where they were shot down and all taken prisoner except for the ball turret gunner, who did not survive the incident. As a further discordant note, they were flying '578, the plane from their first mission that had managed only a total of four before this loss.

Pilot James Baird's story is a little more cheering in that he crash-landed his plane successfully on a Belgian airfield in an Allied-occupied area and returned to Knettishall with his crew. Unlike Resch, luck was on his side and he completed thirty-seven missions in total. For the trophy story, Baird's crash on the Cologne mission has a little more to it than plain statistics. Baird's plane that day was Dong Ong's beloved *Betty Ann* and her loss reverberated down through memories even seventy years later.

The end of the Colburn crew tour was approaching and they flew a mission to Hanover on 26 October in a deputy lead role. The PFF equipment was well in use that day as autumn had taken hold. The target was probably a tank works although other groups were attacking an oil refinery in Hanover too.

It was nearly three weeks later that the Colburn crew embarked on their last combat mission, on 16 November. Fittingly, it was one of the heaviest strategic bombing raids of the war and, like D-Day, it was a maximum effort mission against German ground forces in the Aachen area. In many ways it was a similar effort to the support provided during the break out of forces at Saint-Lô. Listed as 'Area 2', the operation was part of a battle that had been ongoing for several weeks, the Battle of Hürtgen Forest. Lying south of Aachen and in Germany, this heavily defended area became a conflict of a number of individual battles. The difference between the battles in France and here was that this was German soil and its commanders were determined not to allow the Allied advance to penetrate further. The battle raged from 19 September to 16 December 1944 and is the longest battle the US Army has ever fought. Operation Queen was the second phase of the Allied assault to push through this hilly and forested district to the Ruhr. The preliminary air attack to soften up German ground forces used a combined USAAF and RAF force. The 8th Air Force used 1,204 heavy bombers to hit Eschweiler, Weisweiler and Langerwehe, attacking between 1113 and 1248 hours. The 388th dropped its bombs at 1130 hours, but all was not plain sailing for the Colburn crew as, due to technical difficulties, the deputy lead had to provide the PFF guidance. Johnnie recalls that as they approached their IP, the point at which the formation would make their final run to bomb, the autopilot stopped working. They pressed on using a method known as PDI, using the signals from the bomb sight as guidance. Just as the flak began, Colburn's bomber took a hit that severed his rudder control cables, but he managed to fly on. The bombs dropped were recorded as anti-personnel devices and, although the strike results of the 388th were confirmed as good, overall Allied commanders were disappointed that the intense air attacks did not accomplish what was hoped.

On the return trip, Colburn discovered a regular habit of his might prove to be his undoing. He later described this mistake as dumb. Rather than relying on heated boots, Johnnie had for many missions discarded them in favour of using the efficient heating system around his feet supplied from the glycol system on engine number two. However, this system failed and Johnnie realized that as his feet were getting colder and colder, he might suffer frostbite. He couldn't believe that he was on his last mission and yet could be risking such a serious condition. Although not being able to feel his feet for quite a time, he was lucky and no damage was done. Light is limited in the UK at this time of year with early darkness, but the RAF reported a four-hour break in the fog during the afternoon and all the 388th aircraft landed safely. As Johnnie touched down, braked and turned off the runway to taxi to the dispersal, there was elation sweeping the crew. They had made it. Most of them did not believe their war was over although they looked forward to their return to loved ones and a break. It was too soon for them to appreciate they would not fly in combat again. Johnnie expected to be called to fly again, maybe in the Pacific, but this landing proved to be his last combat mission. Others of the crew were to fly in combat again, but not in this war. They received congratulations and, in time, added medals to their tally with an oak leaf added to their Air Medal for every six missions they had flown. Perhaps most touching is the certificate they received and later cherished, their 'Lucky Bastard' certificate.

Chapter 19

The Later Story

History never really says goodbye. History says, 'See you later.'
— Eduardo Galeano

With the completion of their thirty missions, a chapter closed for both the Ong and Colburn crews. There were many reasons to celebrate and each man had his own set of priorities. For the married men, the trip back across the Atlantic could not come fast enough. Dong Ong and co-pilot Earl Lippert had promised to return for their second tour, so their leave in the States was somewhat tempered by the need to return to their unit. Their first tour had been a rapid affair finishing in August, whereas the Colburn crew were slightly more measured, finishing in November 1944. The invitation to return to unit was a voluntary affair, and one that Johnnie Colburn and crew decided not to pursue.

The Ong crew, those other than the pilots, fully expected to be recalled once their leave period in the States was completed. It seems they did not realize their pilots had specifically requested their crew was not recalled. As their new postings arrived, they realized they were being sent to training schools and non-combat roles in the US. New aircraft, particularly the B-29 Superfortress, were arriving into service quickly and most aircrew assumed in the absence of a recall to Europe their destiny was to be an appointment in the Pacific. For some, their war was effectively over, others would be caught up in new conflicts after the Second World War finished.

Although the last B-17 did not roll off the production line until July 1945, there was a sense, even as the trophy crews were flying, that come the end of European operations the B-17 would not be a front line aircraft. The crews could be retrained readily for new aircraft and new types of operation, but even as 1944 came to a close the end of the war was anticipated. Training schools were still producing gunners, engineers, radio operators and pilots in large numbers. The jet age was being born and, even as the first hesitant steps were taken in fighter development, the planners wanted a jet bomber.

In short, the Allied war effort by the end of 1944 was awash with experienced and qualified aviators, but not necessarily on the aircraft types that had longevity of service. This was in direct contrast to their German opponents, who had exploited new developments in aircraft design, but did not have enough experienced pilots to realistically make use of their achievements. The Messerschmitt Me 262 jet fighter had made an appearance almost at the same time at the trophy crews started their combat tours. It was faster than anything the Allies had available but suffered from low engine life, which hampered its availability. Although sometimes seen at the edges of 388th formations, it did not appear in numbers until March 1945 when its potency was demonstrated on 18 March, when a group of thirty-seven shot down twelve bombers and one fighter for the loss of three of their own. However, it was too little too late and many Me 262s were destroyed on the ground as the Allies exerted their air supremacy. To the great frustration of the RAF pilots of 616 Squadron, who flew the Allies' first combat jet, the Gloster Meteor, they were never allowed to fly against the Me 262. Instead, they were assigned to a home defence role to catch and kill V-1 weapons.

In the race for technological breakthroughs, the B-17 was subject to a number of experimental projects. In relation to the 388th Bomb Group, which operated from its home base at Knettishall, it also had a satellite station at RAF Fersfield used for Operation Aphrodite, a secret project to develop radio-controlled bombers. The activities at Fersfield must have been known in part by most crews because Fersfield aircraft operated freely out of Knettishall. Aphrodite was set up on 26 June 1944 using older B-17 and B-24 aircraft. These were modified to carry large explosive charges and were to be guided to their targets by a mother ship, another B-17, which would steer the bomber as a weapon into the target. Although the idea is now well developed utilising drone and missile technology, these early attempts were well intentioned, but fairly crude in their execution. The 'flying bomb' B-17 was initially flown by a pilot for take-off purposes and for getting the bomber trimmed and ready for longer range flight before he would bail out and leave the accompanying mother ship to control it. In this rather hazardous environment, accidents could happen as the leaving pilot would also prime the explosive charge. On a mission to Heligoland, a B-24 blew up killing its pilot, Lieutenant Joseph P. Kennedy Jr. elder brother of future US president John F. Kennedy. With damage being caused on the ground over a wide radius, it was decided to scrap the project in early 1945. However, the research continued and led to other later applications of remote-controlled B–17s in nuclear testing.

As mentioned earlier, Ong is quite open in his accounts that he delayed his return to his unit by taking advantage of the delays in processing the large numbers of servicemen passing through the system on their way to Europe. His thirty-day leave was somewhat elongated and, as a result, his co-pilot had departed to go back to Britain before him. Writing to Earl 'Corky' Lippert's wife, Betty Ann, on 28 October 1944, Dong said:

> *I just passed my physical examination so I guess it won't be long before I get my shipping orders. From the way things look here, we have a good chance of flying across. If we do, I will more than likely beat Corky across. He left from the same port of embarkation that we sailed from the last time.*

Dong took the opportunity to recount his return experiences in a short chapter of the book *388th Anthology Vol 1* (2001). Interestingly, the physical examination at the processing unit in Atlantic City was nearly Dong's undoing as it appears his eyesight was not up to standard. He recalls the incident with his usual enthusiasm:

> *During my physical examination, I encountered difficulty with my eye test. The doctor told me he would have to ground me; however, when he reviewed my papers he found, stamped in large letters, 'Combat Returnee'. He slapped me on the shoulder and said, "You are a borderline case," and passed me.*

Ong's hopes of an air crossing came to nothing and he was allocated to RMS *Queen Elizabeth* for the transatlantic sea crossing. He and another 388th colleague, John Dupray, were somewhat burdened by extra baggage that they had been equipped with by the authorities including blankets, gas masks and canteens despite their protestations that their unit already had the necessary provisions. Preparing for their train journey to the pier and laden down with kit, Dong gives us a snapshot of a scene probably repeated dozens of times in those days:

> *Those of us returning were at the head of the column. Behind us were thousands of troops who gave us the raspberry every time we stopped to rest.*

Earl Lippert was perhaps less canny. He arrived back at Knettishall in early-mid November and was allocated to Loren Johnson's crew from 4 December 1944, some three weeks before Ong was back and flying. The Johnson crew were part of 560th squadron but had lost their co-pilot, Francis Green, due to injury in late October. They were moved up into a lead position just as Green was injured and flew through until 7 April 1945. In this leading process, the 388th brought the PFF aircraft and crews together by moving them into 562 Sqn. The Johnson crew were new arrivals as the original Ong crew were finishing their tour, so Lippert had not had much time to make their acquaintance before he left on leave. Earl flew a total of sixteen missions in his second tour, most against targets in the heart of Germany. At times, they had Ted Heslam with them as Mickey operator; Ted had flown previously with Johnnie Colburn and his name is engraved on the trophy for September.

Dong's return was greeted with enthusiasm at Knettishall as communications during this period were a lot less developed. Men returning to operations would often arrive without warning following their Atlantic crossings. With the sheer quantity of movements, little information was passed on to receiving units about those about to arrive. By 24 December 1944, Dong was ready to fly his first mission of his second tour and with a new crew, including a new co-pilot. The story of the second crew, a further twenty missions and a role in leading, is almost a separate story, although some interesting facets stand out. The war had moved on and, with France and most of lowland Europe either liberated or taking little or no part in the conflict, the missions were concentrated on Germany. With an experienced pilot on hand such as Dong, it seems a certain amount of fluidity was introduced into the crew. Most obvious is the role of co-pilot, which appears to have changed regularly with nine different men sitting in the right-hand seat during the twenty missions. Add to this the visiting command pilots and the cockpit is a place of change. After seven missions, the Ong crew became a primary lead aircraft carrying PFF equipment and a regular Mickey operator arrived in the form of Arthur Fixel. Other names were regulars and one, John Schweikert, was one of Johnnie Colburn's original waist gunners. He had trained with them and flown the Atlantic with them but, as the shape of the missions progressed and the Colburn crew became a PFF crew, he had not been able to stay with them and finish when they did. Along with ball turret gunner Robert Ryan, he had to look for other roles.

Schweikert obviously continued in training and, as most gunners had dual roles as engineers, he was able to complete twenty-seven missions, his last fifteen with Ong's second crew as his engineer.

Another outstanding name on Ong's second crew was John Dupray, who had completed thirty missions in August at the same time the first Ong crew finished their tour. He teamed up with Ong on their return trip on RMS *Queen Elizabeth* and carried his friendship on into Ong's crew as bombardier to complete, like Dong, fifty missions. Dupray had survived two previous aircraft losses on his first tour with the Fitzpatrick crew, one at Poltava and one at Knettishall when his plane was hit by an aircraft coming in from nearby Fersfield. On both occasions, the aircraft was on the ground and the crew were safe.

Ong's fiftieth and final mission was on 18 March 1945 to Berlin. With the Russians approaching Berlin's eastern side, the 8th Air Force launched its biggest raid to Berlin to date with 1,250 heavy bombers striking the city. With the bombs dropped, Dong did something unusual, but also typically flamboyant. Dropping out of formation he got the B-17 down to the deck and raced back to England at very low altitude all the way. Mickey operator Arthur Fixel later mentioned this in an oral memoir of February 2000:

> *He decided he wanted to come back in style. So we dropped down on the deck, and I think we were flying at an elevation of about twenty feet, full out. Fortunately, nothing blew up and I swear ... of course, you can't see anything on radar under 3,000–4,000–5,000 feet. So I was standing back in the waist, and we went by several houses where people on the second floor were higher than we were.*

After fifty successful missions in which his aircraft did not turn back once and many times returned with damage, it seems this outstanding record was something Dong could rely on; permission for his low-level return had been granted. The flak around Berlin that day was particularly heavy and, as the Nazi capital was under threat from Russian land forces too, more anti-aircraft guns had been moved to try to defend the city in what was increasingly looking like a last stand. There were guns in streets, parks and even directly outside the ruined Reichstag building. Perhaps, given the lack of German fighter strength outside the area of the capital, Ong made the decision that he faced greater risks staying in formation as it was certainly no guarantee of safety. In February 1944, two B-17s had collided over Reedham marshes on their return leg to the 385th's base at Great Ashfield in Norfolk, killing both crews. One of the crews was on their last mission and a neighbouring crew reported they had seen the pilots had already broken out some large cigars as they were a few short minutes from final safety. They were struck from below minutes later by a B-17 that had lost control in light cloud and was trying to recover. However, Dong Ong's decision to fly back home in this manner was not entirely based on a rationale of self-preservation, otherwise a safer altitude would have been chosen. This was a character deeply appreciated by all who served with him; he was a 'lucky' guy and a young man of spirit. Dong was coming back in style.

This second tour of Ong and Lippert with their respective crews was against a backdrop of incredible European drama. The Nazi empire with all its cruel extensions was collapsing before their eyes. They had returned to flying duties right about the time of the Battle of the Bulge, the German counter-attack through the Ardennes forest in southern Belgium. Although a huge surprise attack that caused great loss and some dismay in its early stages, once the weather lifted that had grounded Allied planes, the attack stalled. The German ground forces, despite being in an area of excellent cover, were picked off by light bombers every time they took to a road. Perhaps with knowledge of past operations and the limitations of heavy bombers in close support, the 388th B-17s continued their conveyor belt of attacks on the German industrial centres.

The day after Dong Ong's last mission to Berlin, Hitler issued his 'Nero Decree' that ordered the destruction of all German factories. This was the declared end, the start of the Nazi suicide procedure, and suggests even Hitler, after the raid of the 18th, finally acknowledged all was lost. It was an illustration of how the actions of nine individuals that day could play a part in forming world history.

Earl Lippert flew on until 7 April 1945 with his last mission with Loren Johnson and crew to Kaltenkirchen, an airfield from which Me 262s operated. The airfield also hosted a number of Arado Ar 234s, a jet bomber and one of a number of aircraft and projects that could have turned the war, or at least extended it, in Germany's favour had they been exploited earlier. Johnson's crew were leading the 388-A formation when they were subject to an attack of extraordinary proportions. A number of Me 109 fighters embarked on apparent suicide attacks on the formation, attempting to ram the B-17s. Tragically for the 388th, Robert Bare and crew were struck by a fighter and were lost on their second mission. Their first was only the day before. The second casualty was Lewis Hickman and crew, who were also rammed although, unlike the Bare crew, some did manage to escape the aircraft. These desperate measures were conducted by a specially formed Luftwaffe unit, *Sonderkommando Elbe*, and 7 April was the only organized attack in numbers with 180 fighters involved. Of fifteen bombers rammed on this day, eight were lost. The attacks are little known of and certainly not as notorious as the Japanese Kamikaze attacks. Unlike the Japanese, the pilots were not specifically ordered to kill themselves, although the operations were labelled as suicide missions. The Luftwaffe pilot who rammed Robert Bare, Obfeldwebel Verner Linder, did not survive the episode.

Just as Ong and Lippert were returning from leave after their first tour, the Colburn crew were finishing their tour. It might be tempting to imagine a champagne-fuelled party to celebrate their achievement. However, the experience of crews nearing their thirty mission target was mixed. With the practice of fielding pilots out on their first mission to other experienced crews, invariably a pilot ended his time on thirty, but the rest of his crew were lingering one mission behind on twenty-nine. In some instances a crew would be told they all qualified for leave, but in others a further mission with another crew would be necessary.

In Colburn's crew the non-pilot officers, Morris Neiman and Bob Simmon, each completed their tour a short time after Johnnie Colburn. Morris flew to Hamm with Robert Hancock's lead crew as group navigator on 26 November. It was Hancock's final mission, his thirtieth, and he had already been promoted to captain. The risks, even on final missions, were just as intense as the first. To Hancock's right in the high squadron, Wayne Daniels and crew were hit badly by flak over the target and their B-17 blew up as they were bailing out. Even on parachutes, they had had the added hazard of the bomb group behind them dropping bombs through them. Five survived despite the explosion throwing them clear and they became prisoners of war. At least one of the crew was killed when his parachute failed to deploy correctly.

Likewise, three days later on 29 November, Bob Simmon also flew on a mission to Hamm with Herbert Moore's crew that passed without serious incident. It's not clear as to the exact timing of each crew member's return to the States. Johnnie Colburn spent some time at the processing centre at Stone in Staffordshire, Station 594, waiting for his turn to be allocated a place on a ship home. With the future of his crew still in his mind, even though they would never fly together again, Johnnie wrote a letter of recommendation for his radio operator, George Kragle, to help him apply for pilot training. George did not manage to realize his aspirations but the letter still exists in his family's hands. Johnnie wrote on 5 December 1944:

To Officer in Charge of Reassignment of Enlisted Men
T/Sgt. George E Kragle, 35052713, was with me from 24 January 1944 until 16 November 1944, as radio operator of my crew. At times, during our training as a crew, I allowed him to fly the B-17. He is smooth on the controls and very interested in flying. It is my opinion that he would make an excellent pilot, if given the training.

After a short period, Johnnie was homeward bound by sea on the former Dutch honeymoon liner SS *Nieuw Amsterdam*, 'Darling of the Dutch'. Launched in 1938, she completed forty-four transatlantic wartime crossings carrying 400,000 Allied troops, 350,000 fewer than the illustrious *Queen Elizabeth*, but nonetheless, a remarkable number. Johnnie arrived at Halifax, Nova Scotia, on Christmas Day 1944. For many making similar homeward crossings, including the rest of Johnnie's crew, their combat war was over. Johnnie had been joined at this point by Bob Simmon and Morrie Neiman on the homeward crossing. Johnnie had been offered a post if he returned flying the de Havilland Mosquito in a reconnaissance role. He decided instead to take the route back to America for a training post. After all, he had a new son whom he had yet to meet.

Johnnie, after his leave, was posted to Hobbs, New Mexico, as a pilot instructor on B-17s. Johnnie was no stranger to Hobbs as he had trained there little over a year before and now he returned newly promoted to captain. He says now he would much rather have faced combat again than this training role with new pilots. Hobbs was one of three main B-17 pilot training bases and, as Johnnie arrived in early 1945, it hit its peak with 162 B-17s stationed there. Hobbs was well equipped and one trainee described it as having a good mess hall, an officer's club and decent sleeping quarters, but that the town was 'small and uninteresting'. The war in Europe had ended and Johnnie's instructor's duties were completed in July 1945, giving him the opportunity to leave the Air Force. Early release was based on a points system and Johnnie qualified due to his combat experience and time served. Johnnie returned to his pre-war job in the Dixon packing company in Texas, taking a pay cut from his captain's pay. Despite the eruption of further conflicts first in Korea and later Vietnam, Johnnie was not recalled, although several of his crew were. He moved to work with Parker Bros. & Co, a building materials and shipyard company, until retirement. He remained in the Air Force reserves as an officer and retired with the rank of lieutenant colonel on 20 January 1979.

Bob Simmon, Johnnie's bombardier, was posted to Midland and Big Spring in Texas as a bombardier instructor. With many of the instructors roles came the opportunity to move wives to their locations and live a less stressful life. Bob was released from active duty in February 1946 and took a job in a car body repair shop in Fort Wayne, but he remained a reserve officer. He and his wife Katie had met in Fort Wayne before the war when they both worked for the Magnavox company, which produced record players and radio equipment. It was a return home but, come turbulent times, any reserve officer knew life could change. Five years later, in February 1951, Bob was recalled as a bombardier on B-29 and B-50 bombers during the Korean War. It seems during this time that service life suited him and he remained in the regular Air orce afterwards. He and Katie had a young family in the 1950s and, given the stability of an Air Force career, opportunities abounded. Bob went on to radar and navigation school, and was posted to RB-47 Stratojet bombers, the first big jet bomber in the US Air Force. Soon he was flying supersonically in the B-58 Hustler, the world's first supersonic bomber capable of Mach II. In his later career he became chief of the Operations Plans Division of the 379th Bombardment Wing, operating B-52H bombers. He retired on 1 September 1974 as a lieutenant colonel having had the role of Director of Operations of the 40th Air Division. With a full Air Force career in the reserve and regular forces spanning thirty-three years, Bob and his wife were able to retire. Bob built a beautiful house that he designed himself set in the rolling hills of rural Arkansas north of Little Rock. Quite a few of their service friends had also retired in that area, where they all enjoyed boating and fishing in nearby lakes and trout-filled rivers.

George Kragle, Johnnie's radio operator, served out his time in the wartime Air Force, returned home to Cleveland, Ohio, and set up a television repair service. He eventually worked for the large RCA group, which engaged him for the rest of his working life. He seemed to specialize in radar and radio communications, particularly for shipping. While in Cleveland, he and a friend bought an aeroplane and enjoyed flying, a privilege the Army Air Force had not been able to provide. He had designs on owning his own aircraft, but the realities of a young family later proved to be a greater priority. In 1956, he moved to New Orleans with RCA to work on shipping where he met his future wife and married in 1958. He appears to have been ever the technician and his son George Jnr recalls:

He became proficient at fixing items around the house, the toasters, stereos, televisions, etc. Nowadays, we throw the toaster away. He had a round contraption that was covered in black electrical tape and plugged into a wall socket. This was used to adjust the color on our RCA TV set with tubes in the back. One hand was holding the round device and moving it in a circular motion in front of the picture tube while his head was in the back of the set, sort of an awkward position. We kept that set, seems long after solid state was introduced.

George served in the US Army Reserves until 1959 and it appears his service was not Air Force related. In common with so many servicemen of the time, George had obtained skills that prepared him well for the demand for new technology through the 1960s and '70s.

With the two trophy crews, there seems to be a distinct definition between those who served and were never called back, and those who returned to the Air Force for a later career. It seems a good number of returnees post-war decided to stay in the services for longer periods. With the outbreak of new conflicts there were immediate tasks in Korea and Vietnam, but the burgeoning demands of European tensions and the Cold War also demanded a strong US Air Force presence in peacetime Europe.

Richard Theodore 'Ted' Heslam, Johnnie Colburn's regular Mickey operator and named on the trophy in September 1944, continued his wartime flying career through until late March 1945 and served on eight different crews. He flew with Loren Johnson's crew on six occasions, four of them with Earl Lippert as co-pilot. Ted stayed on in the Air Force after the war and, training as a navigator, he served on B-47 and B-52 bombers in a twenty-eight year career and finished as a lieutenant colonel. Interestingly, sometimes the choice of post-war careers was simplified by pre-war experiences. Growing up in Fitchburg, Massachusetts, the Heslam family farmed and had crops growing under glass when a hurricane swept through in 1938 and decimated the business. The 'Great New England Hurricane' was the worst experienced since 1869 and was a category five storm, making landfall as a category three. Across Massachusetts, winds picked up to 186mph, the strongest ever recorded in the USA. Heavy rainfall contributed to extensive flooding, although Fitchburg was largely spared by a government flood defence programme completed only two years earlier in 1936. Nevertheless, the destruction combined with the effects of the Great Depression introduced a good deal of uncertainty. Twenty-five miles away in Lowell, a poultry farmer reported that his cages and birds had been blown away. When the police asked why he was not out looking for them, he said he needed time as he wanted to find the roof of his house first.

Born in 1921, Ted's enlistment record of March 1942 shows he had one year of college education and was listed as a 'salesperson'. The decision to resume with an Air Force career was undoubtedly affected by the difficulties of trying to make a living in his still recovering home area.

The first fifty years of the twentieth century were tumultuous in experiencing two world wars and a savage economic depression. There were many linking and contributing factors in all the events, but the young men serving in the 388th were children of the Great Depression. Unlike those born in the 1930s, those born in the early 1920s had the grim opportunity to witness the change in fortunes of their parents' generation. Their futures were formed, not only through surviving the greatest conflict ever witnessed, but by the economic fortunes of a global market.

Dong Ong's crew experience followed a similar pattern to the young men of Colburn's. Co-pilot Earl Lippert did not return immediately to the States when he finished his combat flying on 7 April 1945 but remained at Knettishall. He flew one more operational mission on 6 May, although the war was certain to finish within days, perhaps hours. The mission was to carry food to Holland as part of the 'Chow Hound' operations. Holland had been in a state of near starvation through the bleak winter of 1944–45 and the transport of much needed food became a priority for aircraft able to take the load. The crew list shows he flew with old friend and former Ong crew navigator, Ed 'Goldy' Goldstein. Writing in the 388th Association's newsletter in 2001, Earl mentioned that he stayed on until the 388th left Knettishall in July 1945:

I stayed with the group and was in the last plane to leave the base along with Maj. Trauth, Maj. Flore, Capt. Phillips and Lt. Goldstein. Goldstein and I were on Ong's original crew; we arrived at the 388th together and left together. It all boils down that it was a great period in our lives and they will never be forgotten.

Having missed three opportunities to fly across the Atlantic, it must have been gratifying to return with a B-17 after all had been achieved. The 388th was formally disbanded on 28 August 1945 at Sioux Falls AAF, South Dakota. The task of selling the B-17 airframes for scrap began shortly afterwards and before long all the stalwarts that carried their men to war were gone.

Earl returned home to his previous work in the oil business in New York State, but in 1951 took a job in alcohol sales, later opening a liquor store of his own.

Dong Ong's engineer, Morris Fleishman, followed his father into farming by buying a farm after the war. His father had farmed, but had latterly taken work in the automotive industry. Perhaps, once again, the Great Depression had altered the lives and prosperity of a family. Before embarking on his post-war occupation, Morris had an important priority. His father, a First World War veteran, had advised him strongly not to marry while in the services. He married Joyce Crystal a week after his discharge from the Army Air Force. They adopted two boys and a girl, and enjoyed a long and happy marriage. Sadly, even as this book was being written, Joyce passed away in October 2014.

All around the United States, returning servicemen were looking for their next steps in life. The story was repeated in Britain, but in continental Europe millions of people were displaced with homes destroyed, families wiped out and the whole pattern of life they knew only six years earlier changed forever. The returning men of the 388th had one element that was perhaps their principal asset; youth. Most were in their early to mid-twenties and some returned to university, some to simple but stable jobs. Others, perhaps not fully able to shake off the excitement and camaraderie of the war, remained in the services. Some families recount that their men did not return the same and, in at least one case, did not seem to settle easily into long-term employment.

Thanks to later interest in Dong Ong's career, he wrote a full account of his time after the Second World War and it is this that provides us with quite a comprehensive picture of his life. Of all the trophy names, it is clear that he created an impression wherever he went, both for his skill and his good fortune. As well as being respected, he was also liked and this quality helped him to progress, but also helped him pull the odd stunt here and there.

After his return to the States, Dong was posted to Kelly AFB in Texas and served for nearly five years with the Base Flight Section. At this point he had become a regular commissioned officer and his duties involved test flying repaired aircraft. This gave Dong a wide experience of aircraft types and he flew the B-29, B-17, B-26, B-25, C-45, C-47 and fighter aircraft such as the P-51. The Cold War had become the West's next hurdle and Dong was posted to Wiesbaden in Germany in 1949 as part of the Berlin Airlift. The Soviet Union, disgruntled and somewhat obsessed by Berlin's position as an island of joint occupation by their former Allies, cut road, rail and canal links to the western half of the city. It was a somewhat incoherent action with the hope that the Western powers would leave Berlin and allow the Soviets to gain full control. Stalin and the Soviet Union also had no desire to see Germany rise from the ashes in the form of an independent country. As in all conflicts, the causes of the Berlin blockade were complex, but centred on the rebuilding and identity of a West German state other than as an occupied land. In a stand-off, the Allies began to resupply Berlin by air with every item necessary for daily life. This huge undertaking saw nearly 9,000 tons of cargo flown into Berlin daily over a period of just over twelve months. Dong's experience as a regular pilot was called upon and he was brought in as a 'qualified' C-54 Skymaster pilot, something he later commented on as he had only flown six hours' transition training on the type. That said, the C-54 was not too different in form to many planes of the day with four radial engines that were not dissimilar to the B-17. Flying daily with cargos that included foodstuffs and coal, Dong recalled he was allowed a three-day pass per month. The flying was not structured into set crews and Dong does not remember flying with the same fellow pilot twice. During this period, Dong also was involved in a peculiar incident with a pilot who completely lost the plot and his senses during a bad weather landing. The engineer, sitting behind the pilots, jumped up and restrained the pilot, whose arms were flailing about, and Dong landed the aircraft safely.

Further postings in 1950 to California and Eglin AFB in Florida saw Dong assigned to the nuclear test programme conducted at Enewetak in the Pacific Marshall Islands. Dong managed to find time to meet and marry his sweetheart, Eva. They married on 3 January 1951 in Andalusia, Alabama, before his Pacific posting. The nuclear tests, four in all, were codenamed Operation Greenhouse. Dong's role was to fly a B-17 as a mother ship and support a radio-controlled drone B-17 that flew through the radioactive cloud and retrieve it on the other side. This operation was similar to the pioneer Aphrodite Missions work done by the 388th Bomb Group at its satellite station at RAF Fersfield in 1944. The Fersfield operation had used pilots in the drone craft to get it airborne before bailing out, but technology had moved on and the drone was now in the hands of ground controllers during take-off. It seems fitting, therefore, that a former 388th pilot was involved so integrally during the nuclear tests. It is likely that Dong would have had little contact with Aphrodite during his time at Knettishall as he was fully occupied with his regular squadron service. Dong recalls some challenging moments during a test when his drone B-17 had the edge on speed over them and it took a throttles wide open attempt to keep up. One of these B-17 mother ships was B-17G 44-83514 *Sentimental Journey*, which is now preserved in flying condition by the Commemorative Air Force Museum in Mesa, Arizona.

A spell flying the B-29 in a search and rescue role escorting bombers towards Korea followed at Okinawa, Japan, in 1951–52, during which time he was promoted to major. Further career postings followed, including a time at Command and Staff College, before he arrived as a squadron aircraft maintenance officer in Maine in 1956 with the first operational squadron of B-52 bombers. He was the first non-aircrew member to qualify to fly the B-52 and he remained with the type into the early 1960s.

Through all of his career, in wartime and peacetime, Dong took whatever opportunities set before him and, out of 2,000 officers, he was selected to work on the Titan II intercontinental missile programme in Arkansas. Promoted to lieutenant colonel, he commanded and supervised the first in-silo firing of the Titan, which impacted successfully in the Pacific.

Following a further and unexpected promotion to colonel, Dong returned to B-52 bombers and embarked on the third war of his career, Vietnam. In 1965 he served as deputy airborne commander on a stream of thirty-three B-52 bombers. His experience in aircraft maintenance and operations led to a posting away from heavy bombers in 1967 and to the 3rd Tactical Fighter wing flying F-100 Super Sabres out of Bien Hoa in Vietnam. His 'luck' was still holding and, after a Second World War dodging flak and bullets,

Vietnam was about to serve up its own form of peril. On 30 January 1968, the Viet Cong and the North Vietnamese People's Army launched a sudden attack, the Tet offensive. The airfield at Bien Hoa came under direct attack and the enemy penetrated the perimeter before being repelled, resulting in 400 American dead. Dong recalled:

> *Throughout the 'Tet', the base was showered with rockets and mortar fire, almost on a nightly basis. My car was destroyed. My office was hit and my chair pierced. The trailer I lived in was also hit. On each incident I was not there.*

By this time, due to Dong's seniority and his knowledge of operations, he was not permitted to fly in combat. In his typical style, he did, on one occasion manage to wrangle his way on to an F-100 for a bombing sortie and he is pictured in the *Seventh Air Force News* smiling as he clambers out of the jet.

In 1969, he was posted once again to Europe and spent three years at Ramstein in Germany with the 26th Tactical Reconnaissance wing as director of maintenance and supply. The aircraft in his care was the McDonnell Douglas F-4C Phantom II. Born just twenty-one years after the Wright brothers took to the air, Dong's career had centred at first around the B-17, an aircraft that cruised at 155 mph and could take two hours of flying over England to reach assembly height at 24,000ft, and had spanned into the introduction of aircraft faster and more complex than a flying student of 1943 could have imagined. The Phantom was capable of more than Mach 2, 1,492mph, with a cruise speed of 585mph, and in many ways was one of the first truly modern jet aircraft.

Dong retired from the Air Force in 1972 after his last posting to Pine Castle AFB in Orlando, Florida. He had served through three wars and one Cold War, and settled down after retirement with Eva in Orlando.

Chapter 20

The Downwind Leg and Final Approach

No man is a man until he has been a soldier.
– Louis de Bernières, *Captain Corelli's Mandolin*

In the 1920s and 1930s, much was written about the First World War. Some of the poetry written still strikes a resonant note, whatever the conflict. One of the most famous extracts is from the poem *For The Fallen* written by Laurence Binyon:

They shall grow not old, as we that are left grow old:
Age shall not weary them, nor the years condemn.
At the going down of the sun and in the morning
We will remember them.

These few lines are repeated many times in services of remembrance around the world, particularly in Britain and the Commonwealth. Normally, we are thinking of those who died so young on a foreign battlefield, but in the context of the trophy story, all our men came home. Seventy years later, all but two have passed away and we can trace whole lives from youth to old age. Those who remain today could be seen as being in 'advanced' old age, if such a thing is definable. They are the men who grew old and, according to the poem, were wearied by it.

Many war stories leave the combatants at the end of their war with perhaps only brief explanations as to what eventually became of them. In the excitement of heroism, it is arguable few want to read of an old man and his ailments, which, in the context of a society that adores youth, is a little sad. The trophy story is about very normal men placed in very extraordinary circumstances. For most, they returned to their normal lives and made the best of what was available to them. In old age they faced their final battles, not through an oxygen mask at 20,000ft while firing at an enemy fighter, but in accomplishing the day to day tasks that many of us take for granted.

While researching the names on the trophy, it became apparent that most, if not all, lived to an age that our forebears would have called 'old' but as life expectancy has risen, we count their ages as younger than we would hope for ourselves. A number of the trophy men died in their sixties, a couple, such as Johnnie's co-pilot Russ Weekes, at 70 exactly. Carl Lindorf, of Dong Ong's crew, died when he was 66. He was one of the youngest to pass away and his death was perhaps the most dramatic of the group, having a heart attack while driving his car and crashing into a tree. Many lived into their eighties, some into their late eighties, so it is fair to say that of the eighteen men of the trophy, the times of their passing was very average. They were, after all, average men.

There are heart-warming stories of happy retirements with many children and grandchildren. Some married but had no children, others married and divorced and remarried. Their lives also reflect the change in society that the Second World War brought about. They came to Britain better dressed, better paid and better fed than their British counterparts, and came away with an understanding of the European conflict and the sufferings of entire nations. For many it was a humbling experience, yet one they could take great pride in. Even as old men they could pull on their A-2 jackets adorned with their squadron badges and enjoy reunions. The 388th Bomb Group Association was formed in 1949 and to this day pulls together those who served, but also provides a framework for research and fellowship for the families. One leading light in the Association was Bob Simmon, Johnnie Colburn's bombardier. He became president of the association through the 1990s and spent many hours taking care of association matters. His sons ensured he relived his wartime training experiences and organized a flight for him in an AT-6, where Bob had the opportunity the fly the aircraft for nearly the entire flight and, according to the cameras on the aircraft, wore a grin for the entire time. In the late 1980s, Bob also hitched a ride in a friend's P-51, *Gunfighter,* owned by Brigadier General Regis 'Reggie' Urschler, in which he sat in the small jump seat behind the pilot.

Also taking to the skies once again in recent years was Johnnie Colburn in B-17 *Thunderbird,* which is now based in Galveston, Texas. Relatives paid for two tickets to fly in *Thunderbird* and Johnnie and his daughter, Darlene, took the flight. Although Johnnie was still confident he could fly the B-17, sadly, the pilots did not take that view – perhaps they were understandably nervous with such a precious aircraft. Johnnie commented: 'They used to pay me to fly these planes and now someone has to pay for me to fly in it!'

Having emphasized the ordinary nature of many of the men, perhaps Dong Ong could be described as an extraordinary man who experienced and achieved much. In the post-war years 'Dong' became 'Don' and to his friends and family he was known by this name. In his later years in retirement in Florida he and his wife Eva faced probably the biggest challenge any couple can encounter. Eva suffered from Alzheimer's for the last twelve years of her life and Don gradually took on a nursing role in looking after her. It was obviously time consuming and a huge effort but, according to his grandson, Justin, Don's devotion was unquestionable. Justin's account of his visits to his grandfather and grandmother's house through these years reveal a touching love story:

I remember how incredibly loyal my grandfather was to her till the day she died. As her memory went so went her speech and it became difficult for any of us to know what she needed. Always though my grandfather seemed to instinctively know what she needed like a glass of water, food, using the restroom, etc. He tried to do everything with the latest medications available on the market to help her and literally waited on her hand and foot all day, every day, and at all hours of the night. It was very heart breaking growing up watching it unfold. I remember she would always call out "Don, Don" and my grandfather would rush to her aid. As her disease worsened her memory faded, sentences blurred together, conversations turned to ramblings, and she began to speak a lot of gibberish. There is one phrase that I remember hearing repeatedly and completely randomly she would say "I love you Don" and he would respond "I love you too." Sometimes she would say, "I love you Don" 10–20 times in a row and my Grandpa always responded with "I love you too." It was very sweet and romantic if you think about it. She was losing her memory and having difficulty remembering, responding, or recognizing anything, but somehow always remembered that she loved her husband. Sometimes she would even forget who Don was and say, "who are you," with which my grandpa would respond, "I'm your husband" and then she would say, "Oh... I love you Don."

Through these years many of Don's photographs, records and even his medals disappeared or were thrown out by Eva, not by any malice, but with the confusion that the disease engendered. Towards the end of Eva's life, Don joined the 388th Association in early 2001. In many ways, this was a late commitment because so many friends and comrades had joined many years before. Partly at the behest of long-term friend and fellow 388th pilot, Paul Patten, Don became a life member. The association newsletter of Spring 2001 announced Don's return from obscurity with the headline 'The Swede Re-Ups after 56 years'. Letters of recognition begin to appear from former crew and close colleagues, and after Eva's death in 2002, Don attended at least one reunion and was pictured with Paul Patten and Gene Peterson.

The onslaught on Don's memories and memorabilia took a further turn for the worse around 2005 as a large tree crashed through his house in Florida while he was away. It took time to track him down, but by that time much of the house was ruined. It is interesting to see that, even at the end of his life, Don was still undertaking adventurous tasks that an 84-year-old should have perhaps thought twice about. A fall from a roof in 2006 led to Don's incapacitation and he died in January 2007.

Dong Ong gained a pleasant notoriety and affection as a pilot with all whom he flew. He is remembered as a man who flew fifty successful missions. The quieter man of the crew, the married man whose wife's name adorned their aircraft, was the co-pilot, Earl 'Corky' Lippert. He flew forty-eight listed missions but, perhaps due to his role as co-pilot, does not have his name in lights.

As mentioned earlier, Morris Gumpel's later years were affected by Parkinson's disease. His brother Roy recounts how Morris found difficulty settling into life and work, but he's not sure how the war affected him.

Some characters are missing from this trophy story, hopefully temporarily, but they proved harder to find than some others. As nearly all the men have passed away, in the context of this book, we are relying on relatives and memories of past, sometimes fleeting, conversations.

One man from the Ong crew who has been difficult to trace was known as John Arvid (listed as Arvid J. Estrom on the trophy). He was the ball turret gunner and flew thirty-two listed missions. His vantage point from below was precarious and his conditions were very confined. His enlistment record of 7 March 1943 shows he was from Middlesex, Connecticut, and he was born in 1916. Other records suggest he was born in 1915, but this kind of disparity often happens. By the time he joined the crew he was nearly 28, so a bit older than some of the others. On enlistment he is recorded as having one year of high school, and that he was a semi-skilled mechanic and repairman. Whether he returned to a similar job after the Air Force, we don't know, but he emerged again shortly before his death in 1983 as a school custodian – a man who looks after the fabric of the school. The school in question was Branford High in Connecticut and, at not much more than thirty miles from John's enlistment office, it begs the question as to whether he lived there all his life. It looks likely as the 1940 census shows him in Branford married to Helen. It seems, on evidence, that he may have worked as a repairman or similar all his working life, before and after the war. He was one of many thousands of course, but one wonders how many pupils of the school in the early 1980s knew the man cleaning floors and stacking chairs spent a number of perilous months high in the sky over Germany suspended below a B-17.

Kenneth Gardner, Dong's radio operator, who was subject to the terrifying night-time parachute drop over Knettishall on 17 July 1944 where the D-handle and ripcord came free in his hand, returned to life as a painter and decorator. He wasn't recalled into the service and continued decorating all his working life. He said little to nothing about his wartime experiences, but was a man who refused to fly again and was described as of a nervous disposition after the war.

In later life as well as through their careers, the quieter men perhaps did not gain the same recognition as some of their peers. Just as Bob Simmon was very well known in the 388th Association and played an important role, his pilot, Johnnie Colburn, is not as well known. This is not to decry Bob, who was known for putting in time and effort for the veterans. When the author mentioned Johnnie, the reaction was often 'who?' Being well known is not the be-all and end-all because, in all walks of life the solid, steady man may get things done more successfully, but cause less of a stir. Johnnie Colburn was 96 at the time of writing and, after time in a retirement home, had a carer and was living with his daughter. Despite a number of strokes and small heart attacks, he soldiered on, although his day to day life was restricted. His memory, too, was not too strong, although he could remember Spanish songs from his youth and sing them. Despite these hardships, he still had an interest in the war and, after reading a recent account of Poltava, commented that perhaps not all their missions were for the best. 'Too political,' he said. In writing this book, it has been possible to pass on information to Johnnie and send him pictures of the places he once knew.

In the sadness of a passing of a generation there are words that are left by those who remain. When Bob Simmon died in April 2008, his best friend wrote the following in the guestbook:

Name: *Johnnie & Happy Colburn*
Message: *Pilot to bombardier: 'Give me a heading to base.' I'll see you again some day. We love you, Bob.*

Chapter 21

The End is Never the End

I can't go back to yesterday because I was a different person then.
— Lewis Carroll, *Alice in Wonderland*

With so many characters and events mentioned in this book, it is hard to know at what point in the story to close. I have no doubt that the publication of this account will bring forward even more information. It will probably help find some of the names I could not find on this first time around. Daniel Visconti's relatives; where are you? Daniel was Dong Ong's loyal tail gunner and, as a man who occupied a lonely vantage point, it would have been good to find his relatives. I know his family is in New York of Italian origin, I know his parents' and siblings' names, but there are a lot of Viscontis in New York. So it is with a few of the names on the trophy but, all told, I feel fairly confident we have the wider story 'in the can'.

A mystery is only a mystery when there are unknown details. I return again and again to the finding of the trophy in Edinburgh, and think through all the possibilities of how it came to be there, adrift for seventy years. In January 2015, I contacted the *Scotsman* newspaper and it printed a feature about the trophy in the *Scotsman on Sunday,* including pictures. Someone in Edinburgh knows in whose cabinet or sideboard it resided for years. There was no word back after that article, even though my email was published alongside the story. There are a thousand possible permutations of how the trophy ended up in Edinburgh. My theory is only a best guess and that somehow the trophy was parcelled up with other Air Force items for shipping back to the States, but perhaps ended up at a depot such as Turnhouse in Scotland. From there, it might have been gifted or even sold in a job lot auction after the war. It is possible that it was entrusted to an officer who was part of the 388th service units that handled everything from postal services to vehicles, and perhaps he ended up in Scotland and left it there. Although I'm certain none of the names mentioned on the trophy had any later link with it, it only takes one man of more than 5,000 Americans who served at Knettishall to have married and settled after meeting a 'wee lassie' from Scotland to solve the mystery. Perhaps it had been in a box in a loft for decades – I suspect we shall never know.

Also unresolved is where the wine cooler originated in the first place. We know it is English, was made between 1880 and 1900, and probably not that uncommon an object. Where it was bought from immediately prior to engraving is unknown, although the suggestion of it originating from a country house seems plausible. Had it been gifted to the 388th by the owner of one of the 'flak houses' used by them? Sadly, all the senior 388th staff who might have remembered have now gone, but maybe, just maybe, a reference may turn up in a diary or notebook one day.

Personally, I'm happy for it to remain a mystery, although I have spent many hours pursuing leads. Sometimes in a good mystery story, you don't find everything out in the end. The cliffhanger aspect adds an element for everyone with which to engage their minds and imaginations. The truth might be very boring indeed.

In many objects of their kind, the historical value or interest is in the eye of the beholder. Trophies can be found all over eBay and they don't cost much – after all, who wants a silver goblet with someone else's name on it? The military trophies can be interesting, but they generally refer to an inter-unit competition, darts, football or running and only infrequently have any bearing on wartime actions. One recent eBay gem was a British Army trophy consisting of two old taps attached to a piece of wood. I confess to having one other artefact that I bought on eBay and it is a darts trophy from HMS *Ark Royal*, the 1960s aircraft carrier, which looks like it was made in the ship's carpentry shop.

I recognize a bigger picture emerging as we say our final goodbyes to a generation that fought in the Second World War. Before too long the number of veterans will be very small and their experiences will be written about as the last survivors. It happened with the First World War and, arguably, interest remains as great as in the early days of the coach trips to the battlefields of the 1920s. The next generation is close to retirement and their sons' and daughters' children wrote school projects about their great-grandparents ten years ago. There is yet another young generation emerging who, prompted by school, are asking all the right questions about their relatives.

If there is one enduring lesson to learn, it is to insist that the older generations label their photographic albums, or at least write on the back of particular photos. As the trove of old memories and photos can mean so much to later generations, they need protecting. Even in our digital age with photos and entries on social media being made at an incredible pace, we must take care to preserve our history carefully. So often I have seen Victorian photo albums in second-hand shops and it is a tragedy to think that some of these earliest photographic images have been lost to their original families.

As the Ong and Colburn crews flew on day by day deep into Nazi-occupied Europe, their story is remarkable. It is remarkable because they returned and seventy years later, in the peace won at such a great cost, we can sit with a book and read something about them. If there is one saying or theme that most of the relatives contacted for this project said, it would be that 'he didn't say much about his Second World War experiences'. Now, with living memory of those who passed through these momentous events in short supply, we are taking stock of history. This does not mean that a plethora of documentaries, books and magazines do not continue to pour out of our media sources on the subject but, with memories frail, the process is about re-examining the existing records. This is not to say that there are not many exciting things to find as we dig deeper, but time and time again I have wished that I could ask detailed questions about the smallest of matters.

Just as the men who flew are now fading like flowers among us, so too the airfields of England are slowly being reclaimed into the landscape they came from. Some survive, many used as airports or landing strips, others have been deliberately erased either through purposeful reclamation to agriculture or for industrial or housing use. There is an enduring sadness about this because these blank strips of overgrown and cracked concrete were the last ever places many young airmen had contact with the earth. As they left, not one intended to die. Many had plans for after the war, careers to resume, studies to finish and sweethearts to marry. They never came back to England. Although we can grasp at a shadow of the past, there are few ways to comprehend the enormity of the war unless you witnessed it first-hand. Now, there are few that can remember the spectacle of a 1,000 bomber raid, few to retell their narrow escapes and even fewer who can recall the names and faces of those who did not come back.

Knettishall is a name few know in Britain, I have been an aviation enthusiast for many years and I had never heard of it. However, when I call family members whose relatives were part of the 388th crews, they, of course, know the name. Each bombardment group is a family and will remain so for many years to come. They carry around the odd names from thousands of miles away that their fathers, uncles or grandfather told them of. Names such as Molesworth, Framlingham, Snetterton Heath, Polebrook and Thorpe Abbotts all spark immediate interest in the veteran who served there – and there were many more. The Royal Air Force also packed a punch with a huge array of bomber and fighter fields. All US Army Air Force bases were prefixed 'RAF' and all bases reverted to their hosts when they left.

Perhaps the peculiarity of this vast mechanized aerial fleet is that there is very little left behind. In the organization of war, when they left they took everything of use and note with them. A few badges and buckles turn up in antiques shops, some old photographs on occasion and even twisted pieces of metal from crash sites scattered throughout the British Isles. This is why the re-appearance of the trophy with its names carefully engraved is a remarkable and unusual occurrence.

To date, the trophy has maintained the anonymity of its previous owners, but has focused minds and research on the men it represents; as it should do. To return to an earlier theme, it is almost as if the trophy had a mysterious spiritual element to reveal itself at exactly the right time to coincide with the seventieth anniversary of the events it represented. Like the plot of any good Indiana Jones movie, it was as if the earth opened and a rare object possessing mysterious powers appeared to the lone searcher. Being a little more objective, one could argue that it was pure chance and good fortune that I, or anyone else with a modicum of aviation knowledge, should 'find' the trophy and pursue an obvious path of curiosity. Being of Christian persuasion, I hold a middle ground belief that there was indeed a purpose to me finding the trophy and investigating it; not because the item itself held any kind of power, but because a higher purpose prevailed. Before I disappear into deep rabbit holes of theology, in simple terms the trophy is a giant finger pointing at names of men otherwise disappearing into obscurity. I am reminded of Dong Ong in such matters because of the onslaught of adverse circumstances in his later life that might have erased much of the detail surrounding his wartime experiences. However, the experience of calling and emailing relatives in America, as a cold caller might sell insurance, has been interesting to say the least. In many families, fresh questions have been asked, old aunties have been consulted, and family records and photographs pored over. We still can't find a picture of Morris Gumpel in uniform and before I stirred the pot it would not have troubled the family; suddenly it matters. My abundant thanks go to all who trawled attics and boxes in a dozen or more houses across America. Forgotten stories, photographs and memorabilia turned up. The phrase, 'I have a *blank* somewhere in the house of his,' was commonplace. Some of the items turned up, others did not and remain a challenge to the relatives who now want to locate them. I would love to see the D-handle of Ken Garner's parachute.

I have made many new long-distance friends and in any friendship it takes time to get to know people. I'm intrigued by the normality or even banal quality of some lives lived. There's nothing wrong with being average and normal. These men were not comic book heroes, but in modern parlance they were heroes. They do not see themselves as that; they simply did what was expected of them and they survived. Unlike the pre-war regular men, many felt they were still civilians but wearing a uniform. Some relatives took little interest in the quest to find out more information. They were curious but somewhat bemused by this strange Englishman asking peculiar questions. This is not to criticize them, for in life there can be few moments to cast a look into family history when there is a job to do, a mortgage to be paid and food to put on the table.

We who are younger by one, two or even three generations from our wartime forebears will soon need to forge a different relationship with the past. The generation who fought will no longer walk among us. The old men on park benches who faced the Germans or Japanese in combat will have no more stories to tell. Time moves on and perhaps we are right to forget some things but, in the noise of modern life, spending moments of reflection is a good thing. Few of us will face the bone-chilling terrors of red hot chards of metal peppering our aircraft or seeing people we called colleagues or even friends die before our eyes. Just as the generation who returned from the First World War to Britain saw huge changes in society as a result, so too in America the generation who travelled and fought brought back an enduring legacy after the Second World War. The phrase 'The Greatest Generation' has emerged in recent years to describe those who lived through the Second World War, yet, I believe in essence, every generation has the intellect, courage and compassion to see through a terrible period of circumstances. Equally, we should not fool ourselves into believing that man is so advanced and superior now that sudden eruptions of intense evil are no longer possible.

For me, the last year has been an amazing journey. It has been a journey of privilege and fulfilment in researching what I enjoy. It has been a year of people watching and people finding. I have played the detective on quiet mysteries and not all questions have been answered fully, but I've discovered that's how history is. To steal and adapt Donald Rumfeld's comical statement on the second Iraq war, there are things we know, things we don't know and unknown things we know will remain unknown. Like a fisherman, my pleasure has been in the 'catch' – finding people, even if they profess to know nothing of value in terms of the 388th trophy.

As with all great journeys of discovery, it has been my personal delight to have found so much from such humble beginnings. What will I do next? One thing is for certain, no second-hand store, car boot sale or antiques shop visit will ever be the same again. The sadness remains that some really interesting and personal items are lost to families who would love to have them. In the online sales world, one can find all sorts of medals, memorabilia and photographs from young men who went off to fight a war and, although we cannot keep everything in our family archives, there's a poignant sense that so much of what we see will mean far more to future generations.

What should become of the trophy now? I've enjoyed its company, and mystery and spent a year of my life having the names engraved in my mind. I don't intend for it to sit on my shelf among the other bits and relics I've collected over the years forever. I don't want history to repeat itself and allow it to be 'lost' again. It is a fascinating party piece but it belongs to all the names engraved and their relatives, it belongs to the US Air Force and it belongs in England, and probably near Knettishall. Perhaps, too, after seventy years of silence, the trophy has more to tell.

David Price
Carlisle, England
June 2015

Acknowledgements

The author wishes to thank everyone who has helped in the research of this book, in particular, of course, the crew, but also family and friends of the crews:

Johnnie W. Colburn
Morris Fleishman
Darlene Colburn Whitt
Robert Simmon Jnr
Ann Kragle
George Kragle
Richard Heslam Jnr
Frank and Blanch Nutt
Wilma Ryan
Terrance Ong
Justin Ong
David Lippert
Penny Warner
Dr Roy Gumpel
John Ganas
Kenneth Gardner Jnr
Robert W. Gardner

For providing such comprehensive records that made this project possible:

Dick Henggeler – 388th Association Historian
Janet Pack and Richard Singer – 388th Anthologies
Dave Sarson – 388th Museum, Hill Top Farm
The 388th Bombardment Group Association and all contributors to the 388th Newsletter.

To those whose foresight in leaving detailed accounts with us we owe a debt of gratitude:

Ed Huntzinger – The 388th At War
Richard Timberlake – They Never Saw Me Then
Dong Ong
Bob Simmon
Arthur Fixel
Gene C. Peterson